Music through Time

An Appreciation of Music in Europe and America

Second Edition

Christopher P. Gordon

Shane R. Porter

John A. Stallsmith, DMA

KENDALL/HUNT PUBLISHING COMPANY

4050 Westmark Drive　　　Dubuque, Iowa 52002

Copyright © 2006, 2007 by Christopher P. Gordon, Shane R. Porter, and John A. Stallsmith

ISBN 10: 0-7575-4096-1
ISBN 13: 978-0-7575-4096-7

Printed in the United States of America
10 9 8 7 6 5 4 3 2 1

CONTENTS

ACKNOWLEDGMENTS

In an endeavor such as this, nothing is accomplished alone and the authors would like to thank the people most responsible for support and encouragement throughout this project. First their families: Pam Gordon, Anna Gordon, Tori Gordon, Dave and Shirley Porter and the "Musical Fathers" of the Tuscaloosa Horns, and Becki Stallsmith, Nellie Stallsmith, and Benjamin Stallsmith.

Secondly, for the help and guidance and skill of the Kendall/Hunt Publishing staff. Specifically, Kimberly Terry, Ray Wood, Cooper Gouge, Paul Gormley, and Greg DeRosa. Thirdly, thanks to the educators who have helped to shape the direction of this project, Dr. Prince L. Dorough and Dr. Devin Stephenson.

1

Philosophy and Aesthetics

What is music? Why does music exist? Is it important? Why are we required to study it? These are just a few of the many questions that make up the mystery surrounding something that is so readily available in today's society. We accept that music is all around us, but in actuality most people know very little of its purpose, its meaning, its value, its development, its content, or its literature. But careful inquiry into these questions can offer a glimpse at the truth lying at the heart of what it means to possess a *liberal education.*

A thoughtful investigation regarding music, its meaning, and purpose requires us to investigate the roots of wisdom in our Western world. Those roots are found in the ideas and practices of the first great society to ask these same questions—the ancient Greeks.

Ancient Greeks

The ancient Greeks contributed much to the basic understanding of the human experience. This society laid the foundations for the first understanding of philosophy, education, athletics, language, logic, mathematics, and yes, even music.

Philosophy and the study of it may be the greatest gifts the ancient Greeks have given the modern world. Philosophy may be defined as the pursuit of truth. The philosopher pursues these truths as they relate to the nature of life and reality. The most valuable outcome of the philosopher's discipline lies in the creation of a process for human action in daily life.

The Greeks valued the training of their youth so highly that they established an educational process that included the pursuit of beauty in the physical body as well as in the mind. Competitions of athletic performance and skill were prized, culminating in the first Olympic games. Each Greek student was also instructed in mental calisthenics pertaining to the areas of reason, deduction, and calculation as related to mathematics and music. Pythagoras, a noted mathematician, investigated the physics of sound and wave vibrations, or pitches, giving the modern world its foundations in acoustics and music theory. So it is that the Greeks established the curriculum content of processes that lead to mature development of the body and the mind.

The Middle Ages

In the Middle Ages and Renaissance similar content for curricular inclusion was emphasized through the **trivium** and **quadrivium**, creating the seven liberal arts. The trivium, the less important liberal arts, contained the subjects of grammar, rhetoric, and logic, forming the basis of medieval university study. The quadrivium, consisting of arithmetic, geometry, music, and astronomy, comprised the higher division of liberal arts. At one time, the trivium was the basis for the Bachelor of Arts degree while the quadrivium was the basis for the Master of Arts degree. To some extent, this broad outline of mental disciplines still defines the liberal arts today. But what is art and why are the degrees in the area of the arts and not science?

What Is Art?

Human beings learn through experience with nature's forms. Nature presents herself to us through complete wholes or forms that people encounter through their five senses. The end product of this sensory experience is knowledge. The knowledge that humans acquire then can be divided into three categories: knowledge pertaining to survival, knowledge pertaining to science, and knowledge pertaining to art.

Experiences that lead to survival in the environment pertain to immediate human needs such as how to gather food, build shelter, make clothing, and thus live another day. This information is vital and is of the highest importance. Interestingly, this knowledge leads to action. Without this knowledge, the individual and the species would cease to exist. Acquisition of this type of knowledge is essential for everyone to obtain.

The second and third types of knowledge, **science** and **art**, belong together because they are completely mental events, abstract in nature, yet they are opposites. Science is a mental and abstract process. This process takes nature's whole forms and mentally dissects them into component parts. This dissection allows for the naming of those parts and the observation of their function within the whole. This, too, is action but an abstract action that results in nature's form remaining dissected for the purpose of knowing and predicting. Therefore, science is a mental process at its core.

Art, too, is a process, an action. Yet, it is an action that requires science before it can be initiated. The individual must first have an understanding of the component parts of a whole before it can begin the abstraction of art. This makes the process of art and the experience gained from it attain a high level of value and meaning to humans. This is known as an **aesthetic**. Aesthetics is the knowledge and recognition of *beauty* in life, in nature, in reality.

The process of art is the manipulation of component parts through skillful technique. This technique, or manipulation, is infused with human desire, feeling, and the need to form a whole that has never been seen in nature before. It is the reverse of science. The assembling of parts into a new whole is a process that bears witness to aspects of its creator when it is finished. Again, art is action, action that results in an artifact or a pure act. It embodies aspects of the creator's technique and character, situation and desire.

Humans regularly employ all three types of experience in their daily lives, and they can do so simultaneously. To do so can result in the greatest artistic creations, scientific laws, or calculations, or it can result in the mere survival in the crowded and confusing world. But each function of experience is interlinked and can be made creative, reflecting each individual.

What Is Fine Art?

Fine arts serve as ornamentation to life. Generally, they do not provide a vital function, yet they become vital because fine arts make life beautiful and they harbor meaning for many individuals. There are several categories that make up the fine arts. Each of these categories varies in that they are perceived through a different sense organ in the consumer or audience member.

Visual art is comprised of artifacts that are created through mediums that can be perceived with the eye, such as painting, sculpture, photography, lithography, and other three-dimensional art pieces. **Dance** is kinesthetic movement designed to be a vehicle of emotion for the dancer through the body's motions, while also designed to invoke emotion in the consuming observer. Drama, too, is kinesthetic motion used to create emotions in the actor through speech as well as body movements. The actor is expert in his/her ability to display emotions and actions necessary to tell a convincing story. **Architecture** is the discipline of design as applied to constructing living spaces or buildings. Through architecture, necessary living and working spaces become beautiful as well as functional.

Music is the greatest form of fine art. It is considered to be the greatest because of the fragileness of its medium—sound. Sound is ethereal and vanishing. It is in real time. While drama and dance are also in real time, they are visual in nature and use external mediums—the body. Music is perceived through the sense of hearing, the most vital of the sense organs. Through sound vibrations, an invisible, untouchable energy, music is perceived as an abstraction of performed symbols, an entirely mental event, making it of the highest order as compared to the other fine arts.

Additionally, music is received into the brain through the ear, connecting to the most sensitive nerve centers in the brain where emotions are processed. Music is the perfect medium for the purpose of communicating and stimulating emotional responses through sound, and the emotional centers can be manipulated through music, causing physiological changes within the body. Music therapy is built on this clinical value of behavior modification as well as physiological effects that can be predicted and prescribed within the body through listening to music. Philosophically and metaphysically speaking, music can cause emotion or reflect emotion within the creator of the music. It is communicative. It is an exchange of energy from the creator to the consumer of the music, and this energy reflects aspects of its creator to its consumer. Feeling will combine with technique in the creator to be released as artifact—music. The listener, or consumer, will receive the artifact, through hearing, evaluate its technical abstraction, and ultimately deposit the same feeling within the listener. This produces the idea of emotion sent, emotion received. No other art form produces such a powerful emotional response in real time in the consumer as does music.

A Need

People have a primal need to make music and also a powerful need to consume it. The development of genre, performance situations, performance ensembles, and the like are byproducts of this need and desire. These will

evolve over time to fit the technologies, market demands, and inspirations of the composers and performers of the various time periods throughout various civilizations, but music making will continue.

In this text, we will become familiar with the genre, people, times, places, and literature that have been produced by many different peoples. But along with that exposure, we will learn why they were motivated to produce in the manner that they did, what lessons we learn from them, and how they apply to our lives today and in the future. We will follow historical developments and great ideas that have marked mankind's march of progress through time as demonstrated through their music, and we will see if this march leads toward the truth the great philosophers of old pursued. Let's begin.

VOCABULARY

Aesthetic	Fine Art	Quadrivium
Architecture	Music	Science
Art	Painting	Sculpture
Dance	Photography	Trivium

WEBSITE

Please refer to the *Music Through Time* site listed in the front of your book to investigate and complete more classroom activities and assignments.

2

The Science of Music

Music exists through the basic elements of pitch, rhythm, melody, harmony, texture, form, timbre, dynamics, and performance ensemble; and music has its own vocabulary to indicate specific elements within these categories. These elements and their references create a language of words and symbols with which a student must become familiar. Understanding these basic concepts and their terms lays a foundation for continued discussion in subsequent chapters of this book.

Pitch

Sound that is musically useful is called **pitch**. Pitches are produced when a vibration in the air reaches a consistent speed. This consistency of speed in a vibration source is what differentiates pitch from noise, where there are random cycles of vibration. Vibrations have a source, and that source can be a column of air, a string that is set in motion, or some other source that possesses a vibrating service material that is a specific length, diameter, or circumference.

Pitches are distinguished as being higher or lower when measured against each other. The degree to which a pitch is high or low and the distance between

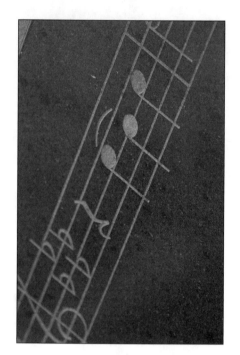

any two pitches is referred to as an **interval**. The smallest distance, or interval, that is musically recognized in Western music is the **half step**. (The interval of two half-steps separating two pitches is called a **whole step**.) There are twelve distinct half steps before there is a duplication of the original pitch at a higher or lower level. This is called the interval of an **octave**. An octave is created in nature when there is a mathematical doubling of the number of vibrations in one cycle of the vibrating source per second. For example, a string of a specific length set in motion may generate 220 cycles per second from top to bottom of the waveform. An octave will be produced of that pitch at a higher level of hearing when the speed of vibration increases to 440 cycles per second. Having many octaves of each of the twelve half steps creates a wide variety of pitches that are musically useful.

Scales

Pitch information used to compose melody and produce harmony in musical compositions comes from scales. A **scale** is a set of pitches that have certain interval relationships between each note in the scale. Not all scales are the same because the interval relationships separating each pitch can change. A **chromatic scale** is a scale that contains only half steps, while all other scales possess differing interval relationships. The **major scale** is commonly used for the composition of melody and harmony, and it has a construction of [W-W-H-W-W-W-H]. Another commonly used scale is the **minor scale**, using an interval construct of [W-H-W-W-H-W-W]. Any one of the major or minor scales that possess seven notes is called a **diatonic scale**.

There are also scales that have more or less than seven notes within them. The **pentatonic scale** has five notes and uses an interval construct of [m3-W-W-m3-W]. Inversions of the pentatonic scale are also used regularly, creating even more variety of melodic content. These types of scales are used a great deal in Asian music, African music, and Afro-American music, especially blues, jazz, and rhythm and blues music.

The ancient Greeks also used a form of scale for their melodic material; however, they refereed to them as **modes**. There were many different modes with varying interval constructs, and there were inversions of these modes that had the prefix *hypo* associated with the name of each mode. The Greeks also ascribed certain emotional qualities to music that was composed from each of the different modes, requiring that they be regulated in society, similar to emotional prescriptions of mood-altering listening material.

Notation

Pitches can be specifically notated in a written system so that music may be read by a performer and expect exact pitch reproduction. Reading and writing music has evolved over time but now consists of a visual graph where specific pitches, high versus low, can be specified on a series of five lines and four spaces called a **staff**. The staff by itself has only a limited range of places where a note, the name given to a specific pitch, can be indicated on a line or space. In order to expand the possibilities of placing many specific notes on a staff, a **clef** sign is added to the staff. The purpose of the clef sign is to specify a range of high or low notes that is to be placed on the staff. There are two common clefs, the treble clef sign and the bass clef sign, in use. When one or the other clef sign is added to a staff of five lines and four spaces, the notes indicated on the staff change in name and pitch level. Two sets of staffs may be linked together, one with the treble clef sign and one with the bass clef sign, forming a **grand staff.** The grand staff allows for many notes to be written in a logical sequence, all

lying in the middle of the hearing range. Most music written for instruments having the ability to play several notes at once, such as the piano, organ, or synthesizer, will be on the grand staff.

Even with the ability to write many notes specified in the grand staff with its considerable number of lines and spaces, interlinked by clef signs, there is still the need to have additional places to write notes that lay outside the staff's capacity. A **ledger line** is a flexible extension of the lines and spaces of the staff at the top or bottom of a staff. These ledger lines are used to extend the range of the staff temporarily upward for the indication of higher pitches or downward for the indication of lower pitches that may fall outside the staff's normal range.

Melody

Melody is a term that refers to musical material of interest that is the most important and memorable, the succession of pitches that fall into units, one after another, of completeness and can contain emotion and meaning for the listener. There are several terms that all refer to melody, differing in the length or formal structure of the melodic material.

A **tune** is a short, memorable melody that is complete in and of itself that needs no additional material, such as *Happy Birthday, Here Comes the Bride*, or *Amazing Grace*. Each of these are easy to remember and easy to reproduce. They make sense in and of themselves. A **theme** refers to a melody, but a melody that is part of a larger formal structure that may contain several different themes or melodies within the whole structure. Themes are used in large structures to deliberately draw their differences to the attention of the listener. In this way, formal structures can be used to organize similar and contrasting melodic material over time. A **motive** usually means a short, incomplete melodic building block. It tends to be short and contain strong rhythmic and/or intervallic qualities. The motive is incomplete but may be used to build a more complete melody through repetitions and manipulations of that melodic material.

Melody uses a **phrase**, or musical thought, to construct a musical sentence. A two-phrase period forms a unit to replicate the function of a paragraph in language. Two phrase periods form enough melodic material to become a complete musical thought. **Cadences** in music are equivalent to punctuation in language, represented by a **half cadence**, where a melody is incomplete and another melodic phrase is required, or an **authentic cadence**, which acts as a period in language, bringing about closure to the melody—usually occurring at the end of the second melody of a two-phrase period.

Texture

Texture in music refers to the number of melodies being heard simultaneously. There are three predominant textures: monophony, polyphony, and homophony. **Monophonic texture** is music that contains one melody sounding alone, without any other supporting material. An example of monophonic music would be if you sang *Happy Birthday* and the only sound was your singing of that melody. Even if a group of singers joined in or a group of instruments played along with your singing and increased the volume or density, as long as only the notes of the melody were played or sung, it would still be monophonic in texture.

Polyphonic texture occurs when more than one melody, of equal importance, sounds at the same time. In this texture, layers of melody battle for the listener's attention, creating density. An example of polyphonic texture would occur when three singers all sing their melodies simultaneously, one singing *Happy Birthday*, another singing *Three Blind Mice*, and still another singing *The Star Spangled Banner*, with each melody complete in and of itself and possessing no other supporting musical material. Polyphony is the first example of historical advancement in textural structure.

Homophonic texture is the newest textural form historically and is the sort that we are most familiar with today. Homophonic texture has one main melody accompanied by other supporting musical material that does not distract the listener from the focus of the primary melody. This would imply a texture using a single melody with chords and accompanying rhythmic material.

Harmony

The word **harmony** refers to more than one pitch sounding simultaneously, or the vertical relationships within the intervals, high versus low, as multiple pitches sound at once. In Western music the basis for our harmony is built on the interval of a third, meaning two alphabet names apart from each other. When three or more notes sound at the same time, it is called a **chord**. The basic chord structure of Western music is the **triad**, three notes, each a third interval apart.

The scale provides the note material for melody as well as harmony. Each scale has a note from which the interval pattern begins in succession. This first note or pitch of the scale is called the **tonic** pitch, meaning the home base or the beginning. The ending note of a scale is the octave duplication of the tonic pitch. Triads are formed from diatonic scales by stacking the notes of the scale upon themselves using intervals of a third. Each note of the scale may be used as the basis for a triad, or root of a triad. This will create seven chords that have different sound qualities and may be useful in adding support, color, and interest to melodies also composed from the scale.

When two or more pitches sound at the same time, their cyclic vibrations are in accord with one another, meaning there is enough room to accommodate each pitch's vibration, or the pitches conflict with each other, meaning their vibrations fight against each other as their cyclic vibrations battle for vibratory space. Pitches possessed of vibrations that are in accord with each other are said to be at rest, or are in **consonance** with each other. Those pitches whose waves conflict with each other are said to be in **dissonance**, or in motion. As pitches intone in the same airspace, their waves alternate between various states of tension, or dissonance, and degrees of rest, or consonance, and it is this dissonance that is resolved into consonance that causes harmony to create a sense of motion—from the tonic pitch, traveling away from it and returning home again.

Keys

As there are twelve chromatic pitches, each of these can be used as a **tonic** on which a scale, usually major or minor, can be constructed. The melody and harmony derived from that tonal area are said to be in a certain **key**. The scale is the basis for melody and harmony, and since all twelve pitches and their corresponding scales can be used, music often does move about from one tonal area, or key, to another. In this way, interest is sustained over longer periods of time, and contrasting sections of music can occur with a maximum of difference between them, setting them apart as distinct and separate. Music may start in one key and progress toward another and even another. When a composer changes from one key to another key, the music is said to modulate. Therefore, **modulation** in music is the process of changing keys, higher or lower, major or minor.

Rhythm

Rhythm is the progression of logically and exactly ordered events through time. As music exists in the combination of time events and sound through pitch, rhythm, and the mastery of it, is crucial to the logical processing of melody and harmony into units of meaning for the listener.

Beats

The way in which time is created in music is through a system of consistently ordered events called **beats**. Beats become useful when multiple events leave the realm of randomness and begin to possess a repeated and consistent amount of time between each event. When these events in sound have reached a regular pattern, they can be grouped together in similar and recognizable units called **measures**.

The process for grouping beats into units of measure is accomplished through a stress

being placed on the first beat of the group within a measure, singling it out and making it more recognizable. This stress is called an **accent**. The number of beats within a measure may vary at will, but preferable patterns have been established in public taste over time, standardizing groups of two, three, or four beats in a measure to be the most common. When an accent is placed on the first of a group of beats, **meter** is produced, with duple meter, triple meter, and quadruple meter corresponding to measures that include that number of beats. Most music selects a meter, and the music remains in that same meter for its duration; however, it is not necessary for music to stay locked into one or another completely.

Tempo

The speed of the beats may vary and is called **tempo**. Historically, tempo indications employed Italian language approximations such as *allegro*, meaning fast, and *adagio*, meaning slow. However, more exact measurements of beats eventually evolved, creating a process of establishing the exact speed of a beat by grouping them in units of beats per minute. The **metronome** is an instrument that allows a musician to accurately establish the speed of a specific tempo, and modern music possesses a tempo marking of a set number of beats per minute rather than the more vague language reference used in past times.

Duration

In addition to the existence and initiation of an event itself, there is also the duration of the event's sound to consider. A sound may be long or short in duration. Over the centuries, a system of symbols indicating length of sound has been established.

Note values vary, but the most common system uses the following table:

Whole Note = four beats

Half note = two beats

Quarter note = one beat

Eighth note = one-half of a beat

Sixteenth note = one-fourth of a beat

As you can see, some notes have durations that are longer than one beat, and they are used to represent sounds that are relatively long. These are the whole note, half note, and quarter note. Note values that represent events that occur within the space of one beat and are, therefore, shorter in duration, include the eighth note and sixteenth note. The eighth note and sixteenth note placement within one beat requires the performer to accurately subdivide the single beat into equal component parts, allowing the performer to place them accurately into the framework of the music's rhythmic scheme and requirements.

Any rhythmic event may also have an accent or stress if so desired, causing irregular attention to be drawn to the event. This is far from a negative event and is often useful in the creation of surprise and variety from the normal stresses of accents within meter. When an accent occurs somewhere inside a measure other than on the first beat, it is called a **syncopation**.

VOCABULARY

Accent	Interval	Pitch
Authentic Cadence	Key	Polyphonic Texture
Bass Clef	Ledger Line	Rhythm
Beat	Major Scale	Scale
Cadence	Measure	Staff
Chord	Melody	Syncopation
Chromatic Scale	Meter	Tempo
Clef	Metronome	Texture
Consonance	Minor Scale	Theme
Diatonic Scale	Mode	Tonic
Dissonance	Modulation	Treble Clef
Grand Staff	Monophonic Texture	Triad
Half Cadence	Motive	Tune
Half Step	Octave	Whole Step
Harmony	Pentatonic Scale	
Homophonic Texture	Phrase	

WEBSITE

Please refer to the *Music Through Time* site listed in the front of your book to investigate and complete more classroom activities and assignments.

CHAPTER

3

Timbre

Since music exists in pitch and within a specific framework of events known as rhythm, the question remains as to what will produce the pitches and perform the events in sound and space. Anything that has the ability to produce a pitch is called an **instrument**, and over the many years of music making there has come to be a wide variety of instruments that vary from one another in their process of producing pitches, the materials from which the instrument is made, and the performance location that is best suited for the instrument. Usually, instruments are categorized in families due to their mechanics or construction.

Instruments are always in a state of flux, seeing manufacturing improvements and usage innovations. This is seen in the present time in the manufacturing of electronic instruments primarily, but innovation and instrument refinement took place in older instruments as well. This chapter will explore the common historical families of instruments and several of the more modern ones.

Human Voice

The oldest instrument is the human voice. Everyone has one, and many enjoy singing and humming. Some even investigate the refining of their voice, making music for a lifetime. There are six categories of human vocal ranges. From highest to lowest they are listed here, with the four most common designations printed in bold:

Soprano

Mezzo Soprano

Contralto

Tenor

Baritone

Bass

The vocal folds, often called vocal cords, in the throat are placed in motion by air moving up from the abdomen. The throat muscles are refined to the extent that they can be trained to focus the vibration of the vocal folds at specific tensions, allowing a wide variety of pitches to be produced. Depending on individual factors such as heredity, hormones, body shape and size, and so on, the degree of highness or lowness of the pitches that can be produced varies from individual to individual, both male and female. And corresponding to the range of the singer, his or her voice will be classified as one of the categories found in the previous list.

Brass

The **brass** family of instruments was originally intended for outdoor and ceremonial use, primarily due to their ability to play a loud volume that can carry over long distances. The brass family all produce their sound in the same manner, through the vibrating of the performer's lips into a metal cup that focuses and intensifies the vibration before it travels into the brass alloy tubing that colors the sound and, depending on its length and diameter, determines its pitch. The longer the tube, and the larger the diameter of the tube, the lower the

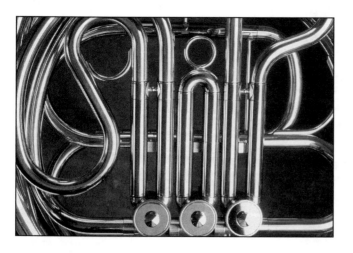

pitch will be. The tube length and diameter forms what is called the "fundamental" pitch, and the performer plays multiple pitches by pushing more air and increasing the tension of the lips, causing the vibration to skip to higher overtones or partials in the harmonic series of a fundamental pitch, allowing several related pitches to be produced. While it is beyond the scope of this text to fully investigate the physics of sound and their corresponding related pitch partials, it will be helpful to know that through the way in which sound is created in waveforms, there is actually more than one pitch that exists within any single pitch. These additional pitches are at a higher interval, or level, than the fundamental tone and also softer than the fundamental, but they do exist in every acoustically produced pitch wave. Performers of brass instruments are quite skilled at using or "surfing" these upper partials, making them sound as pure as the fundamental pitch on which the instrument is manufactured.

There are many instruments within the brass family, but the main four categories from highest to lowest include:

Trumpet

French Horn

Trombone

Tuba

Each of these sub-families of brass instruments has multiple versions, creating a body too numerous to list here.

Woodwinds

The woodwinds are among the oldest wind instruments, and the main categories of woodwinds differ in the manner in which they produce their tones. The four common families of woodwind instruments are listed here from highest to lowest:

Flute

Oboe

Clarinet

Bassoon

The flute, a descendant of the recorder, was originally built of wood and had mild, warm tone. The modern flute is built of metal to increase its volume and flexibility. The mouthpiece is an open hole which the player blows across causing the air to split. The air inside the flute vibrates and sound is created. The player opens and closes holes and keys to manipulate the pitch.

The oboe and the bassoon belong to the **"double reed"** category because they produce their sound in the same manner. Using two cane reeds fixed together, placed in the performer's mouth with air blown in between the two reeds, causing them to vibrate against each other, a tone is then produced within the body of the instrument where that tone is colored, focused, and lengthened or shortened via a set of keys that cover holes cut into the body of the instrument.

The clarinet family belongs to the **"single reed"** category of wind instruments, which uses only one reed affixed to a flat-surfaced

mouthpiece. The end of the mouthpiece and reed is placed in the performer's mouth, and air is forced between the reed and the base of the mouthpiece to create a vibration, the timbre or color of which is less brittle and more warm than that of the double reeds' more nasal quality.

The saxophone family of instruments is also a member of the single reed group. The **saxophone,** like the clarinet, has a wide variety of ranges, including the soprano saxophone, the alto, the tenor, and the baritone saxophones, as well as more exotic variations less commonly seen. The newest of the established woodwind instruments, the saxophone was originally a hybrid of both the brass and woodwind families. Adolph Sax, who invented the instrument, originally desired an instrument that had the flexibility of motion, speed, and range control of the clarinet family combined with the volume of sound that was produced by the brass family. The end result was a louder, faster woodwind that evolved too late to be completely accepted as a full member of the European orchestra, but it found a home in the military bands of Europe and America and in the American popular music that would come from the nineteenth and twentieth centuries.

Strings

This family of instruments produces its sound primarily through the vibration of a length of gut or metal string set in motion through the use of a bow affixed to a wooden body that possesses a sound hole allowing the vibration to enter and spin around inside the body of the instrument, coloring and amplifying it. This family is the primary grouping found in a **symphony orchestra** (the common group of instruments for which most of the European music designed to be performed by large ensembles of the past was intended.)

Most often the bow is used to put the string in motion, but these also may be plucked with the fingers. Again, there are four ranges of instruments, with ranges of highest to lowest.

Violin

Viola

(Violin) Cello

Bass (Viol) (or Double Bass)

Plucked Strings

String instruments also include those that make their sound from the plucking of the strings. These are very old instruments that evolve into various sizes and shapes, having four, five, six, or even as many as twelve strings. Each possesses a different timbre because of the shape of the instrument, the body design, the length of the neck and strings, and the materials from which the strings are manufactured. Fingers and picks of different kinds are used to increase speed of the notes capable of being produced and affect the timbre of the sound when the strings are plucked.

Some instruments common to all of us and often used in "folk" music include those in the following list:

Guitar

Mandolin

Banjo

Ukulele

Pedal Steele Guitar

Electric Bass

Twelve String Guitar

Percussion

Percussion instruments are those that produce their sound by means of striking. The striking of the instrument may be through the hand, stick, mallet, or any other method that may produce a musically useful timbre. Percussion instruments fall into two categories, those that produce pitches, called **melodic percussion** instruments, and those that do not produce a pitch, called **non-melodic percussion** instruments.

The melodic percussion instruments produce pitches from which melody may be played through varying lengths of blocks or tubes made of wood or metal. These will also be of varying densities. Because of the exactness of their lengths and densities, they can produce a consistent pitch in their vibrations.

These are still considered percussion instruments because they are struck with a hammer, mallet, or stick, and the timbres produced give the instrument its uniqueness. A list of some of the common melodic percussion instruments includes:

Marimba

Xylophone

Celeste

Vibraphone

Glockenspiel

Chimes (or Tubular Bells)

Bells

Hand Bells

Non-melodic percussion instruments fall into two large categories, drums and cymbals. A **drum** is of ancient origin and may be made of anything that can produce a cone or shell. A membrane will be fixed to the top of the cone or shell, stretched across it in a taunt manner. The sound is produced from the striking of the membrane with the hand or stick. The timbre of the drum will be a result of the diameter, length, and material from which the cone or shell is constructed as well as the degree of tightness in the membrane.

Cymbals are usually in the general shape of a saucer and are made from metal alloys. Originating from Turkey, cymbals produce a unique splash or crash of sound that can accent and highlight a particular event. They come in various sizes and densities, from the very small finger cymbals to the very large crash cymbals. Both the drums and cymbals are useful in creating time and producing polyphonic layers of sonorous events.

Almost anything can be used as a percussion instrument, providing the timbre is musically useful. Music literature has displayed many unconventional devices used in the percussion section, including an anvil, a war canon, and even birds chirping.

Keyboard Instruments

Over the centuries there have been many keyboard instruments designed and built. The popularity and usefulness of these instuments has reflected changes in public taste and institutional goals. However, due to the many keys and many note capacities of keyboard instruments, they have been ever popular with the public and have attracted the most outstanding of performers.

The first great keyboard instrument was the **pipe organ.** Designed for use in Europe's cathedrals of the Christian church, they are marvels of design and craftsmanship. Often using hundreds of pipes of varying diameters and lengths and built into the building itself to properly store and organize them, the pipe organ used moving air as its sound source. This air would be pumped in a console, or keyboard, which acted as a direction switcher, or terminal, for the air that allowed the performer not only the option of what notes to play, but also what timbre of pipe to send the air to, often having many different timbre possibilities for every single pitch! It was the technological equivalent to a musical computer for cathedrals in the fifteenth century. Needless to say, the pipe organ was the king of instruments, capable of producing massive amounts of sound.

The **harpsichord** was a staple of seventeenth century instrumental music. Used in both large and small ensembles and possessing a high degree of aural

clarity and dexterity, the harpsichord had a brittle timbre due to the strings within it being actually mechanically plucked rather than struck, as is the case of our modern piano. The harpsichord had a sound that would cut through the timbres of a large ensemble and be heard despite not being a very loud instrument. The volume of the instrument was consistent and could not be changed by the performer in most cases.

The **piano-forte** (later the name was shortened to **piano**) became popular in the eighteenth and nineteenth centuries due to the change in mechanics of the keyboard. This instrument used a hammer to strike the strings within, allowing the performer to vary the weight pressing on the key, and thus affecting the volume of sound produced. This was a terrific innovation and was very popular with the public. It also allowed for performers to create their own distinct sound on the piano, leading to more notoriety particularly for performers that could not just be replicated by anyone.

The synthesizer is a modern marvel that has transformed all of music making. It resembles a computer more than it does an instrument, but its usefulness is amazing, allowing one person the palette of sound possibilities that once could only be produced with dozens of performers. It also allows for control and accuracy of sound and pitch that has never been possible before. There are many praises that can be attributed to the synthesizer, and there may be as many curses as well because no other instrument in all of history has caused so many to rise up in love or hatred—the pros and cons of which cannot be argued in the scope of this chapter.

VOCABULARY

Cello	Glockenspiel	Single Reed instrument
Banjo	Guitar	Soprano
Baritone	Harpsichord	Strings
Bass	Human Voice	Symphony Orchestra
Bassoon	Instrument	Tenor
Brass	Mandolin	Trombone
Celeste	Marimba	Trumpet
Clarinet	Melodic Percussion	Tuba
Contralto	Mezzo Soprano	Tubular Bells
Cymbal	Non-melodic Percussion	Ukulele
Double Bass	Oboe	Vibraphone
Double Reed Instrument	Percussion	Viola
Drum	Piano-forte	Violin
Flute	Pipe Organ	Woodwind
French horn	Saxophone	Xylophone

WEBSITE

Please refer to the *Music Through Time* site listed in the front of your book to investigate and complete more classroom activities and assignments.

CHAPTER

4

Form

Form is a term that describes design or shape in music—shapes created through logically related sections of melody and harmony, centered in certain tonal areas. Related melodic and harmonic materials form identifiable sections in the ears of the listeners that can be remembered when repeated. Repetition is vital to music because it creates stability and recognition; however, too much repetition becomes boring and leads to disinterest. Therefore, form in music is the art of creating aural stability balanced with surprise and contrast.

Over many years, composers have developed designs that are balanced and successful at creating logical cognitive flow in music. Historically, these designs share in a cycle of development. The formal shape is created with the solving of a design problem through a composer's brilliant new idea and then moves along to a stage that sees the refinement of the shape's details by others. Further down the road is the stage where the shape's whole is perfected in the hands of a master composer or group of composers. Still further down the road is the stage that sees the expansion and additional tinkering of the shape by composers wishing to break new ground in rebellion against the creative tyranny of the "traditional" shapes, and finally a return to a brilliant new idea stage again as "progress" is made and music is once again made "modern."

In actuality, design is timeless, and the use of a model is not limited to a specific time period. A composer may choose any form from any time period in

which to work and the music, if well crafted, can be successfully received by an audience. But it is the audience that chooses its favorite designs in any current age, and it is in and by these very choices that musical consumers define style and ultimately culture; for culture is defined as the collected artifacts and created works of a civilization, and to some extent the popularity of a form plays a role in its survival.

There is, then, a body of standard forms in which we must become familiar. Some of them are listed here:

Strophic Form (A, A, A ...)

Theme and Variations (A, A1, A2, A3, A4 ...)

Binary (A, B)

Rounded Binary (A, B, A, B)

Ternary (A, B, A)

Fugue

Ritornello

Sonata

Minuet

Rondo

These shapes may be orchestrated in endless ways, calling for varying numbers and timbres of performance forces. They may also be intended for different performance venues, such as the church, theater, concert hall, or small intimate room. When a formal shape, performance force, and performance location are all combined, the specific **genre** name is given the work. For example, music written in sonata form that is intended for a large orchestra to perform in a large concert hall would be called a **symphony**; whereas, a piece written in the same sonata form intended for only two violins, a viola, and a cello to perform in an intimate performance space would be called a **string quartet.** Both works are in the same formal structure but have differing names. The term sonata refers to the shape, while symphony or string quartet is the genre.

The list that follows includes several commonly used genre names:

Chant

Organum

Motet

Mass

Madrigal

Opera

Trio Sonata

Dance Suite

Fugue

Concerto Grosso

Cantata

Organ Chorale

Oratorio
Symphony
Concerto
String Quartet
Lied
Song Cycle
Overture
Character Piece
Program Symphony
Symphonic Poem
Song

Summary

Artifacts and their popularity and usages change over time, and those artifacts that are similar fall into eras. Eras in music and other arts are overarching periods of time that produce artifacts that are an outgrowth of similar philosophies, politics, science, economics, and lifestyles of the people who share them. When a point is reached where the differences outweigh the similarities, a new era begins and is named by historians looking backward in time. The units of chapters that follow investigate the common periods or eras of time in musical terms. Prevailing ideas and practices are discussed, along with discussions on the popular genres of the time and a highlighting of the people who produced them. Remember as you read further that regular people create art, and their lives and circumstances are not altogether different from the consumers of their art. These artisans chose to create with their lives, however, and the results of their efforts have marked them as great in their own time and for all time.

VOCABULARY

Binary	Mass	Sonata
Cantata	Minuet	Song
Chant	Motet	Song Cycle
Character Piece	Opera	String Quartet
Concerto	Oratorio	Strophic Form
Concerto Grosso	Organ Chorale	Symphonic Poem
Dance Suite	Organum	Symphony
Form	Overture	Ternary
Fugue	Program Symphony	Theme and Variations
Genre	Ritornello	Trio Sonata
Lied	Rondo	
Madrigal	Rounded Binary	

WEBSITE

Please refer to the *Music Through Time* site listed in the front of your book to investigate and complete more classroom activities and assignments.

CHAPTER
5
Listening

Music is an exchange of energy from the performer(s) to the audience. Through the constructions of symbols (by the composer) and the performance of those symbols in real time (by the performer), in combination with the performer's unique feelings and interpretations, music is created and consumed. The result of the exchange is ethereal in that it can alter one's mood, heighten emotions, calm or incite, and effect body chemistry through its waves. When created and performed well, music can communicate abstract feelings and ideas that cannot be duplicated in words. It even has the power to communicate the same emotional state to many through one performance, providing a host with a common experience. Because of these mystical effects, music has remained popular over eons, even necessary.

However, as Wynton Marsalis has said,

You have to come to art, art will not come to you. You have to accept it on its own terms, through its own rules, and be willing to receive what it has to give to you. Beethoven is not going to walk up to you and tap your shoulder and say "Hey man, check this out."

To reap the benefit of what art has to offer, you have to open yourself and be willing to investigate, to be curious. In time, with effort, art will feed you, nourish you, and enlighten you. Therefore, a student must establish an efficient

process for the experience of listening, providing the most result in the allotted time.

A person should attend concerts in real time as much as possible. In a live concert, all the senses are involved in the processing of the experience, allowing for the full effect to be realized. This is the way that music had to be experienced historically, and only recently has technology been developed for the transference of this energy in a delayed fashion, through recordings. Yet, sadly, the ease and popularity of the recording has almost caused the demise of live performance, making it now a luxury rather than a common event, while at the same time people can experience music more readily than ever before.

How to Listen

When you listen to music that is new to you, and is outside your normal consuming taste, you must actively listen. You must focus your attention and attempt to comprehend the structure that is presented for you. This may require effort, more effort than you may be used to summoning when listening to music. Most people only listen to music in the style of which they are familiar, and, therefore, allow their innate ability to actively listen to degenerate and decay. Develop a respect for the experience and charge yourself with the task of fully investing in the listening experience. Develop the ability to concentrate and intensify your listening over longer periods of time. Most music takes longer than the three minutes that a popular song takes to consume.

It will help you to focus if you use a model as you listen. This model will help to provide guideposts for listening, keeping your thoughts on task.

Rhythm

1. Identify the meter. _____
2. Identify the tempo of the meter. _____
3. Are there tempo changes within one piece? _____

Texture

4. How many melodic ideas are sounding at the same time? _____
5. Does the texture change periodically? _____
6. If so, where and how often? _____

Melody

7. Is the melody easy to identify? _____
8. Can I remember it if I hear it again? _____

9. How many differing melodic ideas are there? _____

10. Are any repeated, recurring more than once? _____

Harmony

11. Is the rhythm of the chords fast or slow? _____

12. Does this change throughout the piece? _____

13. Does the key change at all in the music? _____

14. If so, where and how often? _____

15. Why do you think a key change was used? _____

16. Was a mode change used, major to minor, etc? _____

17. When and where did it occur? _____

Timbre

18. What instrument is producing the sound(s)? _____

19. Is there more than one timbre employed? _____

20. Are the timbre choices effective? _____

21. What families of instruments are represented? _____

22. Acoustic, electronic, or a combination? _____

Texts

23. Are there words in this piece? _____

24. What language is used? _____

25. Is there more than one layer of text? _____

26. Can you comprehend what is being sung/said? _____

27. Are you supposed to comprehend it? _____

Form

28. Can you identify the formal structure? _____

29. Can you name it? _____

30. If there are melodic repetitions normally occurring in this formal shape, can you identify the melodies as they reappear? _____

31. What is the name of the form? _____

32. What is the name of the corresponding genre? _____

Musicianship

33. Was the performance clear and effective? _____

34. Were the rhythmic elements clear and precise? _____

35. Were the notes performed in tune? _____

36. Were the performers energetic and enthusiastic? _____

37. Were the performers skillful? _____

Personal Response

38. How do you feel during the performance? _____

39. How do you feel after the performance? _____

40. In your opinion, what were the composer's intended reactions? _____

41. Did you experience what the composer and performers intended? _____

42. Why or why not? _____

43. Do you need to hear this piece again in order to comprehend it more fully? _____

44. Will you invest your time and energy into the experience of this music again? _____

45. Why or why not? _____

WEBSITE

Please refer to the *Music Through Time* site listed in the front of your book to investigate and complete more classroom activities and assignments.

6

Medieval Music

Music and musical instruments existed throughout many ancient times and places; however, it is unknown what most of this music sounded like. Singing predates the Medieval Age. Music is evident in Ancient Egypt as far back as 3000 B.C. and in Ancient Greece as early as 800 B.C. The Psalms of the Old Testament refer to the singing of David and the use of musical instruments played in Jewish Temples.

The Roman Empire was a vast and powerful force. For centuries, the Romans ruled much of central Europe and the surrounding areas of the Mediterranean Sea. In the fourth and fifth centuries, a decline of the Roman Empire was initiated by the attacks of the Huns, the Persians, the Visigoths, and the Vandals. Because of a constant struggle for power, their family members and their associates routinely murdered the new rulers. Through threats of death or kidnapping, some popes were forced to recognize new rulers, while other popes formed alliances to broker military unions. Thus, the Frankish

Kingdom was divided in 511 and remained in turmoil for many of the ensuing centuries.

The Medieval Age is an immense period in history, extending from the fall of the Roman Empire to the dawn of the Renaissance. Preceded by the suppressive and tyrannical empire of the Greco-Roman culture, the Medieval Age encompasses more than 1,000 years of turmoil, war, and unrest throughout Europe. The Medieval Age is divided into two large periods of time. The **Romanesque period** encompasses the years 400 A.D. to 1100 A.D. The **Gothic period** encompasses the years of 1100 A.D. to 1430 A.D. These two historic periods are reflected by the styles and attitudes concerning art, music, philosophy, architecture, and religion.

Romanesque Period (400 A.D.–1100 A.D.)

The term *Romanesque* is used to describe architecture that has been influenced by the Roman Empire. In large-scale buildings, Romanesque architecture incorporated into stone-vaulted structures decorated with sculptures. Romanesque art copied existing forms, such as animals or religious icons, and did not embody many original works.

Romanesque also refers to a large period of human history extending from the decline of the Roman Empire to the revival of society in the Gothic Period. During this time, Europe became a conglomeration of farms, manors, and estates controlled by secular lords or local Catholic Church leaders. Throughout this period, people were consumed by conflict, invasions, wars, and inconsistent government. Life became a matter of survival; therefore, most people did not travel beyond the perimeter of their local community, halting the exchange of knowledge and ideas.

The Catholic Church became the only conservator of culture and knowledge. In the height of the Romanesque confusion, Pope Gregory I is born (540).

Pope Gregory initiated the notation of the earliest church music that had been in practice for some time.

Through Christian values, the Church prompted the decline of the vulgar, materialistic Roman Empire. The monasteries became the principal patrons of art, music, and architecture. Throughout this period, the Catholic Church maintained a common language, doctrine, and purpose, thus becoming the only stable element of life. The Catholic Church emphasized personal holiness through withdrawal and reflection.

The Catholic Church preached the rules of salvation, restoring the promise of heaven at the end of earthly existence. Religion became a source of hope to those who had little reason to hope. However, religion did not address or improve human conditions.

Musical Style

The Catholic Church recorded the earliest, most significant notated sources of music. This music is labeled **monophonic**

plainsong or **chant**. These chants emerged as a practical means of making words audible. The priests **intoned** words so that the sound would carry farther than a speaking voice. The act of intoning became necessary as the churches grew and became the local, centralized areas for worshipers. The Abbey Church of St. Vincenzo was constructed in 809 and was 330 feet long. These large structures predate the great cathedrals by 200 years.

Early chant was characterized by syllabic structure and free rhythm. Syllabic structure represents the melodies free of metric influences and containing one note for each syllable of text. Free rhythm represents the melodies that do not contain a regular, recurring pattern of accented and unaccented beats that creates meter.

Early chants were written in Medieval modes. Each mode possesses a unique and definite set of characteristics and intervals. Each mode possesses a **reciting tone**, which carries the bulk of the melody. The reciting tone, usually a fifth above the **final** or **resting tone**, reflects the rule that ascending melodies create tension and descending melodies release tension. Therefore, chants tend to begin on a tone, ascend to the reciting tone, and then descend to the final. Early chants do not attempt to be artistic or expressive but functional and practical.

The Mass

The Catholic Church in Europe developed an intense, systematic method of worship called the **Mass**. The Mass is the most important service within the Catholic Church. The term *Mass* is also applied to musical settings of the texts of the Ordinary of the Mass. The Mass is concise and broad, predictable and comprehensive, and is divided into two sets of texts, the **Ordinary** and the **Proper**. The Ordinary contains the texts that remain constant in every service, regardless of seasons or occasions. The Proper contains the texts that change each week, following a three-year plan called the **Liturgical Year**.

The Liturgical Year is a calendar highlighting all meaningful passages of the Bible, important events in the life of Christ, and the essential doctrines of the Catholic Church. Therefore, the resulting service is a blend of well-known texts and changing texts that are responsive and passive and with little activity from the congregation. Priests, soloists, and/or small choirs are the primary singers.

Text of the Ordinary

Kyrie—*Lord, have mercy. Christ, have mercy. Lord, have mercy.*

Gloria—*Glory to God in the highest and peace to his people on earth ....*

Credo—*I believe in one God, the Father, the Almighty ....*

Sanctus—*Holy, Holy, Holy, Lord, God of power and might ....*

Agnus Dei—*Lamb of God who takest away the sins of the world, have mercy upon me.*

Text of the Proper

Prayers—Season specific and spread throughout the service

Old Testament Lesson

Psalm

New Testament Lesson

Gospel Lesson

Hymns—May or may not be congregational

Homily—Sermon

Liturgical Year

To some extent, most Christian denominations follow the Liturgical Year calendar. The focal points of the calendar are outlined in the following list as they pertain to the important events in the life of Christ.

Advent—The forty days of preparation before Christmas.

Christmas—The birth of Christ.

Epiphany—The season of celebration immediately after Christmas.

Ash Wednesday—The church holy day that begins the season of Lent.

Lent—The forty days, not counting Sundays, of preparation before Easter The forty days recount the forty days of Christ's preparation before his crucifixion.

Palm Sunday—The Sunday before Easter Sunday marks the day Christ entered Jerusalem and is welcomed as the one who will over throw the Roman Empire.

Maundy Thursday—In the afternoon, Christ shares the "Last Supper" with the apostles. Christ then goes to the garden to pray and is arrested.

Good Friday—The day of Christ's crucifixion.

Easter Sunday—The day of Christ's resurrection.

Ascension Day—The forty days following Easter, celebrated the sixth Sunday after Easter and marks the day of Christ's ascension into heaven.

Pentecost Day—The Sunday after the Ascension marks the day the Holy Spirit descended on the apostles.

Secular Music

The Romanesque secular music evolved from the hands of traveling minstrels or entertainers. Each region of Europe had their own traveling minstrels who would compose songs and dances and perform for local wealthy patrons. The minstrels were named according to the region of their residency: the **Troubadours**, from southern France; the **Trouveres**, from northern France; and **Minnesingers**, from German-speaking regions. The music is distinguished by the varying languages and musical elements, but it provides the same entertainment for their patrons. Much of this music has disappeared due to the lack of written traditions.

In several ways, secular music evolved faster than sacred music. Minstrel songs possessed regular rhythmic patterns, strong downbeats, and melodic shapes that were contrary to the free rhythm of the sacred chants. The musical texture of the minstrel songs was generally homophonic, meaning one melody with supporting harmony. Most often, the lute or some other plucked-string predecessor of the guitar presented the harmony.

The subject matter of the minstrel songs included a few consistent topics. The ever-popular love songs reflected the basic human aspiration to give and receive love. Dawn songs described a knight's chivalry in preparing for battle and leaving his maiden in the morning. For the wealthy patrons, songs of flattery assured the singers of a good payment.

Summary

The Romanesque period was characterized by conflict and disorder. The Catholic Church maintained a steadfast hold on society by providing the only stable element of culture. Therefore, throughout this period, the Catholic Church was the primary agent of musical development. Music was first created for practical purposes. Later, music became more artistically inclined.

VOCABULARY

Advent	Gothic Period	Ordinary of the Mass
Agnus Dei	Homily	Palm Sunday
Ascension Day	Hymns	Pentecost Day
Ash Wednesday	Intone	Prayers
Chant	Kyrie	Proper of the Mass
Christmas	Lent	Psalm
Credo	Liturgical Year	Reciting Tone
Easter Sunday	Mass	Resting Tone
Epiphany	Maundy Thursday	Romanesque Period
Final Tone	Minnesingers	Sanctus
Gloria	Monophonic Plainchant	Troubadours
Good Friday	New Testament Lesson	Trouveres
Gospel Lesson	Old Testament Lesson	

WEBSITE

Please refer to the *Music Through Time* site listed in the front of your book to investigate and complete more classroom activities and assignments.

CHAPTER
7
Gothic Period (1100–1430)

The Gothic period pertains to the last three centuries of the Medieval Age. These centuries gave birth to a revival from the oppression of the previous centuries. People became independent and intellectual. Cities were built around trade and commerce from the exchange of knowledge and ideas. For the first time, religious authority was viewed with skepticism as logic ruled every area of life and religion.

Humanism, the prevailing philosophy of the Gothic period, shifted the emphasis of daily life to secular notions. Religion and politics were greatly affected by the shift, forcing them to become more relevant to common life. Religion had long ignored the brutalities of life and prescribed only a salvation-based practice. Worshipers began to seek a more relevant style of religion that underscored human needs. The new humanism emphasized beauty. This new emphasis lead to struggles between the Catholic Church and society that continued well into the Renaissance.

The Gothic period also had turmoil and change. The Mongols conquered Eastern Europe and the 100 Years War between France and England disrupted the fourteenth Century. At the end of the fourteenth century, the Catholic Church was divided by a great Schism, meaning that two people were claiming to be Pope. Improvements gained through humanism were contradicted by the terror of the Black Death, or Bubonic Plague, which spread across Europe in the fifteenth Century.

Gothic art became more realistic and three-dimensional. Pointed arches, ribbed vaulting, and flying buttresses characterized architecture. These characteristics allowed for larger structures, higher ceilings, and wider spaces for windows and stained glass decorations. During this period, the great cathedrals of Europe were constructed and stood as a monument to Gothic intellect and industry. Construction of these great edifices took decades or longer.

Musical Style

Musical developments of the Gothic period led to artistic presentations of the monophonic chants. Syllabic chant gave way to **Neumatic chant,** groups of five or six notes per syllable, and **Melismatic chant,** groups of many notes for each syllable of text. Composers used melodic and rhythmic patterns to create more artistic gestures.

Abbess Hildegard von Bingen (1098–1179) developed a unique and personal style that used melodic patterns recurring in different modal positions. Her music was spiritual and more artistic than her predecessors. Hildegard's works are imbued by her deeply religious faith and optimistic spirit. She was a prolific composer and poet whose works are currently receiving high praise.

The Gothic secular music possesses rhythmic figures, accents, and regular metric patterns. Church musicians longed to bring these techniques into their sacred music without sacrificing the integrity of the chant. Their solution was to create **polyphonic music.** New musical styles occurred in secular music first and in sacred music last.

The most significant development of the Gothic period was that of polyphonic music, known as **organum.** The composers Leonin and Perotin worked at the Church of Notre Dame, Paris, predecessor to the cathedral, where early polyphony reached its highest development.

The simplest form of polyphony is **parallel organum**; the chant is accompanied by a second vocal line above. This parallel line moves at specific intervals above the chant and generally follows the shape and rhythm of the chant.

Florid organum allows the newly composed voice to move independently above the chant melody. Church composers could apply popular secular melodic techniques to the free voice. Altering the rhythm of the original plainchant allowed greater freedom and the addition of a second free voice. The resulting organum gave the melody of the chant to the lowest voice, which was the tenor, and lengthened one or more of its notes so that the original

Hildegard von Bingen's Liber Usualis cover
©Gianni Dagli Orti/CORBIS

chant became lost under the rhythmic and melodic voices occurring above.

Organum is not employed for the entire text of the Mass, but rather for select phrases. To worshipers, the result is a musical service maintained by the ancient chants with the addition of modern polyphonic styles before returning to the chant. This satisfied the desire of composers and worshipers to hear the modern sounding music in their church services.

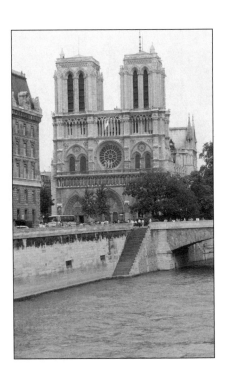

The style and technique of organum spread into other areas of music. Similar in style to the organum settings of the Mass is the **motet**. The motet is similar to organum by its multiple voices with a chant melody in the tenor voice. The motet is distinguished from organum by each of the upper voices having a different set of texts than the tenor-voiced chant. Composers used the motet as a means of expression and experimentation.

The fourteenth century, known as the **Ars Nova**, or New Art, seized upon opportunities to display technical prowess in compositions. The simple-minded predecessors, the **Ars Antiqua**, or Antique Art, were being rejected. Compositional techniques such as **hocket** and **isorhythm** were being developed in the motets of such composers as **Guillaume de Machaut**.

Machaut was a brilliant-minded composer with a myriad of skills. He composed one of the earliest polyphonic settings of the complete Ordinary of the Mass, as well as over 100 other compositions. His motet "Ma fin es ma commencement" is a musical palindrome, written the same forward and backward. This is the equivalent of writing a paragraph with a word order that inverts in the middle, but is still intelligible.

Machaut employed hocket and isorhythm in his motets, using different texts and languages for each individual part. The complexities of these compositions often obliterate the text and all meaning is lost under the burden of technique.

Instrumental Music

Instruments, instrumental forms, and instrumental techniques evolved more slowly than vocal genres. Stringed instruments developed the fastest, producing a family of sound through plucked instruments such as the lute and vihuela. These stringed instruments were primarily used to accompany singers of secular songs. Some sacred music employed brass and wind instruments to double voice parts. These instruments were not employed for individual performances. Instruments were combined to perform for entertainment, such as dances and various other secular compositions.

During the Gothic period, instrumental dances were improvised by the players. Many dances were cast in pairs, beginning with a slow duple meter dance, followed by a fast triple meter dance using the same melody. These improvised pieces have been lost due to the lack of written traditions.

The **estampie** is recognized as the most common dance of the thirteenth and fourteenth centuries. The dance consists of a number of phrases that are

immediately repeated. This formal structure directly relates to secular vocal music, which followed the same patterns.

Summary

The Gothic period created new emphasis on beauty and relevance. The music of this time was not only functional but also artistic. This period develops the first forms of polyphony, and it inspires composers to develop great technical skills. The detriment of evolution was that texts became subservient to skill and the meaning of the texts became lost under rhythmic and melodic complexities.

VOCABULARY

Abbess Hildegard von Bingen	Florid Organum	Motet
Ars Antiqua	Guillaume de Machaut	Neumatic Chant
Ars Nova	Hocket	Organum
Estampie	Isorhythm	Parallel Organum
	Melismatic Chant	Polyphonic Music

WEBSITE

Please refer to the *Music Through Time* site listed in the front of your book to investigate and complete more classroom activities and assignments.

CHAPTER

8

Renaissance Period (1430–1600)

The term *Renaissance* is recognized as meaning "rebirth." The historical period that bears the Renaissance name is marked by a renewed interest in the ideals and forms of classic antiquity, including new literary and design values. The writings of Ancient Greece and Rome became the measure for literature and new philosophies. Capitols and domes replaced the Gothic pinnacles, towers, and vaults. Interest in dignity and the value of man was an extension of Gothic Humanism. Worldly excellence and activity replaced the meditative reflection of earlier generations. Faith became subservient to reason and intellectualism. The Protestant Reformation, the English Reformation, and the Huguenot uprising divided the Catholic Church. Political rule was consolidated into powerful monarchs and aristocrats.

The church remained a leading patron of the arts, even through the growing population of secularists. Wealthy rulers and aristocrats became important

St. Peters

patrons as well. Music printing, especially of secular music, became more widespread. Publishing music was generally at the expense of the composer who did so to broaden his own reputation and to insure that the music was preserved long after his death. These elements reflect a broadening interest in music, along with a growing audience.

Renaissance art concentrates on the beauty of human forms such as works by Raphael and da Vinci. These works are refined, three-dimensional, and more realistic than those of the Gothic era.

The Renaissance was an age of discovery as well. Columbus discovered the new world in 1492, Copernicus studied the heavens to more accurately describe the movement of the planets and stars, and the first English colonies were established.

For the first time in history, the Catholic Church was traumatized with division. Martin Luther, a Catholic Priest, posted his infamous ninety-five theses in Wittenberg in 1517. He hoped to convince church leaders that certain Catholic practices were not Biblical and needed to be dissolved. Church leaders saw Martin Luther and his theses as a threat to their authority, thus renouncing Luther. However, Luther's congregation sided with their young priest and began to observe his teachings. This rebellion throughout central Europe became known as the Protestant Reformation.

A second division occurred seventeen years later, as King Henry VIII of England sought a second divorce. The Pope refused his request. Not willing to be denied, Henry declared all churches in England to be no longer Catholic, but the "Church of England." Henry proclaimed the English ruler, whether King or Queen, to be the new ruler of the church, and therefore proceeded to grant himself a divorce. The English Reformation was the beginning of conflict between Catholics and Protestants that continues today.

The sixteenth and seventeenth centuries experienced a third and less traumatic event involving French Protestants known as the Huguenots. The Huguenots were involved in political and religious turmoil and were driven out of France in 1685. Many of the Huguenots came to the English colonies in America and integrated into the British population, abandoning their separate churches and French language.

Both reformations that separated the Catholic Church were assisted by previous practices of allowing towns to build, maintain, and own their church structures while Rome supplied the priests. This allowed individual congregations to determine which doctrine to follow.

The reformations allowed new developments within music and precipitated changes within the Catholic Church. Composers could choose between the two denominations, however, some composed for both. The new Lutheran Church began to shift the emphasis of their services from passive and responsive to active involvement. Martin Luther generated additional congregational singing through the creation of Lutheran hymns or **chorales**. These hymns became well known to worshipers and provided a musical genre for Lutheran composers.

Musical Style

Renaissance music reflects a common style that became highly refined and widespread. Although tempos were not yet indicated, rhythms are notated in regular meters. Differing forms of vocal music are emphasized and involve a blend of **imitative polyphony** and **homophony**. Southern European imitation is not as strict as in the Franco-Flemish School of composition to the North. Composers tend to develop short ideas and points of imitation that can generate forward motion without extended **canons**. These points of imitation start the voices in a passage and then blend into homophonic harmony, creating a change of texture or highlighting the text. Many complex devices of the Gothic period, such as hocket and isorhythm, were replaced by beauty and purity in the vocal lines. Various vocal compositions were performed with instrumental accompaniment while other compositions were performed **a cappella**.

The last generation of Gothic composers refined the Ars Nova ideas into a convincing style. **Guillaume Dufay**, a master of secular and sacred music, led the Burgundian School, the first generation of Renaissance composers. He sang in the Papal choir and held several important positions. He significantly contributed to the development of **faux-bourdon** and the **cyclic mass**.

Dufay harmonized hymns from chant melodies. First, he set the melodies into regular metric patterns. Secondly, he added melody notes to cover skips and create a gentle flow. Thirdly, he used faux-bourdon to create a harmony part. Lastly, he added a third line to complete the harmony. Performances of the harmonized hymns were in alternation of the original chant, creating a blend of old and new and maintaining a sacred quality.

The Franco-Flemish School of Composition, in Northern Europe, stressed **strict imitation**, or canon, as a means of developing vocal lines. This style was culminated in the works of **Johannes Ockeghem** (1410–1497). Ockeghem composed the *Missa prolationum*, prolation mass, as a series of double canons, two canons occurring simultaneously. Ockeghem wrote only two original parts and provided performer indications for how and when to begin. The opening of "Sanctus," from the *Missa prolationum*, is a clear double canon. The bass and **tenor** begin simultaneously as two leaders, the countertenor then imitates the bass, and the soprano imitates the countertenor. Both imitators are a sixth interval above their respective leaders. All four parts continue until the imitators reach their final notes.

Josquin Desprez (1445–1521) was master of the Renaissance style. His music is a blend of imitative polyphony and homophony. His vocal lines are beautiful and singable. His points of imitation are only a few measures in length, avoiding long lines of canonic imitation. Josquin's setting of "Ave Maria" displays his attention to these elements. His points of imitation overlap, creating polyphonic interest and forward motion. To balance these elements, he composes two-part textures that are imitated in the two remaining voices. The performance is a cappella.

The Catholic Church reacted to the Reformations by forming the Council of Trent (1545–1563). The Council was a gathering of Catholic Church leaders to discuss problems, correct abuses, and return to sacred causes. The church leaders eliminated the addition of texts to the Mass, purged the service of secular

Giovanni Pierluigi de Palestrina
©Michael Nicholson/CORBIS

contents, and corrected other non-Biblical practices of the church. They considered returning service music to the original chants of the sixth and seventh centuries but were convinced to retain polyphony by a Roman composer.

The composer **Giovanni Pierluigi da Palestrina** worked as a singer and composer in Rome. He wrote a Mass dedicated to Pope Marcellus, which convinced church leaders to retain polyphony but clarify the text. Palestrina achieved clarification of text through the use of homophonic texture, imitative polyphony, and texts that do not overlap. Points of imitation were designed to declare each syllable of the phrase before the next voice would enter. Palestrina emphasizes the beauty of vocal lines and their textures. He composed unique choruses of five and six voices, echoes, and provocative harmonies.

Orlando di Lasso, sometimes known as Orlandus Lassus, was born in the Netherlands. He became a prolific composer and international figure by writing sacred masses, motets, and Italian, French, and German secular songs. His musical style was shaped by secular music that possessed emotional content and text painting. Lasso followed the natural accentuation of words. He also created gentle moving patterns of accents in separate and contrasting voices. Counterpoint is present, but not strict.

Few great composers resided in England, therefore art and music was generally imported from central Europe. **William Byrd** was one of the great composers in England during the Renaissance period. Because of his great composing skill, he was given preferential treatment by the royal family to produce works for the Anglican and Catholic churches.

The **madrigal** was a secular song, cultivated in Italy, and popular throughout Europe. Because of the highly developed form, the madrigal is similar to the sacred motet. The text, serious or amorous, revolved around love or the pursuit of love. Madrigals often employed "fa-la-la" choruses and possessed **text painting**. The madrigal "Fair Phyllis I Saw" by John Farmer (1565–1605) is based on a short love poem. Text painting depicts the words "all alone" with a single voice, "up and down he wandered" with wandering lines of imitation, and "fell a kissing" with a metric shift, evoking a spontaneous fall together. The texture consists of four voices.

Andrea Gabrielli and his nephew, **Giovanni Gabrielli**, were musicians at the great Cathedral of St. Mark's in Venice. The cathedral enjoyed rich traditions of musical excellence and embraced the use of musical instruments accompanying voices. To achieve large sounds, Giovanni Gabrielli composed music employing **polychoral** writing. The stereophonic effect would have been majestic as it rose from the galleries of St. Mark.

St. Marks

VOCABULARY

A Cappella
Andrea Gabrielli
Canons
Chorales
Countertenor
Cyclic Mass
Faux-bourdon

Giovanni Gabrielli
Giovanni Pierluigi da
Palestrina
Guillaume Dufay
Homophony
Imitative Polyphony
Johannes Ockeghem

Josquin des Prez
Madrigal
Orlando di Lasso
Polychoral
Strict Imitation
Text Painting
William Byrd

WEBSITE

Please refer to the *Music Through Time* site listed in the front of your book to investigate and complete more classroom activities and assignments.

CHAPTER

9

Baroque Period (1600–1750)

Life and Times

In musical terms, the period of time between 1600 and 1750, the death date of J. S. Bach, is considered to be the Baroque period. Musically, the Baroque reflects many elements of all of European life during those years. It is a time dominated with opulence, pomp, ornamentation, and excess. Much of this influence comes from the example set by the dominant political monarch of the period—**Louis XIV** of France (1638–1715). Known as the "Sun King," Louise XIV enjoyed a seventy-two year uninterrupted reign beginning in 1643 at the age of five. It was the longest in European modern history.

In historical terms, however, this period of time is known as the Age of Absolutism. This name refers to the absolute power that Louis XIV held over his people and nobles. He brought France to its peak of political power and he

Louis XIV
©The Art Archives/CORBIS

declared, "L'etat c'est moi" which translates "I am the state," expressing the reality of his absolute power.

In the Palace of Versailles, Louis began to embody French political power, economic growth, and military might. He lavished upon himself and his sumptuous palace the finest designs in architecture, painting, sculpture, and even gardening that could be acquired. All the gilded excesses were justified as a representation of the power and superiority of the French people—and he as their head. The process of his getting up in the morning and dressing became so ritualized and excessive that it required several servants and almost two hours!

France's economy, led by **Jean-Baptiste Colbert**, was the envy of all of Europe. France increased its wealth and influence over its neighbors with its colonies in the "New World" of North America, constantly sending back to the Motherland riches in goods and trade. Louis' neighbors, Spain, Great Britain, the Ottoman Empire, the Holy Roman Empire, and the Austrian Empire, all followed his lead in the patronage of artisans and craftsmen, thus creating an environment of monarchial patronage of the arts that would result in an explosion of created works and artifacts throughout Europe.

Science

Investigations into science led to expanded ideas and developments throughout this time period. Historic and familiar names of scientists and their achievements fill these years. The mission of these bold explorers was to break away from the model of scientific assumptions that dominated the old world's thinking, and instead, use a system of observations and experiments to create hypotheses about the reality of nature and its lawful workings. Much of what these people "discovered" shook the foundations of religion that depended on the older models of scientific assumptions as proof of dogma, belief, and the infallibility of church doctrine.

Galilei Galileo (1564–1642), born in Pisa, Italy, is regarded as the founder of modern science. Condemned by the Catholic Church for his discoveries using his refracting telescope that could see craters on the moon, observe the moons of Jupiter, and the phases of Venus, he developed the notion that the planets revolved around the sun rather than the Earth. His science was considered religious heresy.

William Harvey was born in 1578 and became an English physician. As doctor to King Charles I of England, he was famous as the discoverer of the function of the heart as a pump and the circulation of blood throughout the body.

Sir Isaac Newton (1642–1727), is one of the great names in history. He was born in Woolsthorpe, England, and graduated from Cambridge, where he would go on to become Professor of Mathematics. Newton wrote *Philosophiae naturalis principia*, supplying a complete proof of gravitational laws. He also developed a new branch of mathematics known as calculus and invented the reflecting telescope.

Galilei Galileo
©Bettmann/CORBIS

The Arts

In the arts, mainly in architecture, painting, and sculpture, there was enormous activity. Due to monarchial patronage as modeled by Louis XIV of France, all countries patronized artisans and gave them the task of creating and adorning the worlds they ruled. Energy, movement, and mastery of space and dimension were primary concerns of these artists as they fulfilled their tasks. Virtuosity, or unusual masterful skill, in all the arts was expected and rewarded.

Sculptors, using the techniques and innovations of **Giovanni Bernini** (1598–1680), found ways to create the illusion of energetic movement in their works. As an architect, sculptor, and painter, Bernini was key to the development of the Baroque style. His most important work is considered to be the colonnade that encloses the piazza outside St. Peters in Rome.

Frans Hals, a Dutch painter born in 1581, is considered one of the greatest portrait artists of the seventeenth century. Living most all his life in Haarlem, he became the portraitist of the Dutch bourgeoisie. Hals created a technique that predates impressionism and is similar in its looseness. He influenced Edouard Manet with his free style and Vincent van Gogh with his subtle range of colors.

Another Dutch painter, **Jan Vermeer** (1632–1675), usually painting middle-class people in simply furnished rooms, created an atmosphere of quiet, timeless happiness in his canvases. His use of soft light and the slightly blurred outlines of his forms highlight his technique that employs his favorite colors, blue and yellow.

Sir Christopher Wren (1632–1723) was a child prodigy, making contributions to anatomy, astronomy, mechanics, and mathematics all before the age of sixteen. As an architect in London, he was chosen to rebuild many churches, including St. Paul's Cathedral after the Great Fire (1666). Wren's attentions were monopolized by this reconstruction project. Taking thirty years, it kept him from his scientific activities.

Writers

Poets and writers also did much influential work during the Baroque period. **John Bunyan** (1628–1688), the English religious writer who became a Baptist and preacher for which he was imprisoned, wrote his famous religious tract "Pilgrim's progress" from jail. **Marie Lafayette** (1634-1693) wrote some of the first early novels from Paris. She chose to publish them anonymously in order to ensure their success and publication. Forming a literary circle there, she wrote her masterpiece *La Princess de Cleves*. Also from France, poet **Jean de Lafontaine** (1621–1695) is best known for his many fables (tales), placing him among the greatest writers of French literature.

London born poet **John Milton** (1608–1674) wrote many pamphlets addressing the radical idea of personal liberties during the Commonwealth period. Much of his life was devoted to poetry which produced the famous *Paradise Lost*.

French dramatist **Jean Baptiste Racine** (1639–1699) was a master playwright of the period. Inspired by the classical Greek tragedy, he began to write plays in 1664. The production of his 1667 masterpiece, *Andromaque*, became one of the most important events of French theater history. Continuing to produce six more epic plays, including *Britannicus*, *Bajazet*, and *Berenice*, Racine became regarded as the master of tragic pathos. The great actress Sarah Bernhardt won significant fame playing the lead in Racine's most famous play, *Phedre*.

Jonathan Swift (1667–1745), an Irish writer born in Dublin, became the greatest satirist in the English language. Moving to England, he became secretary to the diplomat Sir William Temple. His writings are almost all political, including the notable work *Gulliver's Travels* which is a biting satire on man in society.

Summary

While much of the created works of the Baroque fulfill the requests of monarchial patronage, writers, artists, and musicians found a way to infuse their functional works with personal ideas. Inspired by the ideas of personal experimentation and observation used by the scientific community, the artists chose paths of creativity that honored craftsmanship as well as personal development and individual statement.

Writers tackled ideas of social change, even though some did so indirectly and fictiously. Painters made the subjects more human, evoking more of the individual's personality in their canvases. Sculptors were able to capture more dramatic action and an increased dimension of depth and space in their pieces. Architects meshed scientific laws with functional beauty in their buildings.

Music would also reflect these individualistic expressions even in an environment of impersonal craftsmanship prevalent during this time period. This would open the doors to experimentation and formal development that are a hallmark of Baroque music, as seen in the next chapter.

VOCABULARY

Frans Hals	Jean de Lafontaine	Louis XIV
Galilei Galileo	Jean-Baptiste Colbert	Marie Lafayette
Giovanni Bernini	John Bunyan	Sir Christopher Wren
Jan Vermeer	John Milton	Sir Isaac Newton
Jean Baptiste Racine	Jonathan Swift	William Harvey

WEBSITE

Please refer to the *Music Through Time* site listed in the front of your book to investigate and complete more classroom activities and assignments.

CHAPTER

10

Baroque Genres

During the Baroque period, the musician and composer earned his living in one of three ways: as an employee of the church, the court, or the opera house—many times in a combination of two or more. Royal patronage of the arts and specifically patronage of musicians was a matter of course. The church, too, both Catholic and Protestant, had an extended history of arts patronage and sponsorship. Even the opera house rose to provide entrepreneur composers and producers the opportunity for commercial profit through ticket sales to the general public.

Instrumental Music

The historical significance of the Baroque period is witnessed in the importance of instrumental music. For the first time, music performed on instruments, most often with dizzying technical skill, became of equal importance and acceptance as that of vocal music. The increase in the importance of instrumental music performance and the complexity and variety of pieces written for groups of instrumentalists, as well as soloists, can first be attributed to the increase in the numbers of instrument makers and in the quality of their work.

More and better instruments were available than ever before, perfecting the craftsmanship of the string instruments as well as the keyboard instruments, and the development of new instruments, especially in the woodwinds, was seen as well. Never before had so much creativity and innovation taken place in the manufacturing sector, giving such a wide variety of color choices to performers and composers.

The composers responded by writing more complex and technically difficult pieces for players to perform. This led to a competition of sorts among players who vied for the attention and praises of the audiences, culminating in an atmosphere of virtuosity among the instrumentalists that was both amazing and wonderful at the same time.

Instrumentalists were expected by their audiences to be skillful and impressive in the technique as well as their mental creativity. Players were expected to improvise or spontaneously create, melodically and harmonically, especially keyboard players of harpsichord and organ, the two most commonly used keyboard instruments. Those players who could think, perform, and impress on the spot in a performance environment were highly valued. Often improvisational competitions occurred among rival players to secure public acclaim and position. Much of the instrumental literature of this time period have elements of virtuosic display embedded in them.

The Orchestra

Composers turned out pieces for instrumentalists at a furious rate to fill the audience's demand for this dazzling display in church music, in the opera house, and in the court. Given the expected improvisational abilities of the keyboard players, composers adopted a time-saving device in the compositional process known as **figured bass** in order to quicken their output of composed works. Since Baroque musical interest is chiefly melodic, and harmony, primarily major and minor tonalities, serves as support and foundation to that melody, composers developed a practice of grouping together those instruments that would provide the harmonic and rhythmic elements of the music in a single unit called the **continuo**. The continuo is comprised of a polyphonic instrument capable of playing more than one note at the same time, most often a keyboard (organ or harpsichord) or lute, and a bass instrument, most often the cello but also seen is the bassoon, trombone, or other low melodic instrument. In tandem, these two are responsible for the chordal harmony, the general rhythm, and the bass line, or lowest melodic voice. Together, these instruments create for Baroque music a similar function as a rhythm section, without drums, in today's music.

Composers would write the music for the continuo instruments in a code known as the figured bass. The figured bass is comprised of a low melodic line combined with numeric symbols underneath the notes of that melody, indicating other notes that would be added to the single note melody provided. The processing of those numeric symbols into a multi-note tonal sonority is referred to as *realizing* the figured bass. The keyboard or lute player executed this realization.

In combination with the harmonic and rhythmic core of the continuo, composers would write polyphonic melodies that would be assigned to various instruments, primarily from the string family, creating the standard orchestra for the Baroque period. On occasion, additional woodwind, brass, or percussion instruments would be added to the orchestra to heighten the ceremonial or theatrical effect.

The Concerto Grosso

One of the most popular and functional forms developed during this period, also serving the public's desire for virtuosic technical display, was the **concerto grosso**. Developed in Italy, the concerto grosso was a multiple **movement** form with a standardized three-movement design using tempos of fast—slow—fast. This formal device used a group of soloists, called the concertino, pitted against the larger remaining members of the orchestra, called the ripieno. Melodic sections of this formal structure would see a battle of these competing forces play out in an energetic or lyrical manner. Vivaldi's *Four Seasons* is a collection of four concerto grossos, each bearing the names of different seasons, Spring, Summer, Autumn, and Winter, comprising his most famous work. Bach also composed a set of famous concerto grossos called the Brandenburg Concertos.

The Dance Suite

Another popular genre for the emerging Baroque orchestra was the **dance suite**. Comprised of multiple dances of varying amounts, using differing rhythmic patterns and meters, and often preceded by a preparatory piece called a **French overture,** the dance suite became one of the most popular instrumental genres for the orchestra. This was music for listening rather than for social dancing even though the rhythmic patterns were taken from popular social dances from prior eras, such as the **allemande**, the **courante**, the **sarabande**, and the **gigue** as a standard grouping. There was also the possible inclusion of the **pavan**, the **galliard**, the **saltarello**, the **gavotte**, the **minuet**, the **siciliana**, the **bourree**, or even the **air**.

Handel's popular *Water Music* and his *Music for the Royal Fireworks* are both suites. Bach and Purcell, too, composed suites in their extensive outputs.

The Fugue

The most complex and purely absolute music genre in this period is the **fugue**. The term *fugue* may refer to a noun, meaning a specific genre of polyphonic music construction, or it may be encountered as an adjective, fugal, meaning in the manner of this polyphonic writing style. In either case, the essence of what is meant by the term is a multi-voiced imitative texture based on a single motive called the **subject.** The fugue's subject will be a short melodic motive that is introduced alone and then reintroduced at higher or lower intervallic levels while continuing to mesh in a harmonious way with the first melodic line that is continuing to evolve and be heard. This layering creates a texture of similar melodies sounding horizontally that also fit together vertically. During a fugue, the introducing of the first melodic motive, the spinning out of the various transpositions of that motive in a given number of voices, and the cadencing of those melodic ideas, all take place in sections known as **episodes**. A fugue uses these larger sectionalized episodes to piece together the logical extensions of the melodic ideas into a cohesive whole. Often, a fugue will be preceded by an unrelated and sometimes lyrical but short piece called a **prelude**.

J.S. Bach was the master of the fugue, employing the specific genre as well as the writing style in many of his vocal and instrumental compositions during his lifetime. He even wrote a treatise now called *The Art of Fugue* toward the end of his life, exploring every conceivable way that a fugue could be composed.

Vocal Music Genres

Opera

The musical experimentation and personal technical skill that composers in the Renaissance thrived upon led the way for the creation of the greatest musical form of the Baroque period—opera. **Opera** is a combination of theater, music, and story. In the early days of development, it often included dance as well. Theatrical techniques of acting, elaborate set design, and costuming combined with elements of singing and instrumental musical performance prowess and mingled with the power of epic story telling to produce the grandest and most emotionally charged entertainment form ever developed.

Opera is the product of differing influences. Its earliest known forerunners (prior to the Baroque period) were medieval church pageants called miracle, mystery, or morality plays. These often included provisions for vocal solos, choruses, instrumental interludes, and theatrical production elements, such as sets and costumes. In Italy, pageants and descendants of the mystery plays began to serve nonreligious purposes. Often employing the device of stringing existing madrigals together within the framework of a loosely attached storyline, subjects often included the Greek myths of Orpheus and Daphne, which later became the basis for several of the earliest operas.

In 1598, **Jacopo Peri** wrote *Dafne*, the first true opera. In 1600, Peri composed *Euridice* for a royal wedding celebration. In Florence, Italy, there existed a society of intellectuals known as the **Camerata**, which included poets, amateur musicians, and scholars. The purpose of the Camerata was to recreate the emotional impact and power that had been mythologized in the storytelling epics of the fabled Greek tragedies. Peri was a member of the Camerata. For twenty years, the Camerata researched the manner in which classical Greek drama had been performed, and Peri made attempts at reviving it. They concluded that the Greek actors had delivered their lines in a declamatory style, halfway between speaking and true singing. They also hypothesized that rather than the vocal chorus, as had been used in church music and in courtly madrigals, it was only through the solo voice that the most powerful emotional impact could be made on an audience. His efforts to recover this lost art resulted not in a recreation, but rather a new type of solo singing, called **monody**, that was performed in free rhythm to simple accompaniment. Peri, in his failure to recreate older performance practice, actually opened the door to the operatic form.

It fell to another man, however, to realize the full potential of this drama through music. **Claudio Monteverdi**, born in Cremona, Italy, composed his own operatic version of the Orpheus and Euridice myth, in his *Orfeo*. Whereas Peri wrote the first opera, Monteverdi's was the first masterpiece of opera. He expanded the orchestra, including strings, harpsichord and organ, trumpets and drums for ceremonial passages, and recorders. He gave each character a dis-

tinctive accompaniment, developed a more extensive recitative style, and included an overture.

Opera meshed into a form that told its drama through musical tools known as **recitative**, **aria**, and **chorus**. While recitative and aria, in the early Baroque period, were vehicles for solo singers, on occasion large groups of singers, signifying many characters on stage, were used for more intensely dramatic or ceremonial scenes.

Recitative

The purpose of recitative is to portray action or dialogue between characters in the dramatic scene. Musically, it involves a solo singer intoning pitches that are in a ratio of one pitch per syllable of text. This singing form of "reciting," while not emotionally moving, is effective in the delivery of dialogue and plot in a manner that can be easily comprehended by the audience. Baroque opera included two types of recitatives—the **secco recitative**, meaning "dry" in that it was accompanied by harpsichord alone and it provided rhythmic freedom and flexibility for the drama in the moment, and the **accompanied recitative**, one that involved a more specific rhythm in the accompaniment from the whole orchestra.

Aria

The aria, also a vehicle for the solo voice, is where emotional reflection on the previous actions and dialogues takes place. Opera is the perfect vehicle for emotional intensity through drama, and it is in the aria where most of the emotion is produced. The aria is the place where the beautiful, memorable melodies occur as well. It provides a pause in the storytelling and allows the character being portrayed to reflect on the story's action and deliver to the audience an insight into his or her thoughts and feelings brought on by that action. This aspect of insight into the mind and emotions of a character is what a mere play cannot do.

Creating a new dimension in the storytelling process through aria, composers enthralled Baroque audiences. Venice, another city in Italy, saw the popularity of opera rise to such an extent that the first public opera house was opened there. Soon, in a town of 145,000 people, there were no less than seven public opera houses, making opera the immensely popular pastime it would become for all, not just the upper class.

The most popular form of aria in the Baroque era was the **da Capo aria**. Not wanting to be left out of the celebrity afforded virtuoso instrumental soloists of the day who were expected to improvise and display dazzling skills, singers also wanted a vehicle to show the virtuosity and uniqueness in their solo voices. The da Capo aria then became the perfect showpiece for them.

Whereas the aria mostly employed a binary, or A–B, form presented in one pass to move the story along singers insisted on repeating the first "A" section, affording them the opportunity to "ornament" the melody, now heard in the instruments. This repetition of a section of music that had already been heard allowed the singers to display their improvisational skills and extraordinary abilities to jump great leaps, trill, and perform fast scale passages. The audiences soon began to have their favorite singers, and these singers took on star status, commanding higher fees and receiving top billing, bringing about the stereotype of the **prima donna** or the **diva**.

Opera Seria

By the second half of the Baroque period, the most popular form of opera was called **opera seria**. Opera seria has a story, or **libretto** (meaning "the book"), that is derived from myths and legends. Portraying lofty emotions and virtuous characters involved in plots demonstrating moral choices of one kind or another, opera seria was designed to inspire the better natures of the audience. The **librettist**, the one who wrote or adapted a familiar tale into dramatic or musical form for the composer to set to music, often tailored a story to heighten just these sorts of emotions while still maintaining a sellable sense of drama to ticket buyers and patrons.

Oratorio

Similar to opera seria in form was the **oratorio**. While sharing the same musical tools of recitative, aria, and chorus, with orchestra to tell a dramatic story, the oratorio differed in the libretto. Most often, Bible stories such as the ones of Daniel, Noah, St. Paul, Jesus, the travails of the Israelites, or some other long and adventurous story would be the inspiration. Even epic tales of Julius Caesar, the Pharaohs, or some other historic character might be employed.

Other differences were evident, also, in that the oratorio was usually not staged, costumed, or acted out, but rather performed in a concert environment. While still using the performing forces of orchestra, solo singers, and chorus, the oratorio gave the church or the church-minded a similar emotional and dramatic form in which to heighten the emotion in stories familiar to them from the Bible. Oratorios would prove to be especially popular in England whose population has long adored choral music.

Passion

Similar to oratorio in that it employs a similar compositional format and similar performing forces, a **passion** differs in that its story or libretto is limited to the story of the life of Jesus, specifically the part of the story where he returns to Jerusalem knowing he will be arrested, tried, and crucified. Therefore, a Passion is in musical terms similar to an oratorio in scope, design, and performance practice, but with a libretto that is limited to the gospels version of the crucifixion. The most famous passions belong to J. S. Bach. He set one as told by St. Matthew and then another by St. John.

Chorale

In Germany, the land that saw the birth of the Protestant movement begun by Martin Luther, significant church music changes occurred. Part of the significance of the Lutheran church's reforms was to include more specific liturgical involvement by the congregation themselves during the worship services. Martin Luther chose the **chorale**, or hymn, as the vehicle for this reform. Protestant congregations vigorously sang chorale tunes throughout each service, many of which Luther composed. The chorale tune then would become a basic source of inspiration for more extended Lutheran church genres as time progressed. The **chorale prelude**, for example, is a solo organ piece built from the theme of a chorale.

Bach spent a great deal of time employing chorale tunes in his church music via cantatas, organ preludes, improvisations, and the like. It is no accident that in dealing with a set body of melodic content from which to draw, he would find ways to make the familiar tunes new and fresh. He did so through the reharmonization of these tunes, adding harmonic interest and freshness to well-used melodies.

Cantata

Another innovation of church music in the Lutheran tradition was the church **cantata**. The cantata is a form that is the musical equivalent of the sermon. Just as a sermon topic changes every Sunday according to the requirements of the church calendar year and its corresponding emphases, the cantata would reflect the sermon topic and calendar directives. It would use as its libretto appropriate scripture texts for that Sunday. Melodically, the tunes of chorales were often used as source material for the choruses, potentially in addition to the recitatives and arias. Bach's cantatas included standard performing forces of orchestra with continuo, vocal soloists, and choir. It was expected that the cantata be newly composed for each Sunday in the church year. With the cantata length being from twenty to forty minutes, this is an astounding compositional achievement. Even more so when you consider that Bach wrote over 200 cantatas alone.

VOCABULARY

Accompanied Recitative	Camerata	Claudio Monteverdi
Air	Cantata	Concertino
Allemande	Chorale	Concerto Grosso
Aria	Chorale Prelude	Continuo
Bourree	Chorus	Courante

da Capo Aria
Dafne
Dance Suite
Diva
Episodes
Euridice
Figured Bass
French Overture
Fugue
Galliard
Gavotte
Gigue

Jacopo Peri
Libretto
Libbretist
Minuet
Monody
Movement
Opera
Opera Seria
Oratorio
Orfeo
Passion
Pavan

Prelude
Prima Donna
Recitative
Ripieno
Saltarello
Sarabande
Secco Recitative
Siciliana
Subject
The Art of Fugue

WEBSITE

Please refer to the *Music Through Time* site listed in the front of your book to investigate and complete more classroom activities and assignments.

CHAPTER

11

Baroque Composers

The art of music in the Baroque period is advanced through the efforts of composers and their attempts to conceive, organize, edit, and produce abstract works of symbols that come alive in the hands of the performers. It is the composer who pushes the limits of the known possibilities as he toils in the reality of his environment—court, church, or public taste in the opera house. This chapter will bring to light a more personal look at some of the major figures in the time period between 1600 and 1750, showing their humanity, their industry, their decisions making, and their personality.

Claudio Monteverdi (1567–1643)

The baroque period actually begins with the work of **Claudio Monteverdi** who lives in between two artistic practices, the Renaissance and the Baroque. He belongs to both periods, becoming a swing figure and a conduit for change.

Born in Italy, he published his first pieces at the age of fifteen. Early, as a court musician, he concentrated on composing madrigals in the style of the "first art," or rather in the style of Palestrina, the giant figure of the Renaissance. Creating great fame for himself through his vocal compositions, it wasn't until he was forty that he composed his first opera, *Orfeo*, in Mantua, in 1607, ushering in what would be called the age of the "second art."

The second art, or the practices that would become known as the Baroque, was centered on an attention to the words in the text and drawing from them every bit of graphic melodic detail, innovative use of timbre, and affective inspiration possible. This was primarily the concern and achievement of Claudio Monteverdi. It was a concentrated extension of the word painting notions of the Renaissance.

In 1613, he was appointed head of choral music at the famed **St. Mark's Cathedral** in Venice, Italy. St. Mark's was a pillar of musical activity in Venice and had been since the Gabrielis had worked there during the Renaissance, expanding the use of instruments in their church compositions and taking advantage of the architecture of the cathedral to sparkling antiphonal effect. Monteverdi would remain in Venice for the rest of his life, working in the city famed for its church music innovations as well as a ravenous hunger for opera.

- Operas, including *Orfeo* (1607), *Arianna* (1608), *Il ritorno d'Ulisse* (*The Return of Ulysses*, 1640), and *L'incoronazione di Poppea* (1642); other dramatic music (1624)
- Secular vocal music, including nine books of madrigals (1587–1651, book nine was published posthumously)
- Sacred vocal music, including Vespers (1610), Masses, Magnificats, spiritual madrigals, motets, and psalms

Arcangelo Corelli (1653–1713)

Arcangelo Corelli was one of the great virtuoso violinists of his day. His skill as a performer allowed him to be employed in several influential court positions during his lifetime. Due to his interest in the performance and teaching of the string instruments, it is no wonder that he composed for them as well. Writing almost exclusively for the violin or string ensemble, Corelli pioneered some of the early Baroque forms such as the trio sonata and early solo sonatas for church usage or courtly chamber performance. His compositional efforts represent a developmental link in the evolution of the concerto grosso and sonata forms. Bach's instrumental style was clearly influenced by them, as was that of Corelli's other students, which included Handel.

Henry Purcell (1659–1695)

Henry Purcell was the most important English composer and keyboardist during the Baroque period. Spending his entire career as a musician for the English royal court, he started as a boy singer in the court chapel then moved along to become the appointed composer to the king. At twenty he became the organist for Westminster Abbey, and at twenty-three, organist to the Chapel Royal.

As composer for the church, he wrote over fifty anthems and other sacred pieces, including his famous *Ode to St. Cecelia*. In addition to his church position, Purcell possessed an interest in dramatic works and composed songs and accompanying music for plays. He would eventually go on to write short operas, which he considered to be royal entertainments, specifically his **Dido and Aenea**s and the larger **The Fairy Queen**.

Works

- Dramatic music, including *Dido and Aeneas* (1689) and *The Fairy Queen* (1692), incidental music for plays
- Sacred vocal music, including a Magnificat, Te Deum, and over fifty anthems
- Secular vocal music, including court odes

- Instrumental music, including fantasias, sonatas, marches, overtures, and harpsichord suites and dances

Antonio Vivaldi (1678–1741)

Antonio Vivaldi was a celebrated violinist as well as a prolific composer of music for strings and even opera. He is important for his establishment and codification of the Baroque concerto grosso, with its three movement—fast, slow, fast design—and its use of the ritornello form, repeating alternating passages between orchestral melody and sections that feature the solos.

Known as the "Red Priest" due to the color of his hair, Vivaldi was born in Venice, Italy, to a violinist appointed to St. Mark's Cathedral. As a child, he learned violin and developed harpsichord skills. Eventually joining the priesthood, he would spend the majority of his life as teacher of violin at the **Pio Ospedale della Pietà**, one of four orphanages for girls in Venice, which specialized in the girls' musical instruction.

The chapel services at the Pieta were more concert-like than religious events and the orchestra of girls who performed there developed a wide-ranging reputation for their skill and musicality. Much of their reputation was attributable to Vivaldi's skill as violin pedagogue and composer of works that fit the skills of the girls he taught there. He composed over 500 works in the concerto design, making him the most famous composer in this medium in all of Europe for a time, influencing even Bach himself. The most famous work in this genre is a set of four concerti grossi known as the *Four Seasons*. This set of works is an early manifestation of the program music that would dominate the Romantic period of the nineteenth century in that these concertos were specifically graphic in their attempts to emulate images contained in the corresponding poems for each.

He was dismissed for a period of two years, probably due to some economic crisis, but so effective were his teaching techniques at the orphanage that the older girls were able to continue the instruction of the younger ones. When he was rehired, Vivaldi held the title of Concert Master, giving him control over the direction of the orchestra and its concerts as well. Soon he would begin to write sacred music for the chapel for which he wrote over thirty motets, Vespers music, and a Mass. Given his more established position and influence at the Pieta, Vivaldi began to travel.

He began composing operas and on occasion traveled to supervise their performances in different cities. The successes of these resulted in acclaim and honorary titles for him, but his position with the church and the Pieta was eventually marred by a continuing suspicion that he was involved with a young woman named Anna, a singer and former pupil of the orphanage who, along with her sister, could often be found traveling with him. A relationship that he denied was improper in any way, it caused his job with the church to be strained, and he was forced to depend on his operatic works alone for income, and these eventually began to fail to support him.

On July 28, 1741, he died in a boarding house in Vienna where he perhaps was attending an opera performance of Anna's. Due to his wildly extravagant lifestyle which left him short of funds in the end, he was given a pauper's burial that same day.

Works

- Orchestral music
  - Over 239 violin concertos, including *Le quattro stagioni* (*The Four Seasons*, Op.8, Nos.1–4, c.1725)
  - Other solo concertos (bassoon, cello, oboe, flute, recorder)
  - Double concertos
  - Ensemble concertos
  - Sinfonias
- Chamber music
  - Sonatas for violin, cello, and flute
  - Trio sonatas
- Vocal music
  - Oratorios (*Juditha triumphans*, 1716)
  - Mass movements (*Gloria*)
  - Magnificat
  - Psalms, hymns, and motets
- Secular vocal music, including solo cantatas and operas

Georg Friedrich Handel 1685–1759

Born in Halle, Germany, only fifty miles from the birthplace of J. S. Bach, **Georg Friedrich Handel** became the most famous and important English composer of the Baroque period. As an organist and harpsichordist and violinist, Handel became violinist and composer at Hamburg's German opera at the age of seventeen. In 1706, he traveled to Italy to study opera and stayed until his return to Germany in 1710 to take a position as Music Director at the Court of Hanover. Requesting a leave of absence very soon after his appointment in Hanover to travel to England to oversee a production of his opera, *Rinaldo*, he would return to Hanover an international success as an opera composer. In 1712, Handel was granted a second leave to England with the order to return in a reasonable period of time. Two years would pass and still see him in England!

During Handel's two-year absence, his employer in Germany, the Elector of Hanover, would become King of England, taking the title of George I. This would make Georg's fame and flexibility in London awkward at best; so, upon hearing the news and hoping to divert his former employer's potential wrath towards his delinquent employee, Handel secretly composed a suite of music for winds, called the **Water Music**, to be performed by the orchestra on a royal river excursion. The king enjoyed the music so much that he asked for it to be repeated and was delighted to discover that Handel had composed it. All was forgiven and the way cleared for Handel to continue his access to the most affluent and influential of English society.

Georg Friedrich Handel
©Bettmann/CORBIS

Handel went on to become the Music Director for the Royal Academy of Music, which specialized in the presentation of Italian style opera, many of which he composed for the company. For several years, he was hugely successful and the toast of London, even becoming a naturalized citizen. A change in the public's taste for opera occurred in 1728, which would affect Handel's fortunes and artistic direction.

John Gay, a popular playwright in London, presented *The Beggar's Opera*, which went on to become the longest running play in the eighteenth century. Gay's opera actually was not an opera, but rather a play with spoken dialogue that had familiar tunes employed within it. These popular songs, some of which were tunes by Handel, had their words replaced by Gay to reflect aspects of his story and further his plot. Gay also used plots and characters that reflected common people, using thieves, whores, jailers, and so on, as chief subjects rather than the mythologies and legends frequently seen in opera seria librettos. The audiences loved it, demonstrating the beginning of the end of opera seria's dominance in public taste, at least in London.

Handel saw the writing on the economic wall and began looking for other genres in which to compose. He found his answer in the oratorio. Shifting his attention to the production of oratorio concerts, especially during specific church holiday seasons, Handel composed several popular oratorios, including *Messiah*—probably the most recognized piece of classical music in the world. Given England's love of choral music, Handel ensured his permanence in the accolades of music history.

Becoming blind toward the end of his life, Handel continued to compose with the aide of an assistant and to perform in public, as he was a celebrated organist like Bach. It is interesting to note that not only were Handel and J. S. Bach born in the same year, but they were born fifty miles apart, and both would be afflicted by cataracts in their declining years and treated by the same physician. He would collapse at the end of a performance of *Messiah* and die within three days.

Works

- Over forty operas, including *Almira* (1705), *Rinaldo* (1711), *Giulio Cesare* (*Julius Caesar*, 1724), and *Orlando* (1733)
- Oratorios, including *Esther* (1718), *Alexander's Feast* (1736), *Israel in Egypt* (1739), *Messiah* (1742), *Sampson* (1743), *Belshazzar* (1745), *Judas Maccabaeus* (1747), *Solomon* (1749), and *Jephtha* (1752); other sacred vocal music, including *Ode for the Birthday of Queen Anne* (c.1713), *Acis and Galatea* (masque, 1718), *Ode for St. Cecilia's Day* (1739), *Utrech Te Deum* (1713), anthems, and Latin church music
- Secular vocal music
- Orchestral music, including *Water Music* (1717) and *Music for the Royal Fireworks* (1749); concertos for oboe, organ, and horn
- Chamber music, including solo and trio sonatas
- Keyboard music, including harpsichord suites, fugues, preludes, airs, and dances

Johann Sebastian Bach (1685–1750)

Johann Sebastian Bach
©Bettmann/CORBIS

J. S. Bach is truly one of the greatest musical geniuses of all time. Born in Eisenach, Germany, into a family of musicians, Bach's parents died in his youth, leaving him to be raised by his older brother from whom he received his early musical training. Bach would excel at the keyboard and become a virtuoso organist and adviser to organ builders throughout his life. In his youth, Bach demonstrated his tenacity and single-mindedness by walking 200 miles just to hear an organ concert by the famed Buxtehude.

As a composer, he regularly studied other composers' works, as he did not travel extensively but rather copied and transcribed other famous pieces, often rearranging them for varying performance groups. In this way he learned the Italian and French styles, all the rage during the Baroque period. He was extremely prolific as a composer, being credited with the equivalent of thirty-two pages of score for every day of his life and all of it being of superb quality and craftsmanship. An admired improviser, Bach could improvise polyphonically in the genres of fugue or invention adding to his reputation as a renowned keyboardist; therefore, he is responsible for much more music than he ever wrote down.

Johann earned his living in the service of the Lutheran church in various German cities. His duties ranged from overseeing the choir schools and vocal educations of the boys who attended them, to composing, rehearsing, performing, and administering service music for as many as four churches simultaneously. Much of his church music output centered on the cantata, or musical sermon, that was expected to be newly composed each week. Bach had the task of conceiving the work, setting the text and having it approved, copying the parts, rehearsing the instrumentalists and vocalists, and performing the work on Sunday—only to begin again by Monday morning. He would compose over 200 cantatas in all but found time to compose in other genres as well. In fact, he composed in all genres of the period, both vocal and instrumental, except opera.

Bach's family included twenty children by two wives, many of whom did not live to adulthood. However, he would have three sons who also became important and famous composers in their day. These sons became instrumental in the changing of musical taste toward what would become the beginnings of the Classical period, leaving their father to languish in an older dying style.

Bach sits atop the entire march of progress and development in polyphonic music, establishing himself as the uncontested master of counterpoint, which would fall from favor even during his own lifetime. Nevertheless, he toiled in the composition and even the preservation of the historic thought established since Leonin and Perotin, polished by Palestrina, and mastered in his own hand. *The Art of Fugue*, *The Well-Tempered Clavier*, the *Musical Offering*, and even his *Mass in B Minor*, all point to the realization of himself at the end of an historic line of thought and his attempts for the preserving and cataloging of the discipline.

An extremely devout man, Bach saw himself as a craftsman rather than an individual personality. He viewed his skills as being of the highest caliber workmanship, but himself as only the humble servant trying to produce good work often in inadequate circumstances. What he achieved is of the highest order of reserved personal feeling, wrapped in the most challenging of forms in such a way as to create some of mankind's highest achievements in the field of music.

So much so in fact, that when NASA planned the Voyager 1 and Voyager 2 spacecrafts for deep space exploration, they included a solid gold recording of languages, natural sounds, and music from Earth. Now having traveled more than 13 billion miles from Earth on a path to explore deep regions where the sun's light cannot reach, Bach has three inclusions on that record, more than any other composer, representing the best of what mankind has achieved.

Works

- Sacred vocal works, including over 200 church cantatas, seven motets, *Magnificat* (1723), *St. John Passion* (1724), *St. Matthew Passion* (1727), *Christmas Oratorio* (1734), *Mass in B minor* (1749)

- Secular vocal works, including over twenty cantatas

- Orchestral music, including four orchestral suites, six *Brandenburg Concertos*, concertos for one and two violins, and for one, two, three, and four harpsichords

- Chamber music, including six sonatas and partitas for unaccompanied violin, six sonatas for violin and harpsichord, six suites for cello, *Musical Offering* (1747), flute sonatas, and viola da gamba sonatas

- Keyboard music, including two volumes of *Das wohltemperirte Clavier* (*The Well-Tempered Clavier*, 1722, 1742), six English Suites (c.1722), six French Suites (c.1722), *Chromatic Fantasy and Fugue* (c.1720), Italian Concerto (1735), *Goldberg Variations* (1741–1742), and *Die Kunst der Fuge* (*The Art of Fugue* c.1745–1750); suites, fugues, capriccios, concertos, inventions, sinfonias

- Organ music, including over 150 chorale preludes, toccatas, fantasias, preludes, fugues, and passacaglias

VOCABULARY

Antonio Vivaldi	Johann Sebastian Bach	*The Art of Fugue*
Arcangelo Corelli	*Mass in B Minor*	*The Fairy Queen*
Claudio Monteverdi	*Messiah*	*The Well-Tempered*
Dido and Aeneas	*Musical Offering*	*Clavier*
Four Seasons	*Orfeo*	*Water Music*
Georg Friedrich Handel	Pio Ospedale della Pietà	
Henry Purcell	St. Mark's Cathedral	

WEBSITE

Please refer to the *Music Through Time* site listed in the front of your book to investigate and complete more classroom activities and assignments.

CHAPTER
12
Classical Period Times and Events

The middle of the eighteenth century is one of the most remarkable times in modern history. New and radical ideas abounded. Most significantly, the Enlightenment, as this period before the French Revolution is called, marks one of the watershed achievements in human thought that would eventually change the world as time progressed. The Enlightenment is a name given to an idea. That idea was the notion that men were born with certain rights ... "life, liberty, and the pursuit of happiness." It was also a time that displayed a faith in human reason and human possibilities. Having been awed by Newton's discoveries regarding the laws of gravity, the notion developed that all of nature could be understood through observation and experimentation. Secular humanism, as this movement was called, was an attack on the stranglehold the church had on scientific thought. Freedom to observe, think, and experiment would provide the knowledge necessary for the building of a better, more enlightened world.

The Enlightenment

At the center of this idea was the French philosopher **Francois Marie Arouet**, who wrote political pamphlets, plays, and articles under the pen name of **Voltaire,** as well as an American statesman, **Thomas Jefferson**. Together with Swiss philosopher **Jean Jaques Rousseau,** who wrote *Discourse on the Origin and Foundations of Inequality Amongst Men* and *The Social Contract*, which introduced the slogan "Liberty, Equality, Fraternity," and the American statesman **Benjamin Franklin,** who was the only man to sign the three most important documents in U.S. history—the Declaration of Independence, the Peace Treaty of Paris in 1783 that ended the American Revolutionary War, and the Constitution of the United States of America in 1787—these four men would play an important role in the development and implementation of a new philosophical concept. Of course, the end result of the Enlightenment politically is the birth of a new nation, the most powerful nation in the world and ultimately the shaper of world events for more than the next 200 years—the Unites States of America.

The United States was born out of the conflict of ideas regarding the tyranny of English sovereign rule and the control and limitation of taxation on the colonists. Thomas Jefferson, who had been a representative to France from the colonies, was very familiar with the written works of the Enlightenment philosophers and used many of the ideas gleaned there in his authoring of the **Declaration of Independence**. The notion of self-rule and government by the people was a deliberate attempt to put enlightenment ideas into practice. As a result of the works of the authors listed previously, many of Europe's monarchs attempted to at least give the impression that they, too, were enlightened in their rule. While many of these rulers provided only lip service to the new ideas, several did seem to rule in a more enlightened way. Chief among these monarchs was the **Emperor Joseph II of Austria**. His rule and his court would open a haven for enlightened politics and artistic creation during the classical period in music.

The Industrial Revolution

The Industrial Revolution also coincided with the Enlightenment, helping to fuel the ideas of the rights of man. The Industrial Revolution refers to a time of manufacturing development and mechanization that made the production of goods cheaper and more plentiful, driving up profits and ultimately creating a middle class of people in Europe who were self-made and not titled or noble holdovers from the Renaissance court social structures. For the first time, there existed a class of workers, manufacturers, and tradesmen that possessed enough money to have leisure time. The luxury of leisure affords people the time to pursue education, entertainment, and personal contemplation over and above the pursuit of the necessities in an individual's life experience. This would be evidenced in the expansion of arts activities and arts consumption during this time period. The patronage and philosophies of this class would directly impact works created by Mozart and influence other composers as well.

Science

Science had spurred the philosophy of the Enlightenment and, given its social implications, science continued to move forward. Pioneers like **James Watt,** a Scotsman who started as an instrument maker and ultimately went on to make improvements to the new steam engine that helped the Industrial Revolution get off the ground, and **Adam Smith**, who is considered the father of modern economics and author of the text *The Wealth of Nations*, which introduced the concept of the capitalist free enterprise system, were active. **Charles Darwin**, author of *On the Origin of Species by Means of Natural Selection* that promoted the idea of evolution in animals through genetic mutation, and **Jean-Baptiste Lamarck**, a French biologist who published *Zoological Philosophy* in 1809 that advocated similar thoughts, were getting noticed for their work and ideas. Perhaps the most prolific mathematician of all time, **Leonhard Euler**, contributed new ideas in calculus, geometry, algebra, probability, and number theory. Through his work, many areas of applied mathematics, such as acoustics, optics, mechanics, astronomy, artillery, and navigation were expanded. A Swedish botanist, **Carolus Linnaeus**, developed a universal system for the naming of plants and animals according to genus and species, while chemist **Justus Liebig's** two books, *Organic Chemistry and its Application to Agriculture and Physiology* and *Organic Chemistry in its Application to Physiology and Pathology*, revolutionized food production. **Joseph Priestly** discovered oxygen, and **Alessandro Volta** developed a forerunner to the electric battery that produced a steady stream of electricity.

Arts

Francesco Guardi and **Francisco Goya** were painters during this time period. Guardi's "The Concert" portrays a scene of Venetian artistic life, while Goya's "The Shooting" portrays a social protest depicting man's inhumanity to man in the brutality of Napoleon's campaign with Spain.

Writers such as **Johann Wolfgang von Goethe**, the greatest of all German poets, wrote the drama, *Goetz von Berlichingen*, which captured the spirit of German nationalism. Also, **Johann Christoph Friederich von Schiller** ranks as one of the greatest figures of the age as dramatist, poet, and historian. His writings strive for human freedom and served as inspiration for German liberals in their fight for liberty during the early 1800s. His poem *Ode To Joy* was highlighted in Beethoven's 9th Symphony as the text for the choral finale in the fourth movement of the work.

Author **Jane Austen** grew up in the emerging middle class and developed the first novel, opening the door to the world of fiction through her works, *Sense* and *Sensibility, Mansfield Park, Emma,* and *Persuasion.* **Charles Dickens**, whose novels include *A Tale Of Two Cities, Great Expectations, Oliver Twist,* and *David Copperfield,* appealed to the public's social consciousness in an attempt to overcome its institutionalized misery. His popular works were attacks on abuses of the courts of law and schools who were not interested in justice or the education of its students, but rather in the lining of the pockets of its administrators.

Philosopher **Denis Diderot**, the chief editor of the French *Encyclopedie,* became a prolific writer, publishing novels, plays, satires, essays, and letters. His *Pensees Philosophiques* (Philosophical Thoughts) was burned by the Parliament of Paris for its anti-Christian ideas, and he was imprisoned for his *Lettre sur les aveugles* (Essay on Blindness). **Immanuel Kant**, one of the greatest philosophers of all time whose works offer an analysis of speculative and moral reason, saw his great works, *Critique of Pure Reason, Critique of Practical Reason,* and *Critique of Judgment,* published as well.

VOCABULARY

A Tale of Two Cities
Adam Smith
Alessandro Volta
Benjamin Franklin
Carolus Linnaeus
Charles Darwin
Charles Dickens
Critique of Judgment
Critique of Practical Reason
Critique of Pure Reason
David Copperfield
Declaration of Independence
Denis Diderot
Discourse on the Origin and Foundations of Inequality Amongst Men
Emma
Emperor Joseph II of Austria

Encyclopedie
Francesco Guardi
Francisco Goya
Francois Marie Arouet
Goetz von Berlichingen
Great Expectations
Immanuel Kant
James Watt
Jane Austen
Jean Jaques Rousseau
Jean-Baptiste Lamarck
Johann Christoph Friederich von Schiller
Johann Wolfgang von Goethe
Joseph Priestly
Justus Liebig
Leonhard Euler
Lettre sur les aveugles
Mansfield Park
Ode To Joy

Oliver Twist
On the Origin of Species by Means of Natural Selection
Organic Chemistry and its Application to Agriculture and Physiology
Organic Chemistry in its Application to Physiology and Pathology
Pensees Philosophiques
Persuasion
Sense and Sensibility
The Social Contract
The Wealth of Nations
Thomas Jefferson
Voltaire
Zoological Philosophy

WEBSITE

Please refer to the *Music Through Time* site listed in the front of your book to investigate and complete more classroom activities and assignments.

The classical period in music, starting in 1750, is filled with instrumental music and opera. The piano was developed during this time as a more expressive keyboard instrument due to particular innovations in the mechanics of tone production. Instead of plucking the string when a key was pressed on a harpsichord, a piano used a small felted hammer that struck the string. This difference in technology enabled the performer to control volume on the keyboard for the first time. The performer's strength and intensity upon pressing the keys corresponded to varying volumes of loud or soft, giving rise to the new instrument's name, the piano forte. The wonder of this new instrument is that it worked perfectly well in both large and small concert environments, becoming a solo instrument in large concert halls as well as the primary accompanying instrument in chamber music genres. In upper- and middle-class populations, pianos were regularly seen in the living room or drawing room. It would become the instrument of choice among the public during the Industrial Revolution.

Musicians continued to earn their income in the service of royal patronage and the church, but for the first time a new venue opened paths to instrumentalists previously reserved only for singers in the opera house. **Public subscription concerts** emerged providing the upper and middle classes the opportunity

to hear their beloved instrumental music and soloists perform regularly. Soloists and/or promoters would advertise and sell tickets to a series of concerts that would be performed over time, most often one concert every three to five weeks. The public would purchase a subscription, or set of tickets, to the advertised concerts, providing a guaranteed income for the promoter or soloist for the duration of the concerts series. Mozart was particularly fond of performing on this type of format, composing many of his piano works for himself to play in concert.

Sonata Form

Given the popularity of the novel during this period, the public was ready for other large-scale works of art, and in music their hunger was fed in the formulation of the **sonata**. The sonata is a large-scale, multi-movement work of instrumental music. The term *sonata* refers to both an entire genre, as well as a specific schematic for the presentation and contrasting of melodic materials.

As to the first reference, "a large-scale, multi-movement work of instrumental music," the term *sonata* refers to several genre names. The names change with regard to the performance forces required and the setting in which the music will be presented. For example, a **symphony** is a sonata designed for performance by an orchestra in a large concert setting. A **concerto** is a sonata for orchestra and soloist in large concert presentation. A **string quartet** is a sonata designed for performance by four stringed instruments—two violins, one viola, and one cello, specifically—in a chamber music presentation. Finally, a sonata, referring to a solo sonata, is a sonata composed for a solo instrument with piano accompaniment, also chamber music.

Sonata Allegro (First Movement)

The sonata form is comprised of three to four movements (primarily four during this time period). Each movement would be related to the others in terms of the key relationships, the contrasts in tempo and meter of each movement (to heighten interest), and formal designs.

The first movement was most often in a paradigm called the **sonata allegro form**. The term *sonata* is used because of its shape and the term *allegro* referring to its tempo—*fast*. The shape of the sonata allegro is in three sections, ABA. The first section is called the **exposition** because two separate melodies were "exposed" to the listener. These melodies were designed to be as different as possible—in key, tempo, meter, and often in mode (major or minor). Possibly there was introduction material prior to the first melodic section, but not always. The first melodic portion of the exposition would be in the tonic key, also the key of the composition's title. After it had been introduced to the listener, some transitional material would occur, modulating to a related key area and setting the new meter is necessary. The second melody would be heard, now usually a slow contrast to the first, followed by either more transitional material or closing "coda" material designed to bring the two melodies to an obvious conclusion.

When the exposition was completed, the **development** would be heard. The development was often short in duration, taking portions of the two melodies, blending them into a homogenous whole through various compositional devices until they were poured out upon the ears of the audience in the section known as the **recapitulation**.

The recapitulation section is where the first melody is performed again, in the tonic key, in the same meter and tempo, followed by the second theme in its same meter and tempo, but now in the same key as the tonic. Most often there is some "coda" material that is designed as reinforcement of the tonic key area.

Second Movement

The second movement of a sonata is usually slow in tempo and the melody is musical and memorable. The form of the movement may be sonata allegro again, as in the first movement, or it may be in a theme and variations paradigm (A, A1, A2, A3, A4, …) where the composer displays differing settings of meter, tempo, key, and rhythmic devices all supporting the same theme.

Third Movement

The **third movement** is usually in a **minuet** form, held over from the dance suite tradition of the Baroque period. The minuet was a very popular social dance, and it remained so during the classical period. This movement allowed for the rhythmic associations of dance music to support and contrast the formal designs of the other movements in the sonata. A minuet possesses a schematic that can be illustrated as a large ABA design. The first A section will possess two melodies, a and b, with each repeated. The large B section, also called the **trio,** will also have two additional melodies that can be labeled as c and d, each being repeated as well. The final A section would present the original a and b melodies, but only once. Therefore, the overall design would look like A=aabb, B=ccdd, A=ab. The third movement, a minuet in triple meter, would provide a more lively contrast to the duple meter opening and closing movements and the slower more melancholy second movement.

Fourth Movement

The fourth movement had several possibilities, depending on the taste of the composer. A sonata allegro format is used, as well as a theme and variations; however, the final movement is where the **rondo** design is most often chosen as the archetype. The rondo is a sectionalized form that shows a recurring A section, alternating with contrasting melodic material. ABABACA is a possibility. So, too, is ABACABA, or any variance the composer chooses, so long as each alternating section is an original A (e.g., ABACADA…).

The tempo of the first "a" section is usually fast and the meter is most often duple or quadruple.

Genres in Sonata Form

The symphony, the concerto, the string quartet, and the solo sonata are all in this same design during the Classical period with the exception that the concerto was often limited to only three movements, avoiding the minuet. The concerto, too, often saw a repeated section in the first sonata allegro movement during the exposition section. The repeat allowed the orchestra to introduce the melodies; afterward, the soloist reinforced those exposition melodies in a different timbre.

During the late Classical period, in the works of Beethoven, there is an abandonment of the minuet and the replacement of it by a more intellectual triple metered form, the **scherzo**. Beethoven saw the minuet as homage to the aristocracy of an older age who first supported the orchestra's development. Beethoven would perceive himself as second to no one and, therefore, desired to change the traditional remembrance of a time that was filled with more severe class distinctions.

Opera

Opera was the most important vocal genre of the era, but it was in the midst of transition. Previous to the Classical period, opera seria, as made famous by Handel's works, was the accepted style. This, too, was the expectation by those royals who patronized the state theaters. This would change due to the erosion of this style during the Classical period.

The arrival of the novel in the hands of Jane Austen and others fueled an appetite for fiction in the public. Eventually, this taste for real characters engaged in plots of intrigue or lust or deception, reflecting the lives of the people of the eighteenth century rather than the ancients, would erode the mythical settings of opera seria. John Gay's *Beggar's Opera* was so popular with the public that it caused an outcry for similar comedic plots for the stage. Also, the popularity of the French philosophers like **Rousseau** who advocated music with real emotion and real plots by natural people in natural environments in his articles on music for the French *Encyclopedie* (the favorite book of the early humanists), played a role in the change in public taste.

The composer Gluck attempted reform of this kind, and he met with some success. But the most successful composer to affect change in the design and presentation of opera was Mozart. In his later operas, starting with the *Marriage of Figaro*, Mozart actively selected librettos that were more in line with the public taste, even though Emperor Joseph II commissioned some of his operas for the Austrian State Theater. Mozart's last opera, *The Magic Flute*, was a comedy more in the vaudeville tradition. It was such a success that it established the firm popularity of **opera buffa**, or comic opera. This type of opera saw the principle voices as bass singers, often portraying silly buffoon-type characters.

Another innovation of Mozart's was the **ensemble.** The ensemble was neither an aria, duet, nor trio, as is the case when multiple singers perform a scene with the beautiful emotive melody following dialogue or action. Rather, an ensemble is a replacement for the recitative in older generations. Mozart developed a way for several characters to converse or deliver dialogue and action in the scene, as was the case in a recitative, now in a more natural way, updated for the times and more interesting theatrically and melodically.

VOCABULARY

Concerto	Opera buffa	Sonata
Development	Public subscription	Sonata allegro form
Ensemble	concerts	String quartet
Exposition	Recapitulation	Symphony
Marriage of Figaro	Rondo	Third Movement
Minuet	Rousseau	Trio
Opera	Scherzo	

WEBSITE

Please refer to the *Music Through Time* site listed in the front of your book to investigate and complete more classroom activities and assignments.

14

Classical Composers

The Classical period has included many composers who may be listed as active, even influential, but only three stand above the rest as important due to their productivity and innovation as well as their popularity.

Franz Joseph Haydn (1732–1809)

Franz Joseph Haydn in many ways typifies the composer during this period. He worked all of his professional life for wealthy court patrons, first Count von Morzin, then the Esterhazy family, one of the most important and wealthy families in the Austrian empire. He is considered to be the father of modern music.

Born in the town of Rohrau on the Austrian-Hungarian border in 1732, he was the son of a wagon maker, a peasant. Franz Joseph was raised with the

Franz Joseph Haydn
©Bettmann/CORBIS

hope that he might become a clergyman. His studies included lessons on wind and string instruments, and, while not a prodigy, his musical skills were quickly evident. He listened to everything around him. Haydn had an even, balanced, and highly industrious temperament that served him well and fit comfortably with the time and situation in which he was born.

At age eight, he was recruited to the boys' choir at St. Stephens's Cathedral in Vienna, where he stayed until he was let go due to his voice changing. After that, he was forced for eight years to earn a meager living as a street musician. But his reputation grew to the point that he was hired by Count von Morzin as music director and composer. Then, in 1761, he was hired as vice-kapellmeister to Prince Paul Esterhazy, who was succeeded by Prince Nicholas, the Magnificent. Nicholas built a new palace, second only to Versailles, just outside Vienna. An ardent music lover, the new palace had a 400-seat theater for opera. When Kapellmeister Gregorious Werner died, Haydn succeeded him, fully presiding over an orchestra of between twenty and twenty-three players. It became one of the best ensembles in Europe and afforded Haydn the opportunity to continually experiment. The majority of his 104 symphonies were composed during this period.

Haydn's duties at the court included the business management of the court's musicians and its musical life, supplying music for the weekly Tuesday and Thursday afternoon concerts scheduled. Prince Esterhazy played the baryton, now obsolete, and Haydn wrote over 200 pieces for him to play. In addition, Haydn conducted 1026 performances of Italian operas alone between 1780 and 1790. His musical life was a full one, and he earned a good salary and was provided a secretary, a maid, a coachman, and time for hunting and fishing. His position was the envy of many a composer during his day, yet Haydn preferred the company of his own class to intimacies with the aristocracy, and he was contented with being a well-paid and appreciated servant.

Haydn was the leading composer in the world. However, he was deeply impressed by Mozart, whom he considered "the greatest composer the world possesses now." They met in 1781 when Mozart was twenty-five, and the respect was mutual.

Prince Nicholas died in 1790. His successor, Anton, kept Haydn in his position but cut back the court's musical activities. This decision left Haydn free to move to Vienna and travel to England upon the invitation of Johann Saloman. London was Europe's most active musical center at this time, and Haydn stayed for eighteen months, enjoying great public acclaim. While in London he composed a set of twelve symphonies known as the "London Symphonies" and received an honorary degree from Oxford.

So successful was the trip, Haydn returned to London in 1794 and stayed through August 1795. Upon his return, Haydn found the Esterhazy orchestra had been restored by Nicholas II but assigned to mainly accompany church services. Haydn resumed his leadership and composed his great Masses.

Haydn retired from his official duties for the Esterhazy family in 1802. He spent his last years suffering from rheumatism and various illnesses. Respected as the senior elder of all music, he enjoyed entertaining visitors. He died on May 31, 1809, and the Mozart requiem was played at his funeral.

The musical significance of Haydn's life as a composer and his prolific output is that he almost single handedly is responsible for the design of the sonata form in all of its current genres—the symphony, the string quartet, the solo sonata, and the classical concerto. Because of his extended time of employment and the luxurious resources at his disposal, he had much time to experiment and try new things. Also, because he was extremely busy and was not afforded the opportunity to travel extensively until later in life, Haydn was forced to be original and follow his own constructive notions. This may well be the single factor contributing to his historic importance and ultimately the source of his fame and stature as a world music figure during his lifetime.

Works

- Orchestral music, including over 100 symphonies, concertos for violin, cello, harpsichord, and trumpet; divertimenti
- Chamber music, including some sixty-eight string quartets, piano trios and divertimenti, forty sonatas
- Sacred vocal music, including fourteen Masses (*Mass in Time of War*, 1796; *Lord Nelson Mass*, 1798); oratorios, including *The Creation* (*Die Schöpfung*, 1798) and *The Seasons* (*Die Jahreszieten*, 1801)

Wolfgang Amadeus Mozart (1756–1791)

People make a mistake who think that my art has come easily to me. Nobody has devoted so much time and thought to composition as I. There is not a famous master whose music I have not studied over and over.

Wolfgang Mozart may be the world's most famous musical child prodigy. Mozart was lucky enough to be born a genius in 1756, at a time when, musically, Franz Joseph Haydn had paved the way toward endless possibilities in the mature classical style. The genres that were abundant seemed to fit Mozart's mental capabilities perfectly. The unlucky aspect of Mozart's life was to be born to an overbearing and ambitious father who desperately wanted to capitalize on his son's highly unusual gifts.

Leopold Mozart was employed as the vice-kapellmeister to the Archbishop at Salzburg, and he was a good enough musician to recognize his son's extraordinary gifts. Wolfgang was playing the piano by age three, and he was composing by age six. From that age through his teens, Wolfgang was almost constantly on the road being showcased as a piano virtuoso in the courts and palaces of Europe, even performing for the Pope in Rome. Virtually denied a normal childhood because of his travel schedule, Mozart also began composing in earnest, producing a symphony and a full opera by age twelve.

His mental capacity was so heightened that he was able to memorize full programs of music in one hearing, able to recall them exactly. There exists a legend of Mozart as a child being so enthralled with the performance of a great organist he had heard perform in concert that when he arrived home again, Mozart transcribed exactly what he had heard from memory in its entirety. So great were his mental skills, he could think and organize music in his

Wolfgang Amadeus Mozart
©Bettmann/CORBIS

head, with no need to check or polish material at the keyboard as other composers do. He could store his work there, leave it, and return as often as needed until the work was finished, only then picking up ink and quill to put to paper the completed work, virtually transcribing it complete and flawless.

Mozart had a strained and confusing relationship with his controlling father, who seemed to adore his son for his value as a commodity. Always in the news and extravagantly praised during his childhood, Wolfgang was acutely aware of the special gifts that left him different from any other person he encountered. He found himself constantly confronted with mediocrity in others, and he was virtually unable to keep his opinions to himself. In his letters to his parents and sister, a rich source of autobiographic material, he wrote detailed and mocking stories of the many court musicians he met in his travels. Unable or unwilling to control himself, he developed a lifelong capacity for making enemies of those with less talent.

Much of Mozart's time and energy was spent searching for a suitable position, one that paid well and afforded him the opportunity to use his tremendous talent and creativity effectively, rather than follow in his father's career footsteps as a mid-level bureaucratic musician in the service of a small-town patron. But, because of his perceived arrogance and impulsive behavior, every opportunity was soon closed, forcing him to pursue an independent and entrepreneurial career outside the mainstream for musicians. Leopold's letters to Wolfgang are filled with self-righteous sermonizing, imploring his son to behave and fit into society. They show a desperate and average musician and simple-minded father attempting to control a rebellious and impatient genius.

Mozart finally moved by himself to Vienna, the music capital of Europe at the time, to seek his fortune as a composer and performer. He moved in with the Webers, a family he had met in his earlier travels searching for a suitable position. He fell in love and married their second daughter, Constanze, news his father did not take well. By all accounts, it was a good marriage, but it led to a cooling in his relations with his father.

This was a fertile period musically with Mozart obtaining commissions and acquiring students, producing masterpieces in every conceivable genre. In 1776, he met Lorenzo da Ponte, a poet who would become his longtime librettist. Mozart crafted Ponte's work into operas commissioned by the Royal Theater of Emperor Joseph II of Austria. Three great operas resulted, *Le Nozze di Figaro* (1786), *Don Giovanni* (1787), and *Cosi fan tutte* (1790). His gift to history is his contributions to the transformation of Viennese opera from the established opera seria style to opera buffa, or comic opera.

Possibly his greatest opera buffa is his last opera composition, *The Magic Flute*, a fantasy tale set in coded Masonic symbol references. This opera was commissioned not by the Royal Theater, but rather by a commercial theater in the suburbs of Vienna that targeted its work toward more common ticket buyers. It was a huge success in contrast to the limited commercial reward he found at the court opera house.

On the 5th of December, 1791, Wolfgang Amadeus Mozart died of unclear maladies, most likely overwork, stress, and possibly kidney failure as indicated by recorded symptoms. During this time he had just finished *The Magic Flute*, and he was feverishly working to complete a secret commission of a *Requiem Mass*. Mozart labored on this work under the feeling that he was writing this

Mass of death for himself. His fears proved correct because he died before he could finish it.

Mozart's struggle for acceptance and dignity as a creative artist forced him to work outside the normal realm of the music industry at the time. He was met with success and failure financially, living in wealth and close to bankruptcy in recurring cycles. At the time of his death, Mozart saw his final resting place to be an open pauper's grave reserved for debtors, unmarked and forgotten. One of the world's greatest geniuses rested in a pit with a hundred others, surrounded by mediocrities forever.

Mozart's compositional style contrasts to that of his Viennese contemporaries, Haydn and Beethoven, in that his work always reflects a theatrical quality, and his melodies, in all of his genres, are songlike, reminiscent of arias. Haydn and Beethoven instead use melodic germs and methodically spin them out into fully developed themes related by rhythmic device and sequence. Mozart's melodies seem to flow effortlessly out into the world as complete wholes, reflecting charm and effortless grace upon every listener, making him one of the most universally beloved and admired composers in all of music history.

Works

- Orchestral music, including some forty symphonies, cassations, divertimentos, serenades, marches, and dances
- Concertos, including twenty-seven for piano, five for violin, as well as concertos for clarinet, oboe, French horn, bassoon, flute, and flute and harp
- Operas, including *Idomeneo* (1781), *The Abduction from the Seraglio* (*Die Entführung aus dem Serail*, 1782), *The Marriage of Figaro* (*Le nozze di Figaro*, 1786), *Don Giovanni* (1787), *Women are Like That* (*Cosí fan tutte*, 1790), and *The Magic Flute* (*Die Zauberflöte*, 1791)
- Choral music, including eighteen Masses, the *Requiem* K.626 (incomplete, 1791), and other liturgical music
- Chamber music, including twenty-three string quartets, string quintets, clarinet quintet, oboe quartet, flute quartet, piano trios and quartets, sonatas for violin and piano, and divertimentos and serenades (*Eine kleine Nachtmusik* K.525, 1787)
- Keyboard music, including seventeen piano sonatas and *Fantasia in C minor* K.475 (1785)
- Secular vocal music

Ludwig van Beethoven (1770–1827)

Ludwig van Beethoven is one of the great giants of the musical world, casting a shadow so far into history that every composer following him will have their output compared to his. He achieved his status through the sheer force of his uncompromising will during times of great change politically, economically, and artistically. He also achieved all his greatness because of and in spite of the worst possible physical ailment for a musician—deafness! Living in the musical capital of the world, Vienna, during these changing, challenging, unstable times, and hindered by the shackle of ever-increasing deafness, Beethoven managed to carve out a creative career that surpassed anyone that came before him and most of those that have come since he left us. He would become an epic heroic figure, forever changing the meaning and perception of what an artist is, does, and should be.

Born in Bonn, Germany, the son of a minor musician and alcoholic, Ludwig van Beethoven showed early signs of music gifts at the piano. His father, desiring to financially capitalize on another potential Mozart, supervised his piano instruction in a brutal manner. Hoping to increase the speed of improvement, he forced Beethoven to practice for endless hours, chaining him to the piano, often locking him in a dark damp basement alone as punishment if he displeased his father when he was tested. It was a common occurrence for Beethoven to find himself awakened in the middle of the night, dragged to the piano, and forced to perform for his drunken father. He received a beating if his father was not pleased.

Ludwig van Beethoven
©Underwood & Underwood/CORBIS

Still, Beethoven endured and found inner solace in the isolated hours of practice at the piano, preferring it to play and interaction with children his own age. During those years, Beethoven honed a confidence and determination to overcome insurmountable obstacles that would serve him the rest of his life.

During his teenage years, his father became so devastated by his alcoholism that Beethoven was forced to pursue legal appointment as head of his household. This maneuver replaced his incompetent father in matters that were financial and obligatory, keeping the family from collapse. He also became responsible for his younger brothers and their rearing, even though he was not yet an adult himself. Desiring to get away and be on his own, Beethoven finally received financial backing from a group of local patrons who served as his sponsors to Vienna and provided him the opportunity to pursue his career as a concert pianist in the great city. He moved to Vienna, soon had to return to deal with more family business, then moved a second time, never to return, even refusing to come back for his father's funeral.

Beethoven immediately took Vienna by storm with his powerful personal playing style at the keyboard. Much more aggressive than other contemporary pianists in Vienna, Beethoven soon became a sensation, moving easily in the salons of the Viennese elite. He even performed for the local Mozart who was impressed and predicted a bright future for the youngster. The famous Haydn also met the young Beethoven in the city, and Ludwig studied composition with him for a time, demonstrating more independence than the master would like and a rebelliously experimental temperament, challenging the formal confines of the period.

While in Vienna, it was common for Beethoven to enter performance competitions among rival pianists, each attempting to out play the other, hoping to secure their public reputation. Beethoven would inevitably win these piano duals. In addition, he would compose much of his early piano sonatas just for these occasions. His concertos, too, were written for himself to perform in public with orchestra, often with himself conducting.

With his performance stature secure, Beethoven was the darling of Viennese elite society. He moved among the salon families with ease, often accepting money from them, not as patronage but rather as support. The wealthy families saw this support as an opportunity to display their access to the famous man, and Beethoven in turn would often dedicate a composition to one of these patrons as confirmation of their relationship. Yet, despite accepting their money, he never accepted their control or suggestion, choosing to always remain separate and apart from the public artistically.

Beethoven was creatively active at a time when political change was sweeping through Europe, making unstable the traditional class structure and economic roles that had taken centuries to establish. The ideas set forth in America by the colonists' winning their independence and establishing a democratic government complete with rights for every land-owning male caused a ripple effect in Europe, challenging the traditional power of monarchies. France would see the promise of its own revolution led by Napoleon Bonaparte only to witness its hero crown himself Emperor of France. Beethoven was caught up in the swelling of brotherhood that spilled out in France and over the rest of Europe, dedicating his Third Symphony to Bonaparte, then feverously scratching out that same dedication when he witnessed Napoleon's ascension to the throne. The ideas of brotherhood, equality, and the opportunity to rise above one's circumstances would dominate Beethoven's thinking all his life.

Beethoven began to have symptoms of a growing deafness, leaving it hard for him to hear his own playing or the sounds of the orchestra he was conducting. He had to leave both of these roles because, during one performance, he and the orchestra got off from each other and were never able to synch back together, causing the performance to melt down in public humiliation for both Beethoven and the orchestra. He instead dedicated his life to composition only, sliding more and more into a world of silence.

Beethoven's social behavior continued to deteriorate. Often he was known to treat others badly and be argumentative. His behavior was due to his anger at his worsening condition as well as his inability to admit his ailment to even his closest acquaintances. Later he was to bear the full humiliation of his malady, forced to use books and tablets for others to write down their conversations to him so that he might read them and thus communicate. His final symphonies and string quartets were composed in complete silence, hearing them only in his head. Yet they are filled with hope and brotherhood for all humanity.

Beethoven is the last classical composer in that he chose to work in the forms and genres of the day, primarily the sonata forms as displayed in the symphony, the concerto, the string quartet, and the piano sonata. However he composed with such power of personality and such personal conviction as to push those very same forms to the limits of conventionality, not conforming his work to the demands and expectations of the genre as Bach or Haydn would have done. Beethoven instead causes the forms and genres he composed to conform to the demands of his will and point of view. This very thing makes him the first Romantic.

The world responded and revered him, lauded him and rewarded him. He was wealthy due to publishing his music all over Europe and his myth escalated as well. The fortitude to create such masterworks while not being able to hear at all is the equal to Leonardo da Vinci or Michelangelo painting their famous works without being able to see the canvas! He died famous, and all of Vienna came to his funeral. The first great man of the modern age, not born of privilege, but rather earning adoration and respect from all through his creative output—this was how Beethoven's life ended. He set the mark and standard for every other artist to follow, creating for the sake of art rather than for the sake of fame.

Works

- Orchestral music, including nine symphonies: No. 1 (1800); No. 2 (1802); No. 3 "Eroica" (1803); No. 4 (1806); No. 5 (1808); No. 6 "Pastoral" (1808); No. 7 (1812); No. 8 (1812); No. 9 "Choral" (1824); overtures, including *Leonore* (Nos. 1, 2, 3) and *Egmont*; incidental music
- Concertos, including five for piano, one for violin (1806), and one triple concerto (piano, violin, and cello, 1804)
- Chamber music, including string quartets, piano trios, quartets, one quintet, one septet, violin and cello sonatas, serenades, and wind chamber music
- Thirty-two piano sonatas, including Op. 13 "Pathétique" (1806), Op. 27, No. 2 "Moonlight" (1801), Op. 53 "Waldstein" (1804), and Op. 57 "Appassionata" (1805)
- One opera, *Fidelio* (1805)
- Choral music, including *Missa solemnis* (1823)
- Songs, including song cycle *To the Distant Beloved* (*An die ferne Geliebte*, 1816)

VOCABULARY

Cosi fan tutte	Leopold Mozart	*The Creation*
Don Giovanni	Ludwig van Beethoven	*The Magic Flute*
Eroica Symphony	*Missa solemnis*	Wolfgang Amadeus
Franz Joseph Haydn	*Pastoral Symphony*	Mozart
Le Nozze di Figaro	*Requiem Mass*	

WEBSITE

Please refer to the *Music Through Time* site listed in the front of your book to investigate and complete more classroom activities and assignments.

15

Romantic Life and Times

During the Romantic period, American events and American history began to play an important role in the development of the arts. Although at first this role is understated and allowed to percolate, America's role and philosophy emerged onto the world stage in time, influencing Europe instead of being influenced by European ideas.

The American ideal was working itself out in the minds and politics of its people. Race and the questions surrounding race would be dealt with for over 150 years. During the 1800s, America expanded its borders, acquired lands, settled them, and eventually stretched from ocean to ocean. In the process, however, the divide between states that endorsed and depended on slavery and those that did not continued to be the key issue separating all the people from philosophic unity. Thus, the War Between the States emerged, a fight to the death over the moral acceptability of one race of people enslaving another. This

central moral question answered by Abraham Lincoln in "The Gettysburg Address" and culminating in the Emancipation Proclamation, which freed slaves in the southern states, would send a beacon of democracy for the world to follow.

Abraham Lincoln "The Gettysburg Address"

Four score and seven years ago our fathers brought forth on this continent a new nation, conceived in liberty and dedicated to the proposition that all men are created equal. Now we are engaged in a great civil war, testing whether that nation or any nation so conceived and so dedicated can long endure. We are met on a great battlefield of that war. We have come to dedicate a portion of that field as a final resting-place for those who here gave their lives that that nation might live. It is altogether fitting and proper that we should do this. But in a larger sense, we cannot dedicate, we cannot consecrate, we cannot hallow this ground. The brave men, living and dead who struggled here have consecrated it far above our poor power to add or detract. The world will little note nor long remember what we say here, but it can never forget what they did here. It is for us the living rather to be dedicated here to the unfinished work which they who fought here have thus far so nobly advanced. It is rather for us to be here dedicated to the great task remaining before us—that from these honored dead we take increased devotion to that cause for which they gave the last full measure of devotion—that we here highly resolve that these dead shall not have died in vain, that this nation under God shall have a new birth of freedom, and that government of the people, by the people, for the people shall not perish from the earth.

In Europe, the idea of representative government took hold and spread, reaching every culture in time. Each would deal with the same concerns regarding monarchies, democratic philosophies, new economic strategies, and civil liberties. It would take many decades for these questions to be answered and new systems established. In tandem with these governmental changes came a sense of pride in each country's origins, traditions, geography, and uniqueness. A sense of nationalism would pervade artistic creations and inspire created works as artists and their people recreated their own lives.

Science

The Industrial Revolution changed the face of economics for Europe and America. Many inventions and innovations made labor easier, more profitable, and more manageable. A true middle class emerged and urban centers were created for the first time all throughout America.

Many scientific discoveries emerged contributing to knowledge and to the manufacturing sector of the economy. Some of the most outstanding contributions in this area came from the following people.

John Dalton (1766–1844)

An English chemist and physicist who determined the relative weights of atoms, **John Dalton** also formulated the atomic theory that all elements are composed of tiny, identical, and indestructible particles. He also developed Dalton's law of partial pressures, stating that the total pressure of a mixture of gases equals the sum of the pressures exerted by each gas independently. Additionally, he found that gases expand as their temperature is raised.

Andre-Marie Ampere (1775–1836)

Andre-Marie Ampere was a French physicist and mathematician who founded the science of electrodynamics. His discovery that an electric current through a coil acts like a magnet was revolutionary and led to the discovery and the invention of the galvanometer, an instrument for detecting and measuring electric currents. With this instrument, he proved that electric current makes a circuit through a battery. The ampere, a unit used to measure the rate of flow of an electric current, is named after him.

Samuel B. Morse (1791–1872)

Samuel Morse was an American painter, but he is best known for his invention of the electric telegraph, conceived in 1832. He constructed an experimental version in 1835 using a homemade battery and old clockwork to move the paper on which dots and dashes were to be recorded. Morse exhibited his telegraph before businessmen and committees of Congress, but he met skepticism that any message could really be sent from city to city over wire. Finally, in 1844, he built an improved system, and, thereby, the first intercity electromagnetic telegraph line in the world. From the Capitol building in Washington, Morse sent a Biblical quotation as the first formal message on the line to Baltimore.

Charles Babbage (1792–1871)

Charles Babbage, an English mathematician and inventor, invented the principle of the analytical engine, the forerunner of the computer. In 1812, the idea of mechanically calculating mathematical tables occurred to him. Later he invented the calculator that could tabulate mathematical computations to eight decimals. In 1834, he envisioned the capability of performing any mathematical operation by instruction from punched cards, a memory element used to store numbers, and most of the other characteristics displayed by modern computers. A shortage of funds prevented him from building his machine; however, another inventor built a mechanical calculator based on his ideas in Sweden in 1855.

Charles Darwin (1809–1882)

Charles Darwin is known as the discoverer of natural selection. Born in Shrewsbury, England, he studied medicine at Edinburgh, then biology at

Cambridge. In 1831, he became the naturalist on HMS Beagle, which was to make a scientific survey of South American waters, and returned in 1836. By 1846, he had published several works on his geological and zoological discoveries, but he devoted most of his time to his major work *On the Origin of Species by Means of Natural Selection* (1859). He postulated that natural selection was the agent for the transmutation of organisms during evolution.

He then worked on a series of supplemental treatises, including *The Descent of Man* (1871), which postulated the descent of the human race from the anthropoid group. At first, Darwin was attacked as an infidel atheist declaring the Bible a lie, but he replied that it increased God's grandeur to believe that the universe had been created with evolution built in.

Louis Pasteur (1822–1895)

Louis Pasteur made one of the greatest medical discoveries of all time when he proved that microorganisms cause fermentation and disease. He showed that microbes can be killed by chemical and physical means and that the spread of disease can be controlled. He originated pasteurization, sterilization, and antisepsis that led to the development of vaccines, saving millions of lives and almost doubling the average lifespan of man.

James Clerk Maxwell (1831–1879)

James Clerk Maxwell, born in Edinburgh, is generally regarded as one of the greatest physicists the world has ever seen. His work united electricity and magnetism into the concept of the electromagnetic field. He discovered that light is an electromagnetic wave, and his theory that when a charged particle is accelerated, the radiation produced has the same velocity as that of light paved the way for Einstein's special theory of relativity.

Alfred B. Nobel (1833–1896)

Alfred Nobel was a Swedish chemist and industrialist who invented dynamite and founded the Nobel prizes. The Nobel prizes are awarded to those who have contributed most to the common good in the areas of physics, chemistry, medicine, literature, peace, and economics.

Karl Friederich Benz (1844–1929)

Karl Friederich Benz, a German engineer who built the first practical automobile powered by an internal combustion engine, founded Benz and Company in Mannheim to manufacture gas engines. He built his first gas engine in 1878, and produced his first motor vehicle in 1885. The automobile was patented in 1886 and had three wheels, an electric ignition, differential gears, and was water-cooled. In 1926, his company merged and became the Daimler-Benz AG, the manufacturer of the Mercedes-Benz automobile.

Alexander Graham Bell (1847–1922)

Born in Edinburgh in 1847, **Alexander Graham Bell** studied at Edinburgh and London and worked as assistant to his father in teaching elocution. In 1870, he went to Canada and later moved to the United States of America, becoming professor of vocal physiology in Boston. Devoting himself to the teaching of deaf-mutes and to spreading his father's system of "visible speech," he carried out experiments to determine how vowel sounds are produced. A book, describing experiments in combining the notes of electrically driven tuning forks to make vowel sounds, gave him the idea of telegraphic speech.

Later, he reasoned that it would be possible to pick up all sounds of the human voice on the harmonic telegraph. After tedious experimentation, the Bell telephone carried its first intelligible sentence in the spring of 1876. Forming the Bell Telephone Company in 1880, he established the Volta Laboratory.

Thomas Alva Edison (1847–1931)

Thomas Alva Edison first learned how to operate a telegraph while selling newspapers as a young boy at railroad stations. In New York City in 1869, as a supervisor in a stock-ticker firm, he made improvements on the stock-ticker. Later, he opened his own laboratory in Newark, N.J., where he made important improvements in telegraphy and on the typewriter, and invented the carbon transmitter that made Alexander Bell's telephone practical. In 1876, he moved his laboratory to Menlo Park, N.J., where he invented the first phonograph and the prototype of the incandescent electric light bulb. Being interested in systems for distributing electric power from central generating stations, he formed his own company that later merged with another to become General Electric Co.

By the time he died, he had accumulated an impressive list of 1093 patents (motion picture inventions, electricity applications, light bulb, electric typewriter development, dictaphone, mimeograph, etc.), but Thomas Edison's most important contribution was that he organized systematic research on a very large scale allowing hundreds of people to efficiently work together.

Albert A. Michelson (1852–1931)

An American physicist who experimentally established the speed of light as a fundamental constant in 1887, **Albert A. Michelson** was the first American to win a Nobel Prize for science. With the help of his colleague Edward Morley, he conducted the Michelson-Morley experiment. This experiment showed that there was no significant motion of the Earth relative to the ether. This result later became the foundation of Einstein's Theory of Relativity. The ether was a hypothetical medium in which light waves were supposed to travel. The notion of this medium eventually had to be abolished.

Writers

Many fascinating authors produced works during this time period, contributing to the literature that we know today.

J. W. Goethe (1749–1832)

Johann Wolfgang von Goethe ranks as the greatest of all German poets, and he is regarded as the most universal German figure. In 1773, he wrote the drama *Goetz von Berlichingen*, capturing the spirit of German nationalism, then followed with the novel *The Sorrows of Young Werther*. He also wrote a great deal of lyric poetry inspired by his relationships with Charlotte von Stein and other women.

Goethe's fame outside of Germany rests mainly upon *Faust*, a dramatic account of man's journey through heaven and hell, with the devil as companion and enlightened wisdom as the final goal.

Jane Austen (1775–1817)

Jane Austen was an important English novelist who spent her life in the middle-class society. She described it intimately and with humor in her novels, the most famous of which are *Sense and Sensibility*, *Mansfield Park*, *Emma*, and *Persuasion*.

George Gordon, Lord Byron (1788–1824)

Lord Byron was a famous English poet who, in 1809, traveled around the Mediterranean and spent some time in Greece where he aided the Greeks in their fight for independence from Turkey. While there, he wrote two cantos of *Child Harold*, which made him famous. His other works include *Manfred* and *Don Juan*.

Victor Hugo (1802–1885)

Victor-Marie Hugo was a French poet and novelist who became recognized as a leading figure among French Romantics through his great novels, including *Notre Dame de Paris* and *Les Misérables*.

George Sand (1804–1876)

George Sand is the pen name of Amandine—Aurore—Lucille Dudevant. Born in Paris and author of over 100 books, she was known as a Romantic novelist. Famous for her numerous love affairs, including Chopin among others, her first novel, *Indiana,* was a passionate protest against the social conventions that bind a wife to her husband against her will.

Hans Christian Andersen (1805–1875)

A Danish writer and storyteller from Denmark, **Hans Christian Andersen** is best remembered as a writer of children's fairy tales, such as *The Tin Soldier, The Tinderbox,* and *The Ugly Duckling.*

Edgar Allan Poe (1809–1849)

American poet, editor, and writer, **Edgar Allan Poe** was born in Boston but educated in Britain. He made his reputation as a master of macabre stories such as *The Fall of the House of Usher* and *Murders in the Rue Morgue*. He is considered to be the father of the detective story and a stepfather of science fiction.

Charles Dickens (1812–1870)

Charles Dickens is the most widely read Victorian novelist. He appealed to social consciousness to overcome social misery. His immense popularity gave importance to his attacks on the abuses of the law-courts and of schools whose object was not the education of children but the enrichment of proprietors.

Fyodor Dostojevski (1821–1881)

Fyodor Dostojevski is, besides Tolstoy, the most widely read Russian novelist. In 1859, he wrote his masterpiece, *Crime and Punishment,* that sets forth a side of human nature never before portrayed with such insight and accuracy. Two other great novels are *The Idiot* and *The Brothers Karamazov.*

Count Leo Nikolaevich Tolstoy (1828–1910)

Count Leo Nikolaevich Tolstoy ranks as one of the world's great writers. He was also an important moral thinker and reformer. Born in Russia, he joined the army in 1851. After fighting in the Crimean War, he left the army and traveled abroad. Upon his return, he wrote his epic masterpiece, *War and Peace,* the story of five families during Napoleon's invasion of Russia. It is considered one of the greatest novels ever written. His next novel, *Anna Karenina,* also ranks as one of the world's great love stories. Experiencing a spiritual crisis, he went on to write *A Confession* and *What I Believe.*

Mark Twain (1835–1910)

An American writer, **Mark Twain** worked for a time as a Mississippi riverboat pilot, an experience that was the basis for his two most popular works, *The Adventures of Tom Sawyer* and *The Adventures of Huckleberry Finn.* He became famous for his humorous lecturing. Some of his books became established among the world's classics, and when he died he was mourned as the most popular American writer of the last century.

Arts

Many familiar names can be found among the artisans of the Romantic period. Great masterpieces and influential ideas, techniques, and designs emerged. Artists of all disciplines strived for individuality and freedom from former constraints. While motivated by certain similar fascinations such as nature, nationalism, occultism, and the supernatural, it is the realm of personal feeling and personal vision that ties all artists together, creating a status for all romantic artists with their audiences that raised them from the bonds of service to the heights of individual thinkers.

F. V. Eugene Delacroix (1798–1863)

Known as the greatest French Romantic, the writings of Shakespeare, Lord Byron, and Sir Walter Scott inspired many of **F. V. Eugene Delacroix's** paintings. Dante's *Inferno* provided the subject matter for his first successful work. Though Delacroix aimed for a balance between the goals of Classicism and Romanticism, his art centered on a revolutionary idea born with the Romantics—that art should be created out of sincerity and express the artist's truest convictions.

Edouard Manet (1832–1883)

Edouard Manet is considered the first modern painter to inspire the Impressionist movement. Born in Paris, Manet gained his real knowledge of art during visits to Italy, Germany, and Holland. These trips exposed Manet to the same masters who profoundly interpreted realism in the past, like Hals, Velazquez, and Goya. Though Manet regarded himself as working in the tradition of the great masters, his approach was to rethink established themes in modern terms.

Edgar Degas (1834–1917)

A French painter who was a master craftsman of the human figure, **Edgar Degas** was born in a wealthy Parisian family. He, therefore, devoted himself exclusively to painting without needing to sell a canvas. He developed his own style of painting out of the neoclassical tradition that incorporated a sense of composition. Degas was primarily concerned with depicting movement and he preferred to work in pastels.

Paul Cézanne (1839–1906)

A French painter who laid the groundwork for modern styles like Cubism, **Paul Cézanne** was born in Aix-en-Provence; he went to Paris in 1861. There he learned from Manet, Monet, and Pissarro but received much criticism from other artists for his rough style. Although in the company of the Impressionists he formed his style, his was more an extension of that movement moving toward something new. Impressionism concentrated on effects of momentary light obtained through small strokes of color. Cézanne wanted an effect implying more permanence and captured basic forms in his paintings. This insistence on form later influenced the Cubists.

Claude Monet (1840–1926)

During the 1860s, **Claude Monet** was associated with Edouard Manet and with the other aspiring French painters destined to form the Impressionist school—Pissarro, Renoir, and Sisley. Monet experimented by rendering outdoor sunlight with a direct, sketch-like application of bright color. As his style became more daring, he seemed to cut himself off from the possibility of a successful career as a conventional painter supported by the art establishment. Deciding to appeal directly to the public by organizing their own exhibition, the group called themselves independents, but the press soon called them impressionists because their work seemed sketchy and unfinished, like a first impression.

In 1890, Monet purchased property not far from Paris and began to construct a water garden, a lily pond arched with a Japanese bridge overhung with willows and clumps of bamboo. Paintings of the pond and the water lilies occupied him for the remainder of his life.

Auguste Rodin (1840–1917)

Auguste Rodin's ability to catch the essence of a person in marble or bronze demonstrates a firsthand knowledge of the sculptures of Michelangelo. In 1880,

Rodin received a commission from the French government to design monumental doors for a proposed new museum, a work that preoccupied him for the rest of his life. His inspiration was Dante's *Inferno*, but the many figures he created in plaster for his "Gates of Hell" came to represent the sculptor's own vision.

Pierre Auguste Renoir (1841–1919)

The French painter who developed the broken color technique of Impressionism, **Pierre Auguste Renoir** is one of history's most prolific artists, with nearly 6000 paintings completed. In 1862, he joined the art school of Charles Gleyre where he met Sisley, Monet, and Bazille. Renoir's connection with these artists led him to meet Degas and Manet. The concepts of Impressionism developed from the times this group spent in the cafes of Paris.

Paul Gauguin (1848–1903)

A French artist and pioneer of Post-Impressionism who was a master of color compositions, **Paul Gauguin** was born in Paris. In 1891, he decided to escape European civilization and chose to sail for Tahiti where he found the color he needed for his increasingly vivid paintings.

Vincent van Gogh (1853–1890)

A Dutch artist whose tragic life and brilliant canvases made him a legend, **Vincent van Gogh's** early work is dark and thickly painted, but under the influence of the Impressionists, his images grew more colorful. His brush began to form thick linear strokes. His art, becoming "expressionistic," released his inner reactions to the world through turning, swirling, brush strokes; thick paint; and brilliant color.

Photography

In the late parts of the nineteenth century, the invention of the camera changed much of the romantic's inspiration. Because of the photograph's ability to capture nature exactly, full of starkness and power, the artistic tendency toward softness and wistfulness found in the early part of the century, morphed into more realistic creations. While the romantic ideal of individual feeling and artistic expression still dominated, realism introduced stoicism to the later part of the century in all the arts, including music.

Music

In Europe and America, nationalism was a strong force of inspiration for musicians and composers, although it occurred at different times and at different rates of speed on both continents. Also, in the middle and upper classes, a fascination with the supernatural and things of the occult or macabre influences were common. In the Romantic period, the Ouija board was first introduced and was wildly popular. Séances and interest in the spirit world were commonplace. Also, the darker aspects of the spirit world and their corresponding images in the macabre were used to the delight of audiences. The beginnings of our love of being frightened emerged.

Program Music

The dominant factor in music for the Romantic period was the popularity of **program music,** or music that brings to mind images or associations other than purely musical notions. Started by Beethoven in his Pastoral Symphony when he attempted to depict a thunderstorm, program music grew in popularity. When music attempts to portray something else, or follows a script or story, called a program by the romantics like Berlioz, it becomes graphic. This type of graphic program music was new and easily digestible by the audience, especially when compared to the absolute music forms of the Baroque or Classical period, like the fugue or sonata. Program music for a while became the rage, drunk with the passion and drama stirred in the listener.

VOCABULARY

Albert A. Michelson	Edgar Degas	John Dalton
Alexander Graham Bell	Edouard Manet	Karl Friederich Benz
Alfred B. Nobel	F. V. Eugene Delacroix	Louis Pasteur
Andre-Marie Ampere	Fyodor Dostojevski	Mark Twain
Auguste Rodin	George Gordon, Lord	Paul Cézanne
Charles Babbage	Byron	Paul Gauguin
Charles Darwin	George Sand	Pierre Auguste Renoir
Charles Dickens	Hans Christian	Program Music
Claude Monet	Andersen	Samuel B. Morse
Count Leo Nikolaevich	J. W. Goethe	Thomas Alva Edison
Tolstoy	James Clerk Maxwell	Victor Hugo
Edgar Allan Poe	Jane Austen	Vincent van Gogh

WEBSITE

Please refer to the *Music Through Time* site listed in the front of your book to investigate and complete more classroom activities and assignments.

CHAPTER

16

Romantic Genres

Music during the Romantic period is deeply personal. The depth of emotion and personal vision demonstrated by Beethoven creates new interest in the composer as an individual artist in the public's eye. His influence dominates the composers who create music in his absence, and this younger generation of composers will fill the void he left with creations of intense feeling, which is the heart of romanticism.

Many new genres appear and capture the imagination of the public. These genres will occupy both the chamber music world as well as the large concert orchestra and opera stages. Chamber music explodes in popularity, however, and much of the new development will be seen in that environment.

©Archivo Iconografico, S.A./CORBIS

The Lied

The **lied** is a chamber music favorite. German for song or art song, *lieder* is a short, usually descriptive piece for a solo singer and piano accompaniment. Franz P. Schubert, a young contemporary of the elder Beethoven in Vienna, was the master of lieder and created over 600 of them. Often grouping several lieder together in "song cycles," he established a lyrical theme in which the individual lieder in the song cycle were loosely connected. His most famous lied may be ***Erlkönig***. Typical of this style of lieder composition, it embodies many of the devices that romantic music audiences found so entrancing.

Erlkönig is a short vocal composition for a male soloist with piano accompaniment based on a dramatic tale of crisis and superstition, two of the favorite romantic themes. In the tale and lyric, a father is riding his horse at night in the woods carrying his young son in his arms hurrying to get to shelter. (It is implied that the son is ill, feverish, and that the father is anxious to get the boy to shelter, either at home or possibly to a physician.) During the swift ride, the son sees a vision of the Erlkönig, or elf king, who speaks to the child and tempts him to come away with him and play with his daughter(s). This is also implied to be a hallucination caused by the fever because the father repeatedly tries to calm and comfort the child as the son tells the father that what he sees frightens him. Each verse of the tale continues the story with the elf king's attempts to entice the boy getting stronger and more insistent. Schubert heightens the dramatic effect by raising the melodic intervals to higher and higher levels, increasing the performance tension. The piano plays the dramatic part of the horse, flying through the night, with its rhythmic accompaniment, painting the mental picture of galloping hoofs. Finally, the father reaches his destination and upon arriving discovers that his son is dead.

The tale, the dramatic vocal presentation, the sense of dread from potential spirit entities interacting with living loved ones, the overwhelming tragedy in the death of a child and the grief of a parent's loss, and the programmatic musical descriptions of the horse galloping through the night all combine in the hands of Schubert to create a perfect example of the type of melodrama that so enthralled the romantic audience. They loved nothing more than to be moved emotionally to the greatest extent possible.

Schubert Among Friends
©The Art Archives/CORBIS

Character Pieces

Robert Schumann was influential in the creation of another genre for solo piano in the chamber music category. The **character piece,** as he called it, is similar to the lied in that it is a short programmatic work for piano that is descriptive of an emotion or feeling, but without the aid of descriptive words in a text like in a lied. The piano and its musical capabilities combine with the power of the composer's skill to produce mental images in the listener. Schumann created many of these character pieces that embodied musical moments of emotion and suggestion, often grouping them together in overarching collections, as was done in the song cycle, in his *Butterflies, Scenes from Childhood,* and *Carnaval.*

Chopin and Liszt, two other pianists possessing spectacular but divergent styles of playing, composed and performed small emotional works in the character piece mold, but they were less specifically descriptive. Chopin's works were more traditional in that they were based on nationalistic dances from his native Poland—like the Polonaise, Waltz, and Mazurka—or entitled non-descriptive generic names such as preludes, etudes (study pieces for his students), ballades, fantasies, impromptus, or the slightly suggestive nocturne. Composed for him to perform in fashionable French salons, Chopin became the emotional darling of the social elite, earning the nickname "the Poet of the Piano." Liszt, too, composed for himself to perform, and like Chopin, wrote character pieces for the piano entitled etudes, nocturnes, waltzes, ballades, and polonaises, making the character piece the favorite emotional vehicle for the pianist in a small performance situation.

Concert Overture

Felix Mendelssohn made the **concert overture** famous, especially with his *Overture to a Midsummer Night's Dream.* The concert overture is part of the tradition of composers creating music for stage plays to be performed in association with a play, such as Shakespeare's *A Midsummer Night's Dream.* This "incidental music," as it was called, served to heighten the sensory effect of a play's performance for the audience. The play, and its corresponding plot and action, served as programmatic inspiration for these musical creations, and this music was performed before the play began and possibly between acts, serving as a Romantic era precursor to movie sound tracks. The concert overture is the piece that is performed at the beginning of the play. Mendelssohn also composed concert overtures entitled *The Hebrides* and *Fingal's Cave.*

Symphonic Poem

The **symphonic poem**, a new program music genre for orchestra in one movement, is similar to the character piece for piano except that it is scored for orchestra and performed in a large concert situation. Franz Liszt created this piece of program music initially, in a collection of six symphonic poems titled *Les Preludes.* In later life, Liszt became a conductor of orchestras and brought to that situation his compositional skills that had been used for piano creations such as the character piece. In essence, he changed the performance medium and expanded the length of the descriptive music and emerged with a new orchestral genre. Tchaikovsky, also, would become famous for his extensive symphonic poems such as his *Romeo and Juliet.*

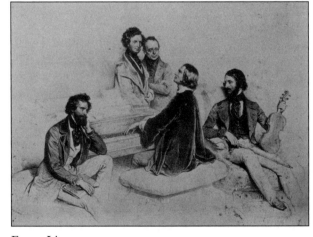

Franz Liszt
©Bettmann/CORBIS

Program Symphony

The **program symphony** is an extension of the symphonic poem in that it is programmatic music composed for orchestra, but it uses multiple movements, like in a symphony, treating these movements descriptively. Hector Berlioz composed the most famous program symphony, *Symphony Fantastique.* His Fantastic symphony follows a story or program of the composer's creation that depicts the transformation of a love affair, growing colder and more morbid in each movement. Formally, Berlioz chose a single melody, which he called his "fixed idea" or *idée fixee.* Berlioz composed additional program symphonies entitled *Harold in Italy* and his own version of *Romeo and Juliet.*

Ballet

While music for **ballet** has a rich history and goes back in time to roots in the ancient world, compositions for ballet became enormously popular as music itself in the hands of program composers such as Tchaikovsky. Ballet is artistic dance with its own set of disciplined body motions and visually stunning steps. Music composed to accompany this type of dance had served primarily as background to the dancers on stage. However, Tchaikovsky, a Russian composer in the late Romantic period, possessed such descriptive skill in a country that was second only to France in its devotion to the art of ballet. He was commissioned to write music for dance companies that resulted in a musical score that provided emotional inspiration for the dancers and memorable and delightful program music for the audiences, intensifying the experience for both. Through Tchaikovsky's efforts in his ballet compositions like *Swan Lake,* *Sleeping Beauty,* and the ever-popular seasonal favorite *Nutcracker,* the doors were opened for composers to enhance the medium of ballet as a vehicle for the composer to excel.

Aida
©NEEMA FREDERIC/CORBIS SYGMA

Orchestral Song Cycle

The **orchestral song cycle** is a development of Gustav Mahler, a late romantic composer and conductor in the opera houses of Vienna and New York. Mahler chose the lied as his vehicle and expanded his accompaniment forces for the solo singer from the traditional piano to the orchestra, with its many timbre choices. Mahler, accustomed to mammoth works in length and performance forces, brought the lied, a chamber genre, to the large concert stage through his song cycles like *Songs* *of a Wayfarer, The Youth's Magic Horn, The Song of the Earth,* and *Songs on the Death of Children.*

Opera

The large vocal genres of the period remained centered in the opera houses. After Mozart, opera buffa, or comic opera, reigned with audiences. In the hands of Italian composers, primarily, opera progressed into a period of flowering that would see a host of works destined to be included in the world's opera repertoire for generations to come. The most famous and prolific of these Italians was Verdi. Verdi bridged the gap between *bel conto* style singing, meaning beautiful singing, and dramatic plot situations. He managed to merge the two styles into a formula whereby the drama is heightened and respected, and the vocal performance style is beautiful, highly resonant, and fluid. He merged these compositional styles with the nationalistic desires of his native Italy and created a force in opera composition that catapulted him to the forefront of opera composers in history.

The only other real challenge to Verdi's style of opera composition was embodied in the work of Richard Wagner. A German who was self taught, Wagner pushed the limits of harmony and the human voice into new directions. Wagner created opera that he called "music drama" in an attempt to unify the story and the music into a cohesive unit under the control of one person—himself. His music dramas created in his middle years consist of four operas together known as the *Ring of the Nibelung.* This set of operas included *The Rhine Gold, The Valkyrie, Siegfried,* and *The Twilight of the Gods.* These mammoth operas, lasting three to four hours each and designed to be seen in successive evening performances, employed German folk tales and mythologies, chromatic harmonies that were new and initially disturbing to audiences, large orchestral instrumentations that forced the singer to develop a singing technique that would allow their individual voice to be heard over an orchestra of close to 100, and had librettos that demanded recurring themes and characters.

Wagner created a means to handle such large-scale works and opened the doors to the tools that would later serve film makers like George Lucas in his *Star Wars* series of movies, as well as *The Lord of the Rings* series. These films have similar components to Wagner's operas in that they have recurring characters that play their roles out over long amounts of time in continuing epic stories. Composers for those film scores, like John Williams, chose to use the same tools that Wagner created for his operas.

The Leitmotiv

The **leitmotiv** is a melody that is associated with an operatic character or a character's emotion, such as love. By branding a melody in the ears of the audience with a character or an emotion, Wagner was able to tell aspects of the story without the use of dialogue, employing purely musical devices and speeding the story along or adding insight into the character's mental state (like aria but without the need for text or singing).

VOCABULARY

Ballet
Carnaval
Character Piece
Concert Overture
Erlkönig
Fingal's Cave
Idée fixee
Leitmotiv
Les Preludes
Lied
Nutcracker

Orchestral Song
 Cycle
*Overture to a Midsummer
 Night's* Dream
Program Symphony
Ring of the Nibelung
Romeo and Juliet
Scenes from Childhood
Siegfried
Sleeping Beauty
Songs of a Wayfarer

*Songs on the Death of
 Children*
Swan Lake
Symphonic Poem
Symphony Fantastique
The Hebrides
The Rhine Gold
The Song of the Earth
The Twilight of the Gods
The Valkyrie
The Youth's Magic Horn

WEBSITE

Please refer to the *Music Through Time* site listed in the front of your book to investigate and complete more classroom activities and assignments.

CHAPTER

17

Romantic Composers

There were many composers active during the Romantic period in music. Most of these pursued their own ideas and emotions in their work, pushing the limits of conventionality and creating new trends.

Franz Peter Schubert (1797–1828)

Dead by the age of thirty-one, **Franz Peter Schubert's** last wish was to be buried next to his idol, Beethoven, in the public cemetery of Vienna. His body rests there now, next to Beethoven's along with a monument in honor of Mozart, a trio of musical giants who worked in that city to change the musical landscape forever.

The son of a schoolteacher, Franz's musical gifts were recognized at an early age. As a boy he sang in the Imperial Court, and as a young man on his own, he followed in his father's footsteps and accepted a teaching post. Continuing his musical activities and interests in his spare time, he surrounded himself with other educated young professionals and artisans of the middle class. With these friends he found an immediate outlet for his music. By 1818, he had turned to full-time composition. Schubert would maintain the support of his friends, even while his success as a published composer was limited. Before long, Schubert had to fight a battle with an illness that was incurable and common in the day. By 1822, at the age of twenty-five, the effects of syphilis began to overtake him, his health and financial condition declined. He continued to compose, however, for six more years, producing some of his most profound music.

Known mostly for his more than 600 songs, Schubert's output is remarkable for a man with so little creative time. More remarkable still is the quality of his works. All aimed toward the Romantic ideal of poetic expression, one of Schubert's innovative contributions to that ideal is in how he structured the accompaniment and the singer with equal roles. His *Erlkönig* is a perfect example, with the piano imitating the horse's thunderous gallop while the singer provides narration and dialogue. Schubert perfected these techniques and used them in his song cycles as well. He composed some of the earliest song cycles, yet they still stand out as some of the finest that have been written.

Schubert also wrote in genres other than lieder. He worked in several sonata form genres, including symphonies and in chamber music. He, like his idol

Beethoven, composed nine symphonies, composed piano sonatas, and they both preferred to compose for the string quartet in chamber ensemble genres. Schubert is distinct from Beethoven in that he approached all his works with a song-like pattern of melodies that sprung forth effortlessly, rather than as a melodic germ developed over time the way Beethoven did. Melody seemed to spring from his pen even during his darkest creative days.

Works

- More than 600 lieder, including *Erlkönig*, and three song cycles, among them *The Lovely Maid of the Mill* and *Winter's Journey*
- Nine symphonies, including No. 8 "Unfinished"
- Chamber music, including fifteen string quartets, one string quintet, two piano trios, the "Trout" Quintet, one octet, and various sonatas
- Piano sonatas, dances, and character pieces
- Choral music, including seven Masses, other liturgical pieces, and part songs
- Operas and incidental music for dramas

Robert Schumann (1810–1856) and Clara Schumann

Robert Schumann embodied the ideals of Romanticism. Son of a bookseller, Robert went to Leipzig to study law, as was his mother's wish. Finding himself absorbed in hours of piano improvisations, Schumann began to concentrate on the piano with a famous teacher there by the name of Friedrich Weick. Blossoming late in life for a pianist, Schumann was in a hurry to make up for lost time and injured his fourth finger in a contraption he designed to isolate and strengthen this weakest of digits. Weick had a daughter named Clara whom he was grooming for the international concert stage, and Robert, nine years her senior, began a courtship of her. Fear of Robert's inability to make a living as a pianist, Clara's father stood in the way of their romance for several years, forcing them to communicate in their compositions.

Finally, after considerable legal wrangling, they married, and Robert became engrossed in composition. Looking for additional avenues for income, Schumann became founder and editor of the first professional journal for musicians, entitled ***Die Neue Zeitschrift für Musik***. With this venture, he single-handedly invented music journalism. Robert used this tool to promote the new music of the romantics, highlighting and reviewing music and performers he admired to the rest of the world. Over the next ten years, he would shape the taste of a generation and help to launch the careers of many. His very first interview was that of Chopin, and his last was Brahms.

Robert accompanied Clara on her performance tours, traveling together and living the life of music professionals. He composed and she performed many of his works for

Clara & Robert Schumann
©Bettmann/CORBIS

piano. On such a trip, he began the first of a series of depressive incidents that would prove to destabilize him. Once, in a fit of depression, Robert threw himself into the Rhine River, an apparent suicide attempt, only to be saved by fishermen. He was institutionalized for mental instability and depression and died two years later, leaving Clara alone with a professional career as the most famous female concert pianist of her day.

Roberts' most significant work was in the field of character pieces for the piano. Here, he applied the spirit of the lied, of which he composed several hundred, to the piano, creating a short programmatic aural image for the solo piano. Even though his controlling father-in-law desired him to compose in more "weighty forms," such as the sonata and symphony, his character pieces flowed from him naturally as an extension of the lied.

Works

- More than 300 lieder, including song cycles
- Orchestral music, including four symphonies and one piano concerto
- Chamber music, including three string quartets, one piano quintet, one piano quartet, piano trios, and sonatas
- Piano music, including three sonatas; numerous miniatures and collections, including *Butterflies*, *Carnaval*, and *Scenes from Childhood*; large works, including *Symphonic Etudes* and *Fantasy in C*
- One opera, incidental music, choral music, and lieder

Felix Mendelssohn (1809–1847)

Felix Mendelssohn is important to the Romantic period and to music history in general because of his diversity of talents. He was a child prodigy on the order of Mozart, yet surpassing him in that he matured musically faster than did Mozart. Felix and his older sister, Fanny, were the children of a Jewish banker in Berlin. Yet seeing themselves as more German than Jewish, the family joined the Protestant church and received an additional often-hyphenated name, Bartholdy or Mendelssohn-Bartholdy. His family summerhouse became the cultural center of Berlin, housing the most popular and important concerts, many of which had the children's compositions programmed for presentation.

Felix studied harmony as a child and piano with his mother, making his performance debut at age nine. Beginning to compose sonatas, a piano trio, a cantata, and two operettas, at age sixteen, he composed the first of his great works, the **Octet for Strings,** and by seventeen, followed with *Overture to A Midsummer Night's Dream*. His output was so sophisticated and prolific that his family hired an orchestra in order for Felix to hear and conduct his works. Through this early work as composer and conductor during his years at home, Felix would go on to become the first great conductor of orchestras, the first to use a baton in his conducting, and the father of modern conducting techniques.

He attended Berlin University, and while there, organized and conducted a concert of J.S. Bach's *St. Matthew's Passion*, its first

Felix Mendelssohn
©Chris Hellier/CORBIS

modern performance, which revitalized interest in the baroque master and reintroduced the forgotten Bach to the musical world. Mendelssohn-Bartholdy would leave Berlin to accept conducting positions in Dusseldorf and then in Leipzig, where he made the Gewandhaus orchestra the best in Europe while making Leipzig its musical capital. There, he programmed works by Mozart, Beethoven, Schubert, Chopin, Liszt, and Schumann, programming considered unusual and unorthodox at that time.

Mendelssohn married while in Leipzig and created the first conservatory, or school for the training of musicians. As founder of the **Leipzig Conservatory** he also persuaded Schumann to come and teach composition alongside himself. The model the Leipzig Conservatory established would be followed the world over for musical training. It brought the master teachers together in one place, attracting many students.

Continuing his conducting career, his teaching career, his composing career, and his festival organizing, Mendelssohn fell victim to a stroke due to exhaustion and overwork. He recovered but had another that left him partially paralyzed. Felix Mendelssohn-Bartholdy died at the age of thirty-eight.

Works

- Orchestral music, including five symphonies (No. 3 *Scottish*, No. 4 *Italian*, No. 5 *Reformation*); concert overtures *A Midsummer Night's Dream*, *The Hebrides*, or *Fingal's Cave*; two piano concertos, and a violin concerto in E minor
- Dramatic music, including one opera and incidental music for six plays including *A Midsummer Night's Dream*
- Choral music, including two oratorios, **St. Paul** and **Elijah**; cantatas; anthems; and part songs
- Chamber music, including six string quartets, two string quintets, piano quartets, one octet, and various sonatas
- Piano music, including *Songs Without Words*, sonatas, fugues, and fantasies
- Organ music, solo vocal music, transcriptions, and arrangements of Bach, Handel, Mozart, and Beethoven

Hector Berlioz (1803–1869)

Hector Berlioz is considered the best French Romantic composer. Son of a physician, his father sent him to Paris to study medicine, but after two miserable years, he enrolled in the conservatory. One of the few Romantic composers who did not play piano, Berlioz was forced to use his intuition and the imagination of his inner ear. In so doing, he is important for his expansion of orchestration, and his text on the subject that would forever alter the manner in which composers heard their works realized in instrumentation.

Berlioz composed in a highly programmatic manner, often using his own experiences as a resource for his works. His famous *Symphonie Fantastique* is based on a "program" he wrote illustrating the intents of each movement of this five-movement symphony. Based on an opium-induced hallucination, the *Fantastic Symphony* roughly follows his love affair with Harriet Smithson, an English actress.

Berlioz loved theater and often attended plays and operas while in the conservatory. There, he saw Miss Smithson in a play and became infatuated with her. A passionate and stormy courtship led to the same in a marriage that eventually fell apart. The fixed idea, the term he used for the same melody that recurred in each movement of the *Symphonie Fantastique*, is the source of musical transformation as the movements progress.

Works

- Orchestral music, including overtures *Waverley, Rob Roy,* and *King Lear;* program symphonies *Symphonie Fantastique,* **Harold in Italy, Romeo et Juliette**
- Choral music, including a **Requiem Mass**, *Te Deum,* **The Damnation of Faust**, and the oratorio *The Childhood of Christ*
- Three operas, including **The Trojans** and **Béatrice et Bénédict**
- Nine solo vocal works with orchestra
- Writings on music, including an orchestration treatise

Giuseppi Verdi (1813–1901)

Giuseppi Verdi is Italian Romantic opera. Practically every one of his compositions for the stage continues to make up the repertoire performed around the world. A composer and politician (Verdi would be selected as an honorary senator to the Italian government), his image and his music are tied to the Italian sense of nationality. In his first successful opera, **Nabucco**, the third act possesses a chorus sung by Hebrew slaves dreaming of freedom from Egyptian oppression. This would be seen as a reference to the Italians struggling under Austrian oppression. Verdi's name would become a battle cry for the Italian resistance, causing him to become an overnight national hero.

The son of a well-off landowner in a small town, Verdi was encouraged musically and eventually returned home from his studies in Milan to become Director of Music for the town. Even though he would become famous, wealthy, and influential (possibly Italy's most famous citizen in his lifetime), he loved nothing better than his small farm there.

Musically, he balanced the *bel canto* solo traditions coming to him from contemporaries Bellini and Donizetti with an expansion of the orchestra and chorus' role in the dramatic elements of his operas.

Works

- Twenty-eight operas, including **Macbeth, Rigoletto, Il trovatore, La traviata, Un ballo in maschera, La forza del destino, Don Carlos, Aida, Otello,** and **Falstaff**
- Vocal music, including a *Requiem Mass*

Franz Liszt (1811–1886)

Franz Liszt was the premier solo pianist of his day, providing captivatingly memorable concerts, creating legions of fans, and changing the performance practices of pianists that exist to this day. He captured the imaginations of his female fans, causing normally dignified upper-middle-class women to act in the most unsophisticated of ways, fainting at concerts and stalking the artist to obtain a memento such as a lock of hair or a button from his coat. He lived his celebrated existence in a similar manner as rock stars and other icons of popular culture today.

Much of the music he composed was for him to perform in concert. He preferred the character piece model provided by the early romantics, such as the etude, nocturnes, waltzes, ballades, polonaises, and so on, and for the first time, chose to memorize them rather than following the customary practice of performing with the music as was typical. In this manner, he gave his audience the impression that his playing was free flowing and divinely inspired adding more frenzy to his image. Also, since his fans thought his best physical attribute was his facial profile, Liszt turned the piano away from the traditional performance position of facing the audience (looking down through the body of the piano toward the audience) to a side angle where the audience could see his hands and his beloved profile. Pianists to this day still perform in this manner and memorize their music, all because of the celebrity of Franz Liszt.

In mid-career, Liszt ventured into the newly developed position of orchestral conductor for the Duke of Weimar. At the podium, he found a venue to continue his musicianship as he had before, but now as leader of many other musicians. In this manner he was visible to the audience, still in control musically, and extended the scope and importance of his concert career internationally. Just as he had composed for himself as a pianist, he composed for his orchestra when he conducted. He had previously enjoyed the musicality of the character piece for piano and now took that concept of program music in one movement and scored it for orchestra, creating a brand new genre perfect for the romantic taste—the **symphonic poem**.

The symphonic poem as a genre opened many doors and possibilities for the orchestra to join into the romantic style as an ensemble as it had been relegated to the classical forms of symphonies, concertos, and opera accompaniments. Liszt first introduced the symphonic poem in a set called *Les Préludes*. These would influence audiences and future composers for generations to come.

In his late years, Liszt took minor orders with the church, becoming an Abbe, and split his time between Rome, Weimar, and Budapest, composing church music including masses, cantatas, and oratorios. He also championed young composers and their new music, using his celebrity to pave their way into cultural acceptance, including his son-in-law, Richard Wagner.

Works

- Orchestral music, including symphonic poems *Les Préludes*, *Dante Symphony*, and *Faust Symphony*; two piano concertos; and *Totentanz* (for piano and orchestra)

- Piano music, including *Transcendental Etudes*, *Sonata in B minor*, *Hungarian Rhapsodies*, nocturnes, waltzes, ballades, polonaises, and other character pieces; numerous transcriptions of orchestral and opera works for piano
- Choral music, including Masses, oratorios, psalms, cantatas, and secular part songs
- One opera; songs with piano

Richard Wagner (1813–1884)

Richard Wagner was largely a self-taught composer. Except for a few private harmony lessons, he was free to explore his own ideas without the influences of traditional musical notions being imparted to him as obligatory. Wagner combined his love of music and his love of theater, writing his first play at fifteen and his first composition at sixteen. Following his own ideas, he stretched the bounds of tonality into the unstable shifting world of the chromatic. Tense and ever changing, his music flows where it wants through seas of dominant harmony in search of a tonal shoreline.

Learning his craft with the operas ***Rienzi, The Flying Dutchman***, and ***Tannhauser***, Wagner left Germany during political upheaval and relocated in Switzerland where he wrote the book for his most important music dramas, as he called them, the *Ring Cycle*, a set of four operas designed to be seen concurrently. These music dramas embodied all his ideas of transforming opera into the "total work of art."

One of his chief innovations was in the expansion of the size and role of the orchestra in opera. The orchestra to Wagner had the power to convey every possible emotion, and he designed his music drama to have continuous music, no recitative or stoppage. In order to do this dramatically, Wagner developed the concept of the *leitmotif*, a melody that is branded with a character, an object, or an emotion in the opera. When this melody is played associating it with a person, thing, or emotion, the orchestra can now play a role in the storytelling, conveying aspects of the story to the audience without a word of lyric or dialogue.

On his return to Germany under the patronage of Ludwig II, Wagner managed to build a special theater in Bayreuth that had the technical facilities necessary to bring about his reformations of the opera tradition, and to this day, the Bayreuth opera house performs only Wagner operas.

Works

- Thirteen operas (music dramas), including *Rienzi; The Flying Dutchman; Tannhäuser;* ***Lohengrin; Tristan und Isolde; The Meistersingers of Nuremberg; The Ring of the Nibelung,*** consisting of ***The Rhine Gold, The Valkyrie, Siegfried,*** and ***The Twilight of the Gods;*** and ***Parsifal***
- Orchestral music, including ***Sigfried Idyll***
- Piano music, vocal music, and choral music

Frederic Chopin (1810–1849)

Frederic Chopin
©Hulton-Deutsch Collection/CORBIS

Frederic Chopin is known as the "poet of the piano." The son of a French father and Polish mother, he was born in Poland, where he studied harmony and counterpoint at the Warsaw Conservatory. After several international concerts, he arrived in Paris, staying until his death. Paris was the center of the musical world during his time there and had many important artists in residence with which he enjoyed friendships. George Sand, pen name for novelist Aurore Dudevant, was six years his senior, yet a relationship began between them that would last for an extended period of time.

After a successful recital debut in Paris, Chopin began to teach lessons to high society offspring, creating for himself an influential and financially successful existence. His performing diminished to small, intimate performances in the salons of his friends, and he composed for his students and for himself. A legendary improviser, many of his compositions came from these improvisations, and they seem to spring from his fabulous yet delicate technique, bringing forth sounds from the instrument that were unique to him in a time that witnessed the likes of Franz Liszt. Chopin would compose exclusively for the piano, and he drew inspiration from much of his native Polish musical heritage. Mazurkas, polonaises, impromptus, nocturnes, etudes, and other character pieces are his genre of choice. His rhythmic devices and tonal references preceded many of the harmonic techniques that would become popular in the French Impressionists like Debussy and Ravel.

He died of tuberculosis at the age of thirty-nine and was considered the first nationalist composer. At the end, his body was buried in Paris, but his heart removed and returned to Poland.

Works

- Works for piano and orchestra, including two piano concertos
- Piano music, including four ballades, *Fantasy in F minor*, *Berceuse*, *Barcarolle*; three sonatas, preludes, études, mazurkas, nocturnes, waltzes, polonaises, impromptus, scherzos, rondos, marches, and variations
- Chamber music, all including piano; songs

Late Romantics

Peter Tchaikovsky (1840–1893)

The name **Peter Tchaikovsky** is synonymous with music of the ballet. Due to the popularity of his dance works and the frequency with which they are performed, many Americans are familiar with his *Nutcracker*, *Swan Lake*, and *The Sleeping Beauty*. However, his creative core is more entrenched in the sonata genres of the symphony, concerto, and string quartet. Also, his romanticism is centered in his work in the symphonic poem.

Born in Russia and trained as a student at the St. Petersburg Conservatory, Tchaikovsky landed a teaching position at the new Moscow Conservatory. There he was torn between different worlds. He was trained in western music but worked in Russia, a gateway to the east. Often, his works were too western for his Russian contemporaries and too modern for his western listeners. Also, his homosexuality conflicted with his social position, and he attempted marriage in hopes of achieving normalcy in his existence only to have that fail miserably. When his marriage fell apart, he left it and his teaching position behind in hopes of a new start. With the aide of benefactress Madame Nadezhda von Meck, who mailed him a stipend, he was able to continue composing.

One of the most performed composers of the late Romantic period, he died of cholera contracted from drinking water that had not been boiled, a commonly known safeguard, leading to the speculation that he committed suicide.

Peter Tchaikovsky
©Bettmann/CORBIS

Works

- Eight operas, including *Eugene Onegin* and *The Queen of Spades*
- Three ballets: *Swan Lake, The Sleeping Beauty,* and *The Nutcracker*
- Orchestral music, including seven symphonies (No. 6 Pathétique), three piano concertos, one violin concerto, and symphonic poems and overtures (*Romeo and Juliet*)
- Chamber and keyboard music, choral music and songs

Johannes Brahms (1833–1897)

Son of a double-bass player, **Johannes Brahms** studied music in his youth, taking lessons in piano, theory, and composition. He, too, was a popular musician, often working in clubs earning money for his family and arranging music for his father's orchestra. In his early twenties, Brahms met Robert and Clara Schumann with whom he became fast friends. Robert championed Brahms' music in his journal, calling him a "young eagle," and it was to Clara that he first brought his new works. Johannes comforted Clara during Robert's mental decline and remained intimate friends for the rest of his life, with her often premiering his works around the world.

Brahms was a classicist in the age of romantics. He composed nothing that was programmatic or extra referential. Instead, he is considered to be the extension of Beethoven, working in symphonies, string quartets, and sonatas. Living and working in Vienna most all of his adult life, Brahms joins his other famous classical contemporaries who worked in that same environment milling that rich creative soil.

Works

- Orchestral music, including four symphonies, **Variations on a Theme by Haydn**; two overtures (**Academic Festival** and **Tragic**); four concertos (two for piano, one for violin, and one double concerto for violin and cello)

- Chamber music, including string quartets, quintets, sextets; piano trios, quartets, and one quintet; one clarinet quintet; sonatas (violin, cello, clarinet/viola)
- Piano music, including sonatas, character pieces, dances, and variation sets (on a theme by Handel; on a theme by Paganini)
- Choral music, including **A German Requiem**, *Alto Rhapsody*, and part songs
- Lieder, including *Vergebliches Ständchen*, *Four Serious Songs*, and folk song arrangements

Gustav Mahler (1860–1911)

Gustav Mahler, last of the great romantic composers, was by trade a conductor. Mahler was born in a small Bohemian town where he studied music with local teachers. In 1875, he went to Vienna to study at the conservatory, where he remained until 1878. Upon finishing his studies, he took a series of conducting posts throughout Central and Eastern Europe, including Budapest, Hamburg, and Leipzig. It was in Leipzig that he first attracted notice with his interpretation of Wagner's *Ring Cycle*. He ultimately ended up in Vienna, conducting the state opera orchestra. His success in transforming the repertory and performance standards of the opera house was nothing short of remarkable, but it came at high personal cost. The constant work forced him to confine his composing to the summer months, and probably contributed to the health problems that would end his life at an early age. In addition, in order to obtain a post in Vienna—a city with deep undercurrents of anti-Semitism—Mahler had to renounce Judaism and convert to Catholicism. In the end it did him no good, and these same anti-Semitic forces compelled him to leave the city.

He immigrated to the United States. In New York, he was engaged as conductor for the Metropolitan Opera, and later the New York Philharmonic. When he died at the age of fifty, he was working on his tenth symphony, a work he had postponed thinking it something of a curse (pointing to Beethoven, Schubert, and Bruckner). His "real" tenth symphony, **Das Lied von der Erde** (a setting of six poems by the eighth century Chinese poet Li Po), serves as a fitting summary of his symphonic style, and one of his true masterpieces.

Mahler's music reflects the same ambiguities as his life. He was intensely tied to the past in many ways, following in the footsteps of the great Austrian symphonists. At the same time, he expanded the forms he inherited to a point that it seemed impossible to go beyond. His works are enormous, both in size and in force. His late symphonies are often more than ninety minutes in length and call for huge instrumental (and often choral) forces. His Symphony No. 8 (called the *Symphony of a Thousand*), for example, calls for five vocal soloists, a boy choir, and an adult choir, along with a gigantic orchestra. He also departed from tradition in his use of tonality. His larger works often ended in a different tonality than they began, weakening the structural role of tonality at the same time that Schoenberg and his contemporaries were moving toward a purely atonal style. The final element we can note in Mahler's music is its wit, often tinged with irony and parody. This often occurs by means of the juxtaposition of incongruous elements to create a jarring, often seemingly banal, mix.

Works

- Orchestral music, including ten symphonies
- Song cycles with orchestra, including *Songs of a Wayfarer, The Youth's Magic Horn, Songs on the Death of Children,* and *The Song of the Earth*
- Lieder

VOCABULARY

Academic Festival
Aida
Barcarolle
Béatrice et Bénédict
Berceuse
Clara Schumann
Das Lied von der Erde
Die Neue Zeitschrift für Musik
Elijah
Falstaff
Fantasy in F minor
Felix Mendelssohn
Franz Liszt
Franz Peter Schubert
Frederic Chopin
German Requiem
Giuseppi Verdi
Gustav Mahler
Harold in Italy
Hector Berlioz
Hungarian Rhapsodies
Il trovatore
Johannes Brahms
La forza del destino
La traviata

Leipzig Conservatory
Les Préludes
Lohengrin
Macbeth
Nabucco
Nutcracker
Octet for Strings
Otello
Parsifal
Peter Tchaikovsky
Requiem Mass
Richard Wagner
Rienzi
Rigoletto
Robert Schumann
Romeo and Juliet
Romeo et Juliette
Siegfried
Sigfried Idyll
Songs of a Wayfarer
Songs on the Death of Children
Songs Without Words
St. Paul
Swan Lake
Symphonic Poem

Symphony No. 6—*The Pathétique*
Symphony No. 8—*Symphony of a Thousand*
Tannhauser
The Damnation of Faust
The Flying Dutchman
The Meistersingers of Nuremberg
The Rhine Gold
The Ring of the Nibelung
The Sleeping Beauty
The Song of the Earth
The Trojans
The Twilight of the Gods
The Valkyrie
The Youth's Magic Horn
Transcendental Etudes
Tristan und Isolde
Variations on a Theme by Haydn

WEBSITE

Please refer to the *Music Through Time* site listed in the front of your book to investigate and complete more classroom activities and assignments.

CHAPTER
18

A Twentieth Century Overview

Whereas the nineteenth century in America is dominated by the expansion of the Industrial Revolution and the expansion of the country from "sea to shining sea," the twentieth century is dominated by differing philosophies and ideas, initiating both from inside and outside of our country with regards to government and politics, science, and the arts. How these philosophies and ideas affected us as a people explains much about the rationale for and the significance of those epic historical events that are so familiar.

In government, the Enlightenment notion of democracy spread throughout Europe in the nineteenth century, causing great commotion in many cases, instability and the rearranging of accepted norms, and it often had its detractors. Democratic governance often displaced power from one group and empowered another, resulting in alternatives to democracy, including communism, socialism, and many splintered "isms." Each of these in turn was seen as a threat to the legitimacy, unabated progression, and supremacy of the Westernized moral "self-evident" core values of the American representative form of government. The century saw these conflicting ideas tested through seemingly constant mortal struggles on the battlefields of the "civilized" world.

Governmental Paradigms with Economic Engines

The American democratic model of government emerged out of the ideas of the eighteenth century Enlightenment philosophy. Its success and perpetuation is dependant on an economic set of ideas that possess a lineage back to the sixteenth century, however. **Capitalism**—the notion that an entity can produce a product or commodity and sell, exchange, or trade that product or commodity on an open free market to those willing to trade or pay for that product—is the economic system on which American democracy is based. Capitalism depends on a free market, on the lawful protection of private property, and on human productivity. Money is exchanged based on a person's ability to produce a good or service that meets the open market's demands. It allows for the ownership and production ability of an entity to expand to a point past an individual's ability to produce, leading to a situation where there is ownership and employees, or hired individuals willing to sell their labor to an owner of a product or service, allowing the owner to expand his/its production capacity, creating wealth through the compounding of profit, while the employee is paid a contracted wage.

The end result of the capitalistic system is a concentration of wealth into the hands of a few while the many labor to survive and risk decline into poverty. The idealistic virtue of capitalism is that it fosters individual development. All are encouraged to participate, and their destiny is only limited by their individual choices and personal industry. In this arena, work is valued, as is innovation and long-range planning. The weakness of this system is that it fosters a class system of wealthy and poor—a veritable survival of the economic fittest. As a response, others throughout the world have created idealistic and philosophical alternatives. The most visible of these is communism and its varied forms.

Communism

Karl Marx and **Friedrich Engels** published their *Communist Manifesto* on February 21, 1848. Its philosophy attempts to form a societal model that theoretically creates a classless society through the abolishment of private ownership of land and property, graduated income tax, and inheritance, while controlling the production and transportation of goods, assigning these to the "state." The end result was to do away with the concept of poverty through the idea of "... from each according to his ability, to each according to his need."

The paradigm selected to establish this ideal state was through the revolution of the proletariat, their name for the labor class who must work for wages. As the revolutionary idea spread and tensions rose in Europe, America saw **communism** and its many variances, including socialism, fascism, and so on, as a primary threat to its survival. The twentieth century priority of American foreign policy was to keep communism as far from our shores and trading partners as possible and to challenge the spread of communism at every turn.

Global Conflicts

World War I (1914–1918) marked the final break with the old world order of the absolute monarchies in Europe. Its outcome would be the catalyst for the Russian Revolution, which gave birth to the Communist ideal and encouraged others in the world to revolt, including China and Cuba, and eventually spawned the **Cold War** between the Soviet Union and the United States.

The Imperialist alliance of the Central Powers—Germany, Austria-Hungary, and Turkey—was in conflict with the Allied Powers—Britain, France, Russia, Belgium, and Serbia. Later Japan, Italy, and the United States eventually joined the Allied Powers in their defense of Serbia in the face of the expansionist policies of Austria-Hungary. At first, America tried to remain neutral, seeking rather to trade with the Allied Powers who needed its manufactured goods and exports such as steel and cotton, among others, in their war effort. American trade vessels were targeted by navies of the Central Powers, hindering trade and endangering ships and crew alike. As a result, the United States entered the "war to end all wars." By 1918, nearly 9 million had been killed and nearly 22 million soldiers had been wounded. It is estimated that twice that amount of civilians eventually died because of the war, causing it to be the bloodiest war ever fought to that time.

World War II would soon make World War I seem like child's play, as between 40 and 50 million people died as a result of this war, with 20 million Russians alone. It was fought over unresolved issues from WWI, expansionist land grab attempts by Germany, Italy, and Japan, and the development of dictatorships in some places. Over 300,000 American soldiers lost their lives, and worst of all, the world's most dangerous weapon of mass destruction was unleashed with the atomic bomb. The threat of planetary destruction looms over subsequent generations as a result.

Ideologies shifted, massive immigration occurred, the establishment of communist states of various sorts emerged, nuclear weapons proliferated, and intense mistrust between capitalistic and communistic governments followed the end of WWII. The **Korean War** and the **Vietnam War** were mid-century developments of this distrust and were expansion and containment attempts in the world order. The Cold War was the longest unofficial war of the century, fought between the Soviet Union and the United States. A standoff of nuclear powers ended only

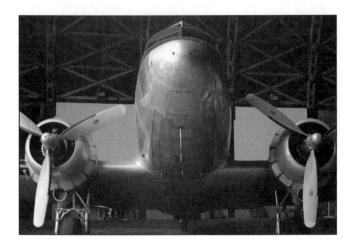

because the arms race it created bankrupted the economy of the Soviet Union. With that, the period of communistic ideology seems to have faded as a major economic and governmental paradigm with only a few countries maintaining any pure communistic orders.

The Civil Rights Movement

Paralleling the many wars that American foreign policy pursued throughout the century, one its most divisive, yet fundamental wars, was an internal struggle between the American citizenry. With unanswered questions of racial equality, civil rights issues reached the forefront of the national conscience, reflecting the continuance of this nations' inability to incorporate racial differences.

Even though slavery was outlawed in the United States in 1865, southern states perpetuated a set of rigid social laws and traditions to keep the Black and White citizenry separated, and, as a byproduct, kept African Americans from voting successfully, ensuring their lower class servitude status. A concentrated and highly organized effort to expose this social inequality, bringing it to the forefront of the American conscience began in **Montgomery, Alabama**, on December 1, 1955.

Rosa Parks, an African American seamstress and **NAACP** volunteer, took a public bus to ride home from work that evening. As the public transportation system of the South was segregated, she took her seat in the back of the bus, squarely in the "Colored" seating section. But as the bus made its stops, the "White" section filled to capacity and one White man had no seat available in his appointed section. The bus driver, attempting to solve the problem for the White male patron, came to the Colored section and asked Ms. Parks to stand and give up her seat so that the White patron could sit. She refused, insisting that she was in her appointed section and that she was tired. As a consequence of her refusal, she was arrested, booked, and convicted of disorderly conduct. The next evening, fifty members of the local African American community met to discuss a public response to Ms. Parks' conviction.

MARTIN LUTHER KING

The group of fifty who met that evening to rectify the injustice of Ms. Parks' situation included a local minister, new to the area, who eventually became the Civil Rights Movement's chief spokesman and architect, **Dr. Martin Luther King Jr**. Born in Atlanta, Georgia, on January 15, 1929, King arrived in Montgomery when he became the pastor of the **Dexter Avenue Baptist Church** in 1954. He helped organize the first public response to segregation in the South when the group initiated the Montgomery Bus Boycott. The African American community in Montgomery at the time depended on public transportation as a way to get to and from their jobs. The collective strategy was to cease to pay for tickets and ride public transportation, which had proven to have policies humiliating to their community. For 381 days, African Americans boycotted the bus system, forcing the White community to use their own cars to individually transport their domestic help to and from work, bringing the ridership of buses to almost nothing, and bringing economic ruin to that sector of the city's budget. The result was a victory for the African American community when the United States Supreme Court ruled that racial segregation of intrastate travel was illegal.

Empowered by their success at the federal level, the group expanded and continued to systematically bring other injustices to the forefront of public discourse. The favorite strategy was to use a form of civil disobedience that was nonviolent, reducing the perception of revolution and anarchy while increasing public sympathy. When resisters were willing to endure beatings from state officials while offering no physical defense and demonstrated the willingness to endure mistreatment as a result of their challenge to "Jim Crowe" social norms they deemed unjust, public opinion began to turn in their favor, forcing a series of Civil Rights Legislation.

Science

During the twentieth century, more discoveries and technological advancements occurred than in anytime previously. From the discovery of penicillin to the mapping of the human DNA structure in medicine, to the theories of physics and the nature and origin of the cosmos, scientists such as **Alexander Fleming, James Watson, Francis Crick, Albert Einstein, Ernest Rutherford, Edwin Powell Hubble,** and **J. Robert Oppenheimer** pioneered developments in physics, time, and space. From the **Wright Brothers** and their first flight at **Kitty Hawk** to the development of **NASA** and its successful missions to the moon and beyond, this century saw more advances in transportation than could even be imagined in previous ones.

Developments in communication, progressing from radio to television to the personal computer and the development of the Internet—all these inventions made the world a smaller place, cross-informing world cultures and populations. The speed of access to unforeseen amounts of information has made life in the modern world fast-paced and uncertain. More possibilities exist now for human development and creation than ever before, yet there is also stress, uncertainty, flux, and dehumanization everywhere. Much of the literature and art created in the twentieth century reflects these uncertainties.

VOCABULARY

Albert Einstein
Alexander Fleming
Capitalism
Civil Rights Movement
Communism
Communist Manifesto
Dexter Avenue Baptist
   Church
Dr. Martin Luther King
   Jr.

Edwin Powell Hubble
Ernest Rutherford
Francis Crick
Friedrich Engels
J. Robert Oppenheimer
James Watson
Karl Marx
Kitty Hawk
Montgomery, Alabama
NAACP

NASA
Rosa Parks
The Cold War
Korean War
Vietnam War
World War I
World War II
Wright Brothers

WEBSITE

Please refer to the *Music Through Time* site listed in the front of your book to investigate and complete more classroom activities and assignments.

CHAPTER

19

European Art and Music in the Twentieth Century

The music of the twentieth century is varied and filled with different influences that led to personal motivations for artistic creation by composers. Europe was conflicted with varying political philosophies that would eventually lead to wars on a global scale. The end result of these conflicts was the forced migration of populations in the eye of conflicts and war. Many scientists and artists would seek safe haven wherever they could find it, and many sought refuge in the United States of America, enriching the creative and scientific capacity of the American society during this time. America then became the cultural leader of the world during the twentieth century, reflecting a "melting-pot" of resources, ideas, and creative capacities. It is necessary, then, to look at twentieth-century music through the dual prism of a European and an American vision.

But before this duality is explored, America's first native composer of note must be mentioned even though he belongs to the ninteenth century.

Louis Moreau Gottschalk (1829–1869)

Born in New Orleans, Louisiana, on May 8, 1829, to **Creole** parents, **Louis Moreau Gottschalk** was America's first great native-born pianist and composer in the Romantic period and style. Trained in Paris, and even praised for his piano skill by the likes of Chopin and Berlioz, Gottschalk would develop an illustrious career as an international piano soloist touring America, Europe, and even South America. He would compose over 100 pieces for the piano, influenced by his European contemporaries as well as his New Orleans heritage. He was the first significant composer to use rhythms and cultural flavors found in the American south where an African culture of African American slaves and European influences mixed in the Creole society of New Orleans. His was the first music to hint at the cultural richness to come from the American south. Most popular of his piano compositions were "**The Banjo**" and "**The Dying Poet**."

Impressionism

In France, a technique in painting initiated by **Claude Monet** led to a school of artistic creation known as **Impressionism**, whose primary objective was to

119

capture the natural outdoors, focusing on how light reflected within the scene. The softening of edges and the blurring of details left a striking and positive emotional response on its audience.

Claude Debussy (1862–1918)

Claude Debussy
©Hulton-Deutsch Collection/CORBIS

Seeking to employ these same softening and blurring effects in music, **Claude Debussy** established the Impressionistic technique in the musical world. Born in France, he would attend the Paris Conservatory and receive his musical education. However, he became more frustrated with the constraints of form used by previous generations of composers and sought to free himself from the tyranny of the sonata allegro form, a very German devise he thought. After winning the prestigious Prix de Rome and spending the obligatory time of study in Rome, he returned to France and intentionally set out to use his own ideas in his subsequent compositions. He favored a more free, formal flow, favoring thematic variations and more complex rhythmic devices. He embraced tonally extended harmonies and employed exotic scales in his melodic materials. These he combined to create a similar effect in music as had been created in the world of painting—the blurring of formal boundaries—allowing freedom and flow in rhythmic ideas and the focusing on orchestration techniques that stretched timbre possibilities. His rhythmic freedom would later influence other twentieth-century composers such as Stravinsky.

His most popular pieces focus on the piano as well as orchestral creations, including: *Prelude à L'après-midi d'un faune* (*Prelude to the Afternoon of a Faun*), *Nocturnes*, *La Mer* (*The Sea*), *Images*, the opera *Pelléas et Mélisande* and the ballet *Jeux* (*Games*).

Maurice Ravel (1875–1937)

A fellow Frenchman and fellow student at the Paris Conservatory, **Maurice Ravel** is often linked with Debussy as a fellow musical Impressionist composer. Sharing traits of rhythmic and melodic craftsmanship established by Debussy to create the French sound, Ravel also excelled in orchestration, often composing works for the piano first then orchestrating them with masterful skill. But he differed from Debussy in that he didn't abandon the traditional concepts of form; rather, he embraced them and thrived in their constraints, placing him as a possible neoclassical composer as well. His most famous pieces include *Bolero,* which is more of a theme and set of orchestration variations, and *Rapsodie espagnole,* reflecting his persistent infatuation with Spanish rhythms and culture.

Expressionism

Musicians of the twentieth century often followed their own creative ideas that were purely musical in nature, having to do with manipulations of harmony, melody, and/or form. However, sometimes composers borrowed creative ideas from the trends and ideas of painters and other visual artists, adapting their overarching concepts in musical terms. An example of this trend in musical composition is the "**Second Viennese School**" of composers headed by **Arnold Schoenberg** and his two disciples, **Anton Webern** and **Alban Berg**. These composers' works are categorized under the visual art term, **Expressionism**. Attempting to create emotional canvases of sound that reflected the intents of artists such as Kandinsky and Munch, these painters attempted to capture a distorted realty, drawing attention to the painter's inner emotions regarding reality, often dark and conflicted due to the times and conditions in which they lived and worked.

Arnold Schoenberg
©CORBIS

Schoenberg, also a painter in the Expressionist style, developed a technique of melodic and harmonic manipulation of pitches called atonality or atonal music, where each of the twelve chromatic pitches had equal importance, undermining the cultural traditions of tonal harmony that had been developed over centuries. This technique, called twelve tone music or dodecaphonic technique, produced a music whose aural effect seemed unstable, harsh, angular, and mathematical, relating pitches to each other in new ways, obliterating the laws of standard motion. This technique created a similar effect in music as did the distortions of reality embraced by the expressionistic painters of that time.

Arnold Schoenberg (1874–1951)

Born in Vienna, Austria, **Arnold Schoenberg,** a Jew, converted to Lutheranism during turbulent times in Germany and Austria; only later did he return to his Judaic heritage. He taught students in composition, including Alban Berg (1885–1935) and Anton Webern (1883–1945), who extended his melodic manipulations to other aspects of musical construction including form and rhythm. Together, these three influential composers are collectively known as the Second Viennese School. Schoenberg's most significant works include *Pierrot lunaire* and *Five Pieces for Orchestra.*

Neoclassicism

The term **Neoclassicism** applies to visual arts, literature, and music. It was spawned as a reaction to the overpowering Romanticism of the nineteenth century, choosing instead to employ emotional restraint and return to the forms and genres of the Baroque and Classical eras, yet infusing them with modern developments in craftsmanship.

Igor Stravinsky (1882–1971)

In music, the neoclassical style was initiated by the Russian-born **Igor Stravinsky**. Insatiably curious and consistently changing musical influences, he initially began composing in the Russian tradition of Tchaikovsky and other Russian nationals when he attended university in St. Petersburg where he studied with Rimsky-Korsakov. Following the Tchaikovsky model of creating music for the ballet, Stravinsky became associated with the Ballet Russes in France

Igor Stravinsky
©Hulton-Deutsch Collection/CORBIS

and its director Serge Diaghilev. He embarked on writing several scores for that company including: *Firebird*, *Petrushka*, and *The Rite of Spring*, whose premiere was so aurally shocking that it created a legendary riot among its well-to-do Parisian audience

Following WWI, Stravinsky lived in Switzerland and became a citizen before moving on to the United States and changing citizenship yet again. In the United States he embarked on a conducting career and recorded many of his works under his own baton.

His compositional style continued to expand, concentrating on rhythmic and meter manipulations, even employing a polytonal harmonic style for a while. Later, he would explore atonality and the twelve tone system of Schoenberg. His most popular works, besides the ballets, are pieces for unconventional combinations of instruments, including *Concerto for Piano and Winds* and *Ebony Concerto*, and operas *The Rake's Progress* and *Oedipus Rex*, and another dramatic work, *The Soldier's Tale*, and the *Symphony of Psalms*.

Nationalism

The **nationalism** of the Romantic period continued to serve as a model for creativity. Several twentieth-century composers drew from the folk elements of their cultures to inspire new art works. **Bela Bartok**, a Hungarian pianist and composer, drew inspiration from Hungarian folk music. Others before him drew upon folk traditions in their works, but for Bartok, it was a respect for the genre as a whole that was significantly new. His fascination with the genre of music was so sincere that he often went out into the country with a wax recording device capturing native Hungarian musicians performing folk material. These recordings and catalogs served as the basis for most of his created work.

Bela Bartok (1881–1945)

Later, Bartok became a Professor of Piano at the Budapest Academy, the same institution where he studied as a young man. In the years prior to WWII, the political environment forced him to migrate to the United States, where he continued to compose in spite of ill health. Bartok wrote in most of the formal genres of his day and especially excelled at string quartets, which remain popular. These formal tendencies can cause him to be legitimately considered a composer in the neoclassic movement. His best known orchestral pieces include, *Music for Strings, Percussion, and Celesta* and *Concerto for Orchestra*, and his piano pieces, *Allegro barbaro* and *Mikrokosmos* remain favorites.

Dimitri Shostokovitch (1906–1975)

Russian-born **Dimitri Shostokovitch's** creative life mirrored the political strife surrounding the birth of the Soviet Union and its socialistic ideal. Stifling creative freedom, and preferring for its artists to glorify the "party line," Shostokovitch found it difficult to freely follow his compositional muse in an environment filled with such government control of taste. Early in his career, he produced works for the cinema, the opera house, and the ballet, but his second opera, *The Lady Macbeth of the Mtsensk District*, received official reprisal. Forcing him to reign in his individuality, Shostokovitch spent several years producing more acceptable works for the local governmental authorities and centered these around the symphony and other sonatas, even though his popularity in the West was rising. In 1953, after the death of Stalin, Shostokovitch returned to a more open creative freedom, sealing his popularity and acclaim in the West.

American Nationalism

In America, the nineteenth century path to success for an American-born musician or composer included study in Europe in order to gain traditional skills as well as artistic apprentice-like acceptability. A favorite path for these artistic crusades ended in France, often with arguably the most important woman musician of the twentieth century—Nadia Boulanger.

Nadia Boulanger (1887–1979)

Nadia Boulanger, a French composer, conductor, and teacher, is more responsible for the success of an American school of compositional thought than any other individual. The daughter of a former Paris Conservatory teacher, she, too, attended that institution and received her education studying with Gabriel Faure. She became the first woman conductor of many major orchestras throughout the world, including the New York, Boston, and Philadelphia Orchestras. In 1921, Boulanger began to teach composition at the American Conservatory of Music in Fontainebleau, France. There she would teach, train, and inspire several generations of young aspiring American-born composers to be "American." The list of her students is a veritable who's who of American art music composers, including Aaron Copland, Igor Stravinsky, Elliot Carter, David Diamond, Philip Glass, Roy Harris, Quincy Jones, Walter Piston, Virgil Thomson, Ross Lee Finney, and a host of others.

Nadia Boulanger
©Bettmann/CORBIS

Aaron Copland (1900–1990)

The son of Russian Jewish immigrants, **Aaron Copland** was born in Brooklyn, New York, on November 14, 1900. By age twenty, he was in Paris studying with Nadia Boulanger, who taught him to use the geographic elements of his native country as inspiration for his creative works.

Aaron Copland conducts his Lincoln portrait with Coretta Scott King narrating
©Bettmann/CORBIS

Upon his return to New York, he discovered a Renaissance of creative activity, into which he plunged headlong. Using voicings, which provides a broad, open, aural quality that mirrors the landscape of his native topography, and combining folk-like images of cowboys, mountain ranges, and significant historical figures as launch points for many of his works, Copland is considered the "Dean of American Composers." He would go on to teach composition at the Berkshire Music Center, where he would help mold several generations of native American art musicians and composers.

His most famous works include the ballets *Billy the Kid* and *Appalachian Spring*, and his orchestral music, including *Fanfare for the Common Man* and *A Lincoln Portrait*. He also composed music for film and songs.

Leonard Bernstein (1918–1990)

The first great international figure of art music who was native born and exclusively trained in American institutions was **Leonard Bernstein**. He remains the single-most important and influential art musician of the second half of the twentieth century worldwide.

Born in Lawrence, Massachusetts, Bernstein attended Harvard University after his high school graduation before continuing to study at the Curtis Institute of Music in Philadelphia. He studied conducting with Fritz Reiner and Serge Koussevitsky, orchestration with Randall Thompson, and theory and composition with Walter Piston, among others. He attended the Boston Symphony Orchestra's summer institute at Tanglewood, where he was Koussevitsky's conducting assistant and where he met Aaron Copland, whose music Bernstein would later champion.

In 1943, Bernstein obtained his first conducting position with the New York Philharmonic as an assistant conductor. In this capacity, his responsibilities included orchestral preparations and the conducting of orchestra rehearsals prior to the arrival of a guest conductor, who polished the final rehearsal before a broadcast performance. Conducting the afternoon concerts for children was also his responsibility. His meteoric rise to fame from musical obscurity came in the midst of these conditions.

On November 14, 1943, Bruno Walter, who was in the height of his international fame as a conductor, was scheduled to lead the New York Philharmonic in a concert broadcast via radio around the country. He suddenly fell ill and could not go on. With only a few hours notice, Bernstein, who was performing a small concert of his own compositions at another location in New York, was summoned to fill in for Walter so that the concert and broadcast could continue. Racing across town, frantically studying music with which he was only scarcely familiar, Bernstein went on stage in the midst of a most stressful and calamitous situation. Not only did he survive the situation, but he was brilliant in his performance and interpretation that evening, leading to a tumult of notoriety and praise for the young novice. He awoke the next morning to find himself an artistic hero as the news leaked out of the conditions surrounding his major conducting debut. Bernstein never looked back, taking his boundless energy and enthusiasm to greater and greater heights. He ascended to the conductorships of several major world orchestras, holding lifetime positions and titles with several. As television became a constant in American life, he became the first figure to use the media to its fullest extent, becoming a major world celebrity through his conducting and educational programs for children.

As a composer, Bernstein worked in several of the standard forms of classical music, including symphonies, orchestral song cycles, and even a Mass. Yet his natural curiosities extended beyond the boundaries of art music alone. Since his Harvard days, where he wrote music for collegiate skits, Bernstein had an active interest in theatre music. He wrote many scores of Broadway musicals and film scores, the most famous example of both being the legendary *West Side Story*. No other American of the twentieth century would have such an impact on world music culture as did Leonard Bernstein.

Summary

American art music activity and consumption reached its height in the 1950s and then began a steady decline in popularity as its audience grew older. While the younger generation became enraptured with what would become the rock and roll era with the emergence of Elvis Presley and others that followed, this new popular music also reflected a more conflicted and confusing world politically and philosophically. As the generations seemed to split over important issues such as civil rights, the Vietnam War, Watergate, the drug culture, and the sexual freedoms that accompanied the rising women's movement, middle America would enter its most internally turbulent period of the century.

The cultural productions and consumptions of the old world seemed to the new generation to be stuffy, out of date, and irrelevant to the day-to-day issues that dominated their conflicted existence. Therefore, the consuming audience for art music fractured, causing economic instability within musical institutions across the country and artistic indifference among those who continued to patronize them. The older generation favored stability and tended to choose literature that was more familiar as its favorite, rather than the new and challenging pieces by young composers who were attempting to expand musical horizons through experimentation in their works. The audience, rather, preferred the tried and true literature of the Classical and Romantic period composers, which seemed to bring release from the chaos of the outer world and reinforced refinement of taste and status.

Thus, modern composers, attempting to establish their own reputations outside the shadows of those same giant composers, toiled in obscurity, seeing their chances for equivalent immortality fade and the opportunity to be truly heard and appreciated decline. Trying to make a name for themselves, many of these young composers attempted styles that would deliberately cause a "Rite of Spring-like" reaction, embracing many avant garde techniques such as minimalism and electronic music compositions—music created with the help of the newly developed computer. Composers such as Philip Glass, John Cage, Pierre Schaeffer, Pierre Boulez, Karlheinz Stockhausen, Edgar Varese, Steve Reich, and others would find their audience primarily limited to the students of music on university and conservatory campuses. Academics and the halls of learning became the new patronizing unit, the new archiver of techniques and taste, and the museum-like celebrant to music made by intellectuals for intellectuals.

While many of these attempts do indeed reach artistic levels or expression and create new aural palettes of sonic design that are noteworthy in and of themselves, the end of the twentieth century marks the final break between the composers and performers of art music and the mass audience of consumers. Art music, with its origins in European heritage and traditions, is "popular" with the masses in America no more.

VOCABULARY

A Lincoln Portrait	*Fanfare for the Common Man*	*Nocturnes*
Aaron Copland		*Oedipus Rex*
Alban Berg	*Firebird*	*Pelléas et Mélisande*
Allegro Barbaro	*Five Pieces for Orchestra*	*Petrushka*
Anton Webern	Igor Stravinsky	*Pierrot lunaire*
Appalachian Spring	*Images*	*Prelude à L'après-midi d'un faune*
Arnold Schoenberg	Impressionism	
Bela Bartok	*Jeux*	*Rapsodie Espagnole*
Billy the Kid	*La Mer*	Second Viennese School
Bolero	Leonard Bernstein	*Symphony of Psalms*
Claude Debussy	Louis Moreau Gottschalk	"The Banjo"
Claude Monet		*The Dying Poet*
Concerto for Orchestra	Maurice Ravel	*The Lady Macbeth of the Mtsensk District*
Concerto for Piano and Winds	*Mikrokosmos*	
	Music for Strings, Percussion, and Celesta	*The Rake's Progress*
Creole		*The Rite of Spring*
Dimitri Shostokovitch	Nadia Boulanger	*The Soldier's Tale*
Ebony Concerto	Nationalism	*West Side Story*
Expressionism	Neoclassicism	

WEBSITE

Please refer to the *Music Through Time* site listed in the front of your book to investigate and complete more classroom activities and assignments.

CHAPTER

20

"Dixieland"

From the influences of the military brass bands of John Phillip Sousa to the syncopated rhythms of Scott Joplin, a new type of music, with those "ragged out" rhythms came about in the late 1800s. Dixieland, headed up by the great cornetist **Charles "Buddy" Bolden**, whose band roared through the historian's agreeable birthplace of Dixieland, **New Orleans**, around 1895. Bolden was considered the first "King" of cornet in New Orleans and the first band leader to employ improvisation as a technique in the creation of his music. He is remembered as one of the finest horn players of the era, with a loud clear tone. Eventually his band rose to become one of the most popular bands in the great city.

In 1903, Bolden became a very paranoid musician and even turned down the offer to be the first person to record this new style music. He believed that other musicians wanted to steal his ideas, and thus, he declined the offer. In 1907, Bolden, a trendsetter of a new style of music and an unforgettable horn player, was institutionalized because of mental illness. He would remain institutionalized for the remainder of his life, never playing again. He died on November 4, 1931, in Louisiana's hospital for the insane.

The Original Dixieland Jazz Band

Instead of Bolden being the first to record this new type of music, **Nick LaRocca** (La-Rock-a) and the **Original Dixieland Jazz Band**, formed in 1914, stepped up to do the honors for the Victor Talking Machine label. On February 26, 1917, the band recorded "Livery Stable Blues," coupled on the "B" side with "Dixie Jazz Band One Step." With this recording, the five-member group (consisting of Nick LaRocca—Cornet, Larry Shields—Clarinet, Eddie Edwards—Trombone, Tony Sbabaro—Drums, and Henry Ragas—Piano) emerged into national prominence by recording the first jazz record and selling over a million copies.

The group also gained a degree of fame that overshadowed their improvisational abilities. When the recording became a number one seller, other Dixieland groups scrambled to record. When the African American musicians recorded the same style of music, their improvisational skills were more adept and their phrasing was more artistic and natural.

Generating much criticism, Nick LaRocca maintained that White men created jazz and African American men were purely imitators of a music that was originated by White men. LaRocca also passionately insisted that his group, The Original Dixieland Jazz Band, played a vital role in the "invention" of jazz in the early twentieth century in New Orleans.

Jelly Roll Morton (1890–1941)

Another self-proclaimed inventor of jazz, **Ferdinand "Jelly Roll" Morton**, one of New Orleans' greatest piano players, was not responsible for the invention of jazz; however, he is the first musician to actually show that jazz can be archived in written form. Being able to write down this newly created style of music, Morton was the first to write arrangements that would fit on one side of a 78-rpm record.

Morton began developing his skills as a teenager, working in the famous red-light district of New Orleans called Storyville. Along with being a pianist, he claimed many other jobs, like vaudeville comedian, gambler, pool shark, pimp, and of course, pianist. Living with his grandmother and lying about his occupation, he was thrown out of her house. This may have been one of the best direction changes of his career. Once Jelly Roll was out, he took to the road and never looked back.

He headed to Chicago where he became one of the most important transitional pianists from the old Ragtime to the new Jazz style. Forming and heading up the band The Red Hot Peppers, Morton and his band became staples in the Victor recording studio, recording an entire series of jazz works for the label in 1930.

Morton was not the first, nor the last, musician to migrate to Chicago. There was a great influx of New Orleans musicians that migrated to Chicago, foreshadowing a new era of music in a new great city. Morton and The Peppers played with such great musicians as Kid Ory, Johnny Dodds, Baby Dodds, and Johnny St. Cyr, and also worked with such great sidemen as Bubber Miley and Zutty Singleton.

The Great Depression soon began, and life became hard for musicians. Morton became particularly taxed during this time period because the new sound of the swing band or big band, was becoming more popular and people were no longer interested in the antiquated sound of Dixieland. Jelly Roll Morton, the great pianist, ended his career performing as a bar pianist in Washington D.C.

In 1938, Morton had the honor of recording a series of interviews with Alan Lomax on early jazz music for the Library of Congress. These interviews caused a revival among Jelly Roll's peers; however, he died just before the interviews were released and the Dixieland popularity flared one last time.

Sidney Bechet (1897–1959)

Sidney Bechet was a clarinetist and a young gun with much the same type of flare as Jelly Roll Morton. Born April 14, 1897, he was considered to be a child prodigy. By his teenage years, he was a featured performer with Buddy Bolden's band as well as many of New Orleans' other great bands. His style of playing clarinet and soprano saxophone was so dominating that many groups gave him the lead lines that were typically reserved for the more powerful trumpet. As a master of improvisation, in 1917, he too faced the migration to the northern jazz powerhouse city of Chicago. By 1919, he was playing with Will Marion Cook's Syncopated Orchestra and then in Europe with Louis Mitchell's Jazz Kings.

In 1923, Bechet had his first break in the recording studio with blues singer Clarence Williams and the Blue Five, which featured Bechet on a recording with Louis Armstrong, whom Bechet knew and befriended as a kid while living in New Orleans. Before moving back to Europe and Germany, Bechet played a brief stint with the Duke Ellington Washingtonians, however, he never recorded with them. In 1952, Bechet made his way back to a warmly receptive France.

While in France, he recorded hit records that rivaled the sales of pop stars. He was acknowledged by his peers and by historians as one of the greatest soloists of early jazz. Bechet, no matter where he lived, was always in on the scene, and he lived a very rich and fulfilling musical life.

Joe "King" Oliver (1885–1938)

Joe "King" Oliver, a young trombonist, was quickly converted to cornet while playing in brass bands in New Orleans around 1907. These bands played the typical hot spots in New Orleans; however, by 1918, he was no longer satisfied with the complacency of music in New Orleans. He, too, packed his horn and moved to Chicago, becoming the leader of his own band in 1920. After a trip with his band to the Bay area of California, he returned to Chicago to begin working as King Oliver's Creole Jazz Band at the Lincoln Gardens in June of 1922. Oliver extended an invitation to a new rising star, cornetist Louis Armstrong, who joined the band a month later.

King Oliver's band consisted of many of the New Orleans greats, like clarinetist Johnny Dodds, trombonist Honore Dutrey, pianist Lil Hardin (who eventually became the wife of Louis Armstrong), drummer Baby Dodds, and double bassist and banjo player Bill Johnson. In 1923, Oliver and the group began recording.

Late in 1924, after touring Midwest towns and some on the east coast, the band grew to include two, sometimes three, saxophones. Soon after the growth of the band and a successful but short commitment to the Savoy Ballroom in

New York (starting mid-1927), the band began to separate in the fall of that same year. Oliver stayed in New York and recorded with many different informal orchestras, but by 1931, he ceased recording. After some minor touring, Joe Oliver retired to Savannah, Georgia, to live out his final months.

He is considered to be one of the most important musicians to come out of New Orleans. He possessed a quick and short melodic style, nicely contrasting to the younger Armstrong. He also used a variety of expressions using rhythm and pitch, as well as novelty effects derived from the vocal blues embellishments. It is hard to measure the influence Joe Oliver had on music. It's been said that the most musical period of his life was never recorded and by the time he began to record, Louis Armstrong, who was hired by Oliver, had a talent that began to outshine not only his, but also almost every other musician of the time.

Louis Armstrong (1901–1971)

Considered the greatest jazz musician by many, **Louis Armstrong** defined what it is to play jazz. Born on August 4, 1901, and referred to as "Satchmo" or "Satchelmouth" (because of the size of his mouth and smiling teeth), his influence of technical ability, happiness and spontaneity, and an inventive, musical mind still dominate jazz music to this day. Louis, also later known as "Pops," hailed from a very poor family. At age eleven, after firing a gun into the streets celebrating New Years Eve, Armstrong was sent to the home for colored waifs. While at the reform school, he learned to play the cornet. When released at age fourteen, he began working selling papers, selling coal from a cart and unloading boats.

Although he didn't own his own instrument at the time, he was insistent on listening to the local bands play at the club that was a church by day and the Funky Butt Dance Hall by night. Joe "King" Oliver, who acted as a father to Louis, was Armstrong's favorite band to watch. Oliver liked Louis' spirit so much, he began instructing him on the instrument and even gave him his first real cornet. In 1917, Armstrong played in dive bars in New Orleans' red light district, **Storyville**, with a group inspired by Oliver. In 1919, Armstrong left New Orleans for the first time as a part of Fate Marable's band from St Louis. Marable led a band that played on the Strekfus Mississippi riverboat lines. Armstrong's musical savvy and astounding sound carried for miles and is the beginning of one tale that still travels the Mississippi Delta. One riverboat passenger recalls:

It was unlike anything I have ever heard. This sound that echoed off the banks of the Mississippi River, it was almost as if the notes filled the air even after the music was done. But on this particular night, something happened that took all the patrons by total surprise. As we were traveling along the Mighty Mississippi, we heard another sound, coming from the distance. We were in awe because the musicians on our boat were on a break. As we traveled down the river, the sound of this music got greater and greater. The lights of another boat came around the bend and the sound of a cornet was wailing. This, of course, caught the attention of our fine musicians as they came back to the bandstand and began to play,

Louis Armstrong
©John Springer Collection/CORBIS

covering up the music in the distance. As time passed and the two boats drew near to each other, they pulled up side by side and what happened next was not to be expected nor has it ever happened with such spontaneity again. The boats stopped, the musicians stared and Marable and Armstrong kicked up the music with unrelenting energy. People began dancing on both boats and at the end of the tune; you could hear the heavy panting by all that were dancing. As if to kindly accept the challenge, the other band struck up a tune and played fiercely almost until dancers collapsed. This continued on for hours and at the end of the night, literally, the sun was coming up, I noticed one odd thing, not only was the music great that was coming from the other boat, the band was led by white cornetist Bix Biederbecke. This was the night that Armstrong and Biederbecke became friendly rivals. It was also the night that made me realize that great music and great performances transcend all racial barriers. It was a mighty night on the Mighty Mississippi (Author Unknown)

Joe Oliver, in 1922, sent a telegram to the young Armstrong asking him to join his **Creole Jazz Band** at Lincoln Gardens in Chicago. Armstrong had dreamed of this moment, and by the time he arrived in Chicago, the buzz was already around. It wasn't long after his arrival that Armstrong's amazing playing soon made him a sensation among other musicians. Playing in Oliver's Creole Jazz Band, Louis met his first wife, Lillian Hardin. An arranger and piano player for the band, she was an ambitious and intelligent woman who believed Armstrong to be wasting his time and talent in Oliver's band. Married in February 1924, she pressured Armstrong to reluctantly leave his bandleader and mentor.

Armstrong then moved to New York to be a part of Fletcher Henderson's Orchestra for thirteen months. In 1925, after his stint with Henderson and recording with many other groups, Armstrong and his **Hot Five** began to record. This was the first time Armstrong recorded using his own name as the bandleader. The recordings of the Hot Five and the **Hot Seven** show evidence of Armstrong's powerful creativity, and these recordings are considered jazz classics.

By 1929, Armstrong had become quite famous and felt it was time to move again. He headed to Los Angeles, where he fronted the band called Louis Armstrong and his Sebastian New Cotton Club Orchestra. However, this was quickly tiresome and he returned to Chicago to assemble his own touring group. In June, Louis, along with his group, returned to New Orleans for the first time since leaving to join "King" Oliver's group in 1922. Armstrong received a hero's welcome but was also greeted by the rampant racism of the time. The White radio announcer refused to mention Armstrong and his group even though he was to play a free concert for the American-African population. The show was cancelled at the last minute.

In 1931, Lil and Louis separated and Louis left on the road for the next three years. He crossed the United States many times before heading to Europe. In 1935, upon his return to the United States, Armstrong hired Joe Glaser as his manager. Although Glaser was allegedly connected to mob boss Al Capone, Glaser and Louis became great friends. Glaser was a trustworthy manager to Louis and remained his manager until Glaser died in 1969.

The Dixieland revival was just beginning when Be-Bop started to challenge the normalcy of jazz. In the environment of this new music, the Armstrong Orchestra was beginning to look tired, with concert and record sales declining.

Armstrong was accused of being too commercial, yet, in 1947, with Louis' well-being in mind, Glaser took it upon himself to fire the orchestra and replace them with a small group that became one of the most popular bands in jazz history—**The Louis Armstrong Jazz All-Stars**. It was this band's popularity and touring schedule (taking them all over the world) that dubbed Armstrong with his moniker, "America's Jazz Ambassador."

In 1963, Louis and the All-Stars knocked the Beatles off the number one spot on the pop record charts with their version of "**Hello Dolly**." In 1969, Louis recorded another sweet tune that landed the number one spot again—"**What a Wonderful World**." This tune went on to become Billboard's "Greatest Song of the Century."

Louis' health began to weaken shortly after that recording, and he was hospitalized several times over the next three years. He continued to record even up to the end. On July 6, 1971, Louis Armstrong—"Satchmo," "Pops," and "America's Jazz Ambassador"—died in his sleep in his home in Queens, New York, hailed as the greatest music influence America has ever produced.

VOCABULARY

Charles "Buddy" Bolden
Creole Jazz Band
Ferdinand "Jelly Roll" Morton
Fletcher Henderson's Orchestra
"Hello Dolly"

Hot Five
Hot Seven
Joe "King" Oliver
Louis Armstrong
Louis Armstrong Jazz All-Stars
New Orleans
Nick LaRocca

Sidney Bechet
Storyville
The Original Dixieland Jazz Band
The Red Hot Peppers
"What a Wonderful World"

WEBSITE

Please refer to the *Music Through Time* site listed in the front of your book to investigate and complete more classroom activities and assignments.

CHAPTER
21

The Blues

What is the blues? Dictionaries define the blues as a melancholy or sad feeling. However, to the people that sing or play "**the blues**," it is not limited to one particular feeling. In fact, it encompasses all emotion and is expressionistic by nature. It is happiness, sadness, anger, nervousness, eagerness, stressfulness, passion, and sexuality; it is everything or just one thing the person is expressing and the blues relies on that moment when expression occurs. As much as music scholars and historians try, blues cannot be easily explained or identified academically like many other genres of music. To put academic labels on the blues is offensive to the creator. Blues music is more an attempt by the performer to cast off the feelings previously mentioned, attempting to overcome them, face them, and survive them. Blues can be among the purest forms of creation because it is so reliant on the nature and soul of the performer.

The Mississippi Delta, the birthplace of the blues, is where this new music was rising at the turn of the nineteenth century. However, the blues pre-dates even the Civil War. It stems back to the capture of slaves off the West African coast, and it can be traced directly to the southern United States where plantations purchased slaves as a labor source and brought them home to work the

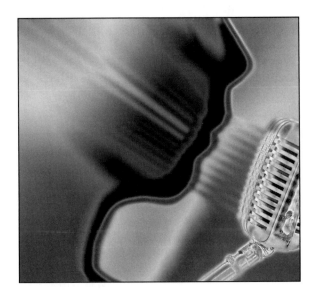

land. Music of the African homeland traveled to America with the slaves. African folksongs and their rhythmic stylings kept the slaves as lighthearted as possible during times of oppression and fear. The traditions of many different African cultures blended together as different tribesmen were forced to work side by side in this new world. **Field hollers**, **work songs** and **spirituals** mingled and the blues began to develop. Those songs were used as means of expression and communication. Because instruments were not allowed by the plantation owners for fear of communicating an uprising among the slaves, frequently only voices and body percussion were used for music making. This use of the voice and the body as a percussion instrument combined with the use of the "call and response" techniques favored by the field hollers, created the early "Delta Blues." The Christian influence grew in the African culture that was forced to adopt the religion of their slave masters. While the Whites would attend church on Sundays, singing the standard hymns, the slaves developed their own methods of church singing, using fervent vocals, call-and-response singing, clapping, and stomping. Not only did this become an integral part of music in the south, it was laying the foundation for the formation of what became known as "the blues."

The term *the blues* wasn't really coined until a Muscle Shoals, Alabama, native, **W. C. Handy** (William Christopher), "discovered" the blues. Handy, while sitting on a train platform in Tutwiler, Mississippi, heard strange guitar music from a passing traveler. Being a trumpet player and a well-rounded musician himself, Handy took note of the form of the music and the chords that supplied its unusual sound. In 1912, Handy's "**Memphis Blues**" was the first song to be published with "blues" in the title. Handy, claiming the discovery of the blues, continued to promote the new musical style, which helped the blues become a viable genre of music.

Early blues musicians in the hot Mississippi delta were often the only source of entertainment, often playing in segregated clubs or after-hours churches that were transformed into juke joints at night. Blues musicians were many times equivalent to the medieval troubadour, traveling frequently, sometimes with a vaudevillian circuit show or a medicine show. With such travels and performances, the enthusiasm for the blues spread quickly throughout the south. The blues often chronicled the African-American experience in the south during the late nineteenth and early twentieth centuries. The music was often passed on orally, occasionally in written form, but not preserved by recording until much later. The earliest known recordings of the blues were created well after W.C. Handy's first publication of "Memphis Blues." Recordings in the delta started around the early 1920s, however there was little interest in the newly recorded music from the south. Musicians like **Charley Patton** and **Skip James** headed north to record. Upon completion of any recording project, they would return to the delta to continue gigging at juke joints, dances, foot washes, and fish fries.

The 1920s and 1930s saw many great blues musicians from the delta develop and spread the blues north. Charley Patton, Son House, and Robert Johnson, all influenced the next generation of blues greats, like Muddy Waters. The music of the delta eventually moved north with the mass exodus of many African American southerners attempting to escape the economic constraints of

"sharecropping." Chicago eventually overshadowed the Mississippi delta as the center for the blues because the recording industry found a market selling "race records" to African American consumers.

W. C. Handy (1873–1958)

Alabama-born **W. C. Handy** is recognized as "The Father of the Blues." Although this declaration was self-proclaimed, his life-long support of the musical genre established the blues as a part of musical history. Handy was steadfast in his efforts of documentation and publication of blues music. W. C., whose musical tastes leaned more toward a polished sound like that of King Oliver's Creole Jazz Band, realized the importance of the blues as a part of the American legacy. Handy was a songwriter and performer before establishing himself as a bandleader, continuing his career in New York City. Handy literally had the blues pass him by one day just before the turn of the twentieth century. A traveling blues musician inspired Handy to begin working with the progression and sound of the blues. His composition and publication of "Memphis Blues" is said by historians to not be a legitimate blues; it was, however, the first tune with "blues" in the title and consequently influenced the creation of other blues tunes such as the historic "Crazy Blues," known to be the first blues tune ever to be recorded by Mamie Smith in 1920. W. C. Handy's cultural contributions have garnered him such honors as the W. C. Handy Park in Memphis, Tennessee, the W. C. Handy Blues Festival in Memphis, and the W. C. Handy Music Festival in Florence, Alabama. The Blues Foundation, www.blues.org, annually recognizes the achievement of blues artists by awarding the prestigious W. C. Handy blues award.

Robert Johnson (1911–1938)

Robert Johnson is probably the most legendary blues musician because of the story that outlines his life and death. Although his blues-recording career was a very short one, the legend of his life has expanded to mythical proportions. In brief, Johnson, in order to fulfill his passion, struck a deal with the devil; exchanging amazing guitar performance ability for his soul, the devil claimed his prize sooner than Johnson was hoping. In rural folklore, an intersection of two roads was often thought of as an evil place, a place of black magic. These stories date back to the folklore of African witch doctors and European pagan rituals.

Born in Hazlehurst, Mississippi, on May 8, 1911, Johnson was the illegitimate son of Julia Dodd and Noah Johnson. Robert would ultimately never meet his father. Because of dire work situations, Johnson and his mother moved quite frequently from Memphis to various parts of the delta. Johnson, as a young boy, began working in the cotton fields of a Robinsonville plantation. Although miserable in his work, his music comforted him and other workers frequently. At age seventeen, Johnson married Virginia Travis, his childhood sweetheart. Although their love was very strong, the romance was short lived because of the ill-timed passing of his wife during childbirth. This was the turning point of Johnson's life. From this point, Johnson was a wanderer and devoted everything within him to his music.

Over time, Johnson diligently worked to hone his skills. He and friend Willie Brown (Blind Dog Willie or Sweet Willie Brown) would often sit in graveyards on tombstones, writing ominous blues melodies while drinking moonshine. Although he couldn't read music, Johnson learned to play guitar by listening to and watching other blues musicians, such as Charlie Patton or Son House, who inspired Johnson to develop his own bottleneck slide technique. Johnson and Brown traveled the roads of the south to perform at juke joints and entered "chopping contests" along the way. Although Johnson received some mild acclaim for his contributions, many blues musicians were envious of his abilities, spreading rumors about Johnson paying "the devil's price" to satisfy his own ambitions.

According to the myth, Johnson longed for fame and fortune to ease the pain caused by the death of his wife and child. He was not satisfied with his own musical abilities and believed he needed more talent to achieve the standard of success for which he'd hoped. Already feeling forsaken by God, he made the monumental trip to the crossroads at the stroke of midnight. He walked down highway 61 to where it intersected with highway 49 in Clarksdale, Mississippi. Reciting an ancient incantation, he called upon Satan to rise up from the fires of hell. In exchange for Johnson's soul, the devil grabbed the guitar from Johnson's quivering hand, tuned it, and returned it to Johnson who received the talent that he desired. From that point on, Johnson played that guitar with an otherworldly style that others had never heard.

The legend of Robert Johnson is intriguing because many blues musicians who have sung about the legend of the crossroads, or covered Robert Johnson's original "**Crossroads Blues**" have had misfortune as musicians. After the group Cream with Eric Clapton, covered Johnson's tune "Crossroads Blues," the band almost immediately separated due to Clapton's ensuing depression and heroin use. The Allman Brothers band had its misfortunes as well. Gregg Allman shot himself in the foot before a tour, to avoid the draft. A couple of other band members had incidents with arrest and heroine, all after they covered Johnson's "Crossroads." The most devastating of all incidents happened to Lynard Skynard who typically toured by bus but decided to do a series of live recordings, one of which included "Crossroads." It ended up becoming one of their greatest selling live albums. Because of its success, the band finally decided to take to the skies to tour instead of using a bus. Shortly after employing a plane for touring, most members of the band died in a fiery crash.

Mamie Smith (1883–1946)

Mamie Smith, born May 26, 1883, in Cincinnati, Ohio, is surrounded by her own blues legend. She was a vaudeville circuit singer that made blues history by being the first woman and singer to record a blues tune. In 1920, "**Crazy Blues**" became a huge hit, selling more than a million copies within the first year of its release. The success of this recording paved the way for future young ladies to record the blues. Although technically a vaudeville singer, she was a groundbreaking and influential young female artist of the blues genre. Her presence on stage was majestic, outlined with ornate costume jewelry; she influenced other young ladies of the twenties.

Ma Rainey (1886–1939)

One of the great female vocalists that significantly influenced the sound of the delta blues around the turn of the last century was Gertrude Pridgett. Born in Columbus, Georgia, in 1886, she became known as "The Mother of the Blues." At age fourteen she began touring and performing in the vaudeville circuit and is considered to be among the first women to perform blues in that circuit. She was an important link between the country blues idiom and the male-dominated genre of delta blues. In 1904, Gertrude married William (known as "Pa") Rainey, and the duo set out performing together as **Ma and Pa Rainey**, also known as "The Assassinators of the Blues." While the duo was out touring, Ma Rainey met Bessie Smith and immediately began to mentor the young vocalist. Not only was Ma Rainey a rough blues woman with a great vocal technique, she was an excellent songwriter as well. Through these skills, she created a prolific legacy within the blues genre and set the bar for many of the up and coming ladies of jazz including, Billie Holiday and Ella Fitzgerald.

Bessie Smith (1894–1937)

Bessie Smith, a Chattanooga, Tennessee native, influenced generations of vocalists, including **Billie Holiday** and **Janice Joplin**. Her life was lived with confidence and self-assurance. Her rich and expressive vocals often leaned on these two traits. Bessie wasn't just a performer, she was a composer as well, writing famous blues tune likes, **"Back Water Blues"** and **"Bessie's Blues."** Her performance travel was practically halted by the Great Depression. It was difficult for many African American artists to find work during that time, but it was particularly difficult for southern African American women. She survived the decline in work, however, and was marking a comeback in 1937. She was scheduled to perform in New York's Carnegie Hall at the legendary John Hammond concert, **"From Spirituals to Swing."** Her performance was pre-empted by a fatal car accident. The concert was dedicated to the woman who had been so vocally influential in the blues.

Son House (1902–1988)

Son House, originally a preacher and greatly influenced by the Baptist church, incorporated intense passion in his delta blues sound. His performances were powerful and emotional; his stage presence was intriguing and sometimes even frightening in his ability to move the listener in such a powerful and musical way. He was always performing and traveling with other blues greats like Charley Patton, Willie Brown, and Robert Johnson. No matter how much he traveled with these musicians and no matter how influential they were, his sound remained his own. Many future blues men and women can trace their roots directly back to the sound of House. Between the early 1940s to late 1960s, Son House disappeared from the blues scene until researchers tracked him down. Once found, he began the second half of his career as a respected blues performer. With his legendary skill and past associations with Charley Patton and Robert Johnson, he was particularly valuable to the history of the blues. Cub Koda, music critic for the blues, stated, "Hailed as the greatest living delta blues singer still actively performing, no one dared called themselves the King of the Blues as long as Son was around."

Charley Patton (1891–1934)

If Son House is going to be mentioned in the history of the delta blues, **Charley Patton** should proceed or follow House's mention; the two were practically inseparable as blues musicians. Their musical lives paralleled, and many times they performed together, along with Willie Brown and Robert Johnson.

Born in Edwards, Mississippi, in 1891, Patton is the uncontested "Father of the Delta Blues." Much like House's passionate performances, Patton's fiery and energetic renditions stirred crowds on a regular basis. His raw vocal style and the ability to be a one-man percussion section with his guitar, combined with his ability to create innovative flows of rhythm, kept listeners tuned into the music, seemingly in a daze. His performances on stage were uninhibited, much like his lifestyle. He was a part-time pimp, a regular womanizer, and a heavy drinker; he never backed away, however, from a playing challenge and many times took another bluesman to the "chopping block."

His ability influenced not only blues performers like Muddy Waters, Johnny Shines, and John Lee Hooker, but he is considered to be a direct pioneer in the genre of rock-n-roll through his influences on Stevie Ray Vaughan and Jimi Hendrix.

Muddy Waters (1913/1915–1983)

McKinley Morganfield, better known in the blues world as **Muddy Waters,** who took his nickname from one of his favorite Mississippi creeks, was a little behind the bar when he started playing the guitar. Picking it up at age seventeen, although not readily skilled in performing, he worked hard and was influenced by seeing passionate performances of both House and Johnson. By 1940, he was quite an accomplished delta blues guitarist. He packed up his cargo and headed to Chicago where, within a few years, everyone knew him and he had completely revolutionized the entire Chicago blues scene. His skill with the electric guitar was one of the many contributions he made to Chicago Urban Blues. His power vocals and compelling songwriting became another staple in

his Chicago blues repertoire. Unlike many bluesmen who liked to maintain a solo or ensemble career, Waters' followed in the likes of Duke Ellington by becoming a bandleader and putting together a sizeable blues band. This band was groundbreaking in that it is solely responsible for establishing the sound of **Chicago Electric Blues**. This electric band would become the model for the rock-n-roll band of the next generation. The Rolling Stones and The Beatles incorporated Waters' music into their repertoire, and the Rolling Stones' name was taken directly from a Muddy Waters song.

John Lee Hooker (1917–2001)

The master of "Boogie" with a sensuous and haunting vocal style, **John Lee Hooker** had the ability to create a groove on just one repetitive chord. Born in Clarksdale, Mississippi, in 1917, his style paved the way for the blues and rock-n-roll jam bands, riffing tirelessly over only a few chords. Admired by many blues and rock artists, Hooker learned to play guitar from his stepfather, who was a student or peer of Charley Patton. Hooker moved to Detroit in 1943, where his gospel and delta-blues influenced sound was welcomed. Hooker worked continuously for the next forty years, including appearances in the move "The Blues Brothers" and a release in 1989 entitled "The Healer," for which he won much acclaim. "The Healer" was one of Hooker's most monumental recordings. Many of the musicians he influenced over the last half century were invited to perform with him on the recording.

B. B. King (1925–   )

The most famous and widely recognizable blues musician transcends all racial and musical barriers. His career as a blues musician spans over five decades and has seen many of the world's finest concert halls as well as small blues clubs. Known as "The King of the Blues," **B. B. King** was born **Riley B. King** in 1925 in Indianola, Mississippi, and he has had one of the most enduring music careers in existence. He is respected as a blues diplomat and deserves most of the credit for the blues genre entering the mainstream.

King wasn't always a blues performer. Although he spent much of his life a musician, he started his career not unlike Sam Phillips, as a disc jockey in Memphis. There he was known as the "**Beale Street Blues Boy**" and eventually shortened his name to "B. B." King. His "single-string" guitar solos blended well with his commanding vocals, and his bends on the strings echo the sound of the gospel church "moaning" during a call-and-response. King's influence on other blues musicians is countless. Some of King's original songs, like "**Stormy Monday**," have been covered by many bands, used on commercial TV and in movies. King is still a performer that travels hundreds of days and thousands of miles per year with the annual "B. B. King Blues Festival," which is one of the few traveling blues festivals left in existence.

Ray Charles (1930–2004)

Aside from B. B. King, there is no other blues musician that is more popular in many different areas of American music than **Ray Charles**. Born in Albany, Georgia in 1923, Charles is well known for his innovation for blending popular music into his performances and recordings. His work reflects inspiration from gospel, blues, jazz, pop/rock, R&B, soul, and country music. As a vocalist, he was originally inspired by pianist/songwriter Nat King Cole, and his early recordings reflect that influence.

In the mid 1950s, Charles entered into his own developed style with the recording "**I've Got a Woman**." The song has a heavy gospel influence, and integrated with the new rock-n-roll, Charles created a new style of African American music—*soul*. Charles' music would continue in this trend until 1959 when he released his signature hit "**What'd I Say**." His ability to merge soul,

rock-n-roll, and even gospel had a huge impact on popular music. His version of "America the Beautiful" is one of the most loved versions in the American culture.

Conclusion

Blues music is the wellspring of all American music in the twentieth century. It provides the source of a unique experience expressed in sound and story, indicative of the land that gave it birth, unable to be duplicated anywhere else in the world. These sounds are produced from the clash of two races, Black and White, adapting to each other on American soil over a 200-year period. Because legalized slavery was allowed to exist in this country in the American south, African Americans hailing from many different places assimilated into a culture of forced labor, Christian religion, and few options. That struggle, injustice, and assimilation, over time, evolved into the most beautiful yet haunting musical salve for the American soul, flavoring everything that follows, forcing everyone to never forget the sweet sound of grace that flows over posterity.

VOCABULARY

B. B. King
"Back Water Blues"
"Beale Street Blues Boy"
Bessie Smith
"Bessie's Blues"
Billie Holiday
Blues
Call and Response
Charley Patton
Chicago Electric Blues
"Crazy Blues"
"Crossroads Blues"

Field hollers
"From Spirituals to
 Swing"
"I've Got a Woman"
Janice Joplin
John Lee Hooker
Ma and Pa Rainey
Mamie Smith
"Memphis Blues"
Muddy Waters
Ray Charles
Riley B. King

Robert Johnson
Sharecropping
Skip James
Son House
Soul
Spirituals
"Stormy Monday"
"The Healer"
W. C. Handy
"What'd I Say"
Work songs

WEBSITE

Please refer to the *Music Through Time* site listed in the front of your book to investigate and complete more classroom activities and assignments.

CHAPTER

22

The Big Bands Swing

In the twentieth century, each generation of U.S. citizens carved out its own popular, rebellious music. Each decade of young people saw their emotions stirred and its taste criticized because of the perceived "lewdness" of the new "hot" music. At the turn of the century, the hot music was ragtime. Then, shortly after World War I, jazz entered the scene with big bands swinging through the "roaring twenties." Indeed, swing music was intended to move your feet, as well as heighten the audience's listening pleasure.

People yearned for the new beat that was found in the big band dance halls, prominently led by such band leaders as Duke Ellington, Jimmie Lunceford, Glen Gray, Chick Webb, and Fletcher Henderson. White bandleaders entered the scene as well, with Tommy Dorsey, Glenn Miller, Woody Herman, and Benny Goodman, all of whom would have great swing bands. Benny Goodman's band was so great that it defined the new era, gaining him the debated title "The King of Swing." These bands still have a special place in the hearts of millions of Americans. The inspiration and love of the big bands guided many Americans through the Great Depression and World War II, some of the darkest times in American history. Swing music fulfilled their desire for sentimental emotion and provided an escape from the mundane, all the while being loved for its excitement and appreciated as a fine art form.

The 1930s

In the 1930s there were big bands, even before "swing" was ever used to describe the music. What the big bands all had in common were outstanding musical arrangers. These were sidemen that wrote for the specific band of which they were a part. These brilliant musicians were able to write charts that had interaction between all sections of the big band in a way that hadn't been done before. This new style of music saw each portion of the band playing completely different parts, yet it had plenty of room for the improvised solos that were developed in the Dixieland era.

Although it's been noted that **Fletcher Henderson** is the father of big band jazz and one of the first arrangers for such a group, there are debatable facts that suggest jazz orchestration can be attributed to three others—Art Hickman; Ferde Grofe, orchestrator of *Rhapsody in Blue* for a young George Gershwin; and Paul Whiteman. The claim is that Hickman's orchestra was the first to use saxophones. Hickman hired Grofe to arrange music for his orchestra, but the band never saw success.

Paul Whiteman (1890–1967)

Paul Whiteman spent a lot of his time around San Francisco's Barbary Coast when he "discovered" jazz. The spontaneity, expression, emotion, rhythm, and spiritual uplifting in the music he heard enthralled him, but he thought that other bandleaders gave lackluster presentations. Whiteman saw the possibilities of arranging this popular music so it could be played by a dance orchestra, using the jazz soloists as a part of that orchestra and allowing the music to have a specific form and identity. Whiteman hired Grofe, who possessed orchestration knowledge and had experience in popular musical forms, to begin arranging "jazz" music for his ensemble. Whiteman, who had a background in classical music, was the bandleader with a ton of ideas, and Grofe was the master craftsman who translated Whiteman's ideas into notes. The result was an incredible sensation in the Paul Whiteman Orchestra.

The Whiteman Orchestra's first recording, "Whispering," sold almost two million copies, an astounding achievement considering there were only about the same number of phonographs in the whole country at that time. Later, the band's recording of "Three O'Clock in the Morning" achieved even bigger public sales.

Whiteman had vision, and all of his associates knew it. It can be said that Paul Whiteman invented franchising in the music business, allowing many orchestras around the country to use the name The Paul Whiteman Orchestra. Consequently, he became wealthy from royalties paid him for the use of the name. In 1924, the Whiteman Orchestra presented a concert entitled "Experiment in Modern Music" premiering George Gershwin's *Rhapsody in Blue*. Critics applauded it as a great artistic success.

Whiteman's ability to recognize outstanding talent allowed him to employ an impressive line up in his orchestra. At different times he had such musicians as brothers Jimmy and Tommy Dorsey, Charlie and Jack Teagarden, Bix Beiderbecke, Eddie Lang, Frankie Trumbauer, and Joe Venuti. He also employed singers like Bing Crosby, Mildred Bailey, Johnny Mercer, and the great Billie Holiday, all of whom he paid very well.

Whiteman's controversy came with the self-imposed title "The King of Jazz" that he used as a promotional tool. This hyperbolic advertising followed in the tradition of previous jazz musicians, such as Joe Oliver titling himself "King Oliver" and Jelly Roll Morton representing himself as the "Originator of Jazz," claiming he was actually able to point to the day he invented jazz. The biggest controversy surrounding Whiteman was the fact that he was White. The great Duke Ellington acknowledges Whiteman in his biography by dedicating a portion of the biography to Whiteman saying, "Paul Whiteman was known as the 'King of Jazz', and no one has yet to come near carrying that title with more certainty and dignity."

Others made better music after Whiteman and his orchestra, but the fact remains that he led the way from Dixieland into the Big Band dance era. The pioneer is most certainly not always the best. He may have been first and one of the most successful, but the intensity needed to put the new music on the map occurred when another young man and clarinetist decided to put his heart and passion into developing this new style.

Benny Goodman (1909–1986)

A young man who would accept nothing from his band except perfection provided the drive needed to divert America's attention to the new style of music. **Benny Goodman,** a bandleader who demanded countless hours of rehearsal to obtain the perfection he was seeking, landed a late night radio spot on the show "Let's Dance." Not only did Goodman have a swinging band, it was also incredibly clean and the soloists were passionate.

At the suggestion of John Hammond, Goodman hired the Henderson brothers, Fletcher and Horace, to be the arrangers for his band. The new arrangements, particularly by Fletcher, became as much of a signature for the band's sound as Goodman's clarinet. Goodman's band took Fletcher's arrangements and made them sound as if they were on fire, something that was missing in Fletcher's own group. Of course, helping to ignite this fire in all swing bands is

the drummer, and Goodman employed one of the best, Gene Krupa. Krupa's style was intense, yet not showy. He drove the band without calling undue attention to himself. He connected the entire band rhythmically and used his hard-hitting style to give the music intensity.

Even though Benny Goodman had one of the most swinging bands in the nation at the time, financial success was eluding him. After losing his radio spot on "Let's Dance" for playing too loud and too fast, John Hammond stepped in and arranged a tour for them in hopes of keeping the band together. However, the band was not being received well in many different places during the tour, and Goodman was ready to give up music as a career and put away his

Benny Goodman and Orchestra
©Bettmann/CORBIS

clarinet. Hammond persuaded him to hang in and finish the scheduled bookings that ended in California, hoping something good would happen.

On August 21, 1935, in Los Angeles, a crowd lined the streets around the block in anticipation of the concert, confusing Goodman and his band into thinking someone famous was in town nearby. At first, Goodman played the same tunes he had performed for polite dancing on the tour and was coolly received by the California teenagers. Then, Krupa suggested to Goodman, "If we're gonna die, let's at least die playing our own thing." Benny agreed and the band played its thrilling "King Porter Stomp." The crowd burst with excitement, filling the isles dancing wildly and cheering hysterically.

The California teenagers had been listening to the "Let's Dance" broadcasts for weeks, unlike the more sedate midwestern audiences, and they were expecting the hard-swinging dance rhythms they had heard on the radio. Goodman, thinking that his style of playing on the broadcasts was too much for the country, was attempting to stave off financial failure by performing more relaxed numbers on the tour. When he finally played full out in desperation in Los Angeles, fate had provided just the right audience. Whatever ensued that night became instantly legendary, and the news of the teenage hysteria spread across the country, creating enormous success for the Goodman band from that moment forward.

In 1938, Goodman's band achieved its highest honor, performing in Carnegie Hall. No jazz had yet graced the walls of that hall, and Goodman and his band lit the place up with a swinging glory, cementing the commercial and artistic achievements of the big band era at the same time.

Count Basie (1904–1984)

During the World War II era, there were literally hundreds of swing bands across the nation. Swing music was a vital part of American culture, and it was such a lift to the nation's spirits. Without its energy and innate optimism, the war effort would have been much harder. **William "Count" Basie** (1904–1984) was one of the leading figures in the swing era. He and Duke Ellington led bands that were the epitome of the big band style.

William studied piano with his mother, and as a young man, left for New York to meet **James P. Johnson** and **Fats Waller,** the reigning giants of ragtime, stride, and early jazz piano. Waller had a great influence on Basie and gave him lessons. Before Basie was twenty, he was working as a vaudeville solo pianist, accompanist, musical director, and he had extensive touring experience. All of this early training helped significantly influence his later career. In 1927, stranded in Kansas City, Basie began playing organ for theaters presenting silent films. In July 1928, he joined the Blue Devils, Walter Page's midwestern legendary group, which also included Jimmy Rushing. Both Page and Rushing would be a vital part of Basie's own band. After leaving the Blue Devils in 1929, Basie entered **Bennie Moten's Kansas City Orchestra**. In 1935, Bennie Moten unexpectedly died and Buster Moten continued the band. Dissent among members of the band caused a split and many left. Basie put together a smaller group of musicians from the Moten group including Jo Jones and Lester Young and became its leader. Known as the Barons of Rhythm, he began playing a lengthy appointment at the Reno Club in Kansas City.

In 1936, after many radio broadcasts, the Decca Record Company contacted them for a recording contract. Soon, the Barons of Rhythm became known as The Count Basie Orchestra and went on to become one of the greatest big bands of the swing era. Toward the end of the 1930s, the Basie Orchestra became well known around the world for playing "One O'Clock Jump," "Jumpin' at the Woodside," and "Taxi War Dance."

In 1950, because of certain financial hardships, Basie led a smaller group consisting of six to nine members, involving great musicians such as Clark Terry, Buddy DeFranco, Serge Chaloff, and Buddy Rich. In 1952, Basie reorganized the full big band, went on a sequence of long tours,

Duke Ellington and Count Basie
©Bettmann/CORBIS

and made recordings that established him as a giant in the jazz world. It made his band a permanent training ground for young jazz musicians.

Serious illness slowed Basie's career, even at times performing from a wheelchair. After his death in 1984, the Basie band continued under the direction of Thad Jones and eventually Frank Foster. Basie's mark on the big band era is still alive as many swing bands try to emulate that sound of the Count Basie Orchestra.

Duke Ellington (1899–1974)

Edward Kennedy "Duke" Ellington is one the most productive and creative composers of the twentieth century. His outstanding number of compositions and variety of musical forms, from big band to orchestral, have been unmatched by any other in the century. His success and development as a musician was an incredible journey and was marked by constant achievement. He is regarded as America's greatest bandleader and composer.

Ellington's contributions to the musical world redefined the forms from which he worked. He used many of the elements of American music in his compositions, from the blues and Tin Pan Alley, to the European orchestral music tradition, combining them all into his own style. The music is complex for the player, yet understandable by the listener. An outstanding feature of Ellington's talent was his ability to musically capture in composition the individual capabilities of his band members. He listened to his musicians as they soloed or warmed up, and if he heard something individual and unique, Duke would incorporate that sound into a new piece of music.

Edward Kennedy Ellington was born in Washington, D.C. on April 29, 1899. He began studying piano at age seven and was greatly influenced by the stride piano greats like James P. Johnson, Fats Waller, and Willie "the Lion" Smith. **The Washingtonians,** Duke's band, assembled in New York City in 1923. By 1930, the "Duke Ellington Orchestra" included twelve musicians and quickly achieved national prominence by recordings, film appearances, and radio broadcasts as the house band from the famed **Cotton Club** in Harlem.

Continuing to grow his career as a band leader and composer, Ellington was responsible for beginning an annual concert series at Carnegie Hall that initially premiered the famed artistic achievement **"Black, Brown, & Beige."** Duke had nearly 2000 compositions in print before his death in 1974, rivaling that of classical composer Wolfgang Amadeus Mozart. He is the first American composer to be archived in the Smithsonian Museum in Washington, D.C., hailed as a national treasure.

VOCABULARY

Barons of Rhythm
Bennie Moten's Kansas
    City Orchestra
Benny Goodman
"Black, Brown, & Beige"
Blue Devils
Cotton Club
Edward Kennedy
    "Duke" Ellington

"Experiment in Modern
    Music"
Fats Waller
Fletcher Henderson
James P. Johnson
John Hammond
"Jumpin' at the
    Woodside"
"King Porter Stomp"

"One O'Clock Jump"
Paul Whiteman
"Taxi War Dance"
The Washingtonians
"Three O'Clock in the
    Morning"
"Whispering"
William "Count" Basie

WEBSITE

Please refer to the *Music Through Time* site listed in the front of your book to investigate and complete more classroom activities and assignments.

CHAPTER

23

From Swing to Bop
The Transition from the Big Band to the Small Group

One of the earliest speakeasies in New York City was named the **Onyx Club**, located at number 35 on 52nd street, opening its doors in 1927. Joe Helbock, who ran the Onyx Club, entertained patrons with many different musical groups, including the Spirits of Rhythm or Joe Sullivan on piano. In December 1933, after prohibition was repealed, the Onyx set the standard for the new jazz clubs that would come to dominate **52nd street**. Due to the quickly rising popularity of the Onyx Club, Helbock made two moves that increased his own popularity. His first decision was to hire **Art Tatum** with the ever-popular Spirits of Rhythm as his main act at the Onyx Club, and his second and best decision was to move the Onyx Club down the street to Number 72, re-opening it as a full-scale nightclub. He didn't close the old Onyx Club, however, leaving Tatum there to perform under the club's new name, the Famous Door.

In time, more clubs opened on the street, and the nightlife quickly spread. Unfortunately, organized crime seems to be a part of jazz history because of the success and popularity of the music, and with the influence of organized crime, the focus of jazz moved to the district of Midtown. During the latter years of prohibition, there were stride pianists holding sway in these clubs. Crime

bosses took care of their musicians, and thus, musicians became very territorial. Each new club, dance hall, and cabaret had its own musicians and big bands and each began as a speakeasy. All the clubs had wild, crazy names like the Mad House, Mexico's and the Nest, and Tillie's and Jerry's, with the majority owned by the gangland bosses of New York City.

Musicians working in the big bands of many Harlem clubs watched the mob quickly control the clubs and 52nd street. Not only were the new clubs downtown set up more lavishly and better equipped, but the mob also hired big name entertainment. Even the Harlem staple Cotton Club would eventually relocate to the downtown area, although the Cotton Club didn't move to 52nd street, but rather to 48th street. As the mob bosses were controlling the new "hot district," they began to control the newspapers, discouraging visitors from going to Harlem and rerouting them to the "**New Swing Street**."

By 1935, The Onyx, **The Famous Door**, **The Hickory House**, **The Yacht Club**, **Leon and Eddie's**, **Tony's,** and the **21 Club** were all in operation on 52nd Street. The new clubs were mainly segregated and not until the end of the 1930s would this segregation begin to dissipate. **Café Society**, a landmark club in Greenwich Village opened by Barney Josephson, was the first to try integration. This was the club that **Billie Holiday** took completely by surprise when she performed Abel Meeropol's "**Strange Fruit**," a strong political song about the brutality of racism in the south. Nevertheless, from the opening, Josephson employed African American waiters and bar attendants. Helbock and many of the other club owners presented mainly African American musicians.

By this time, there were more than a half dozen new clubs on the street, and a similar music policy took effect for those clubs offering entertainment. The bands were to be small, usually only quartets, led by famous bandleaders. The bands only played fifty-minute sets, alternating with an intermission act like pianist Nat King Cole. This marked the decline of the big band.

As the number of clubs increased and the bands became smaller, more and more African American musicians gained employment. Many made a solid living moving from one club to another, one band to the next, creating a homogenous style in the new club scene. Differing from the old New Orleans style where a band was fronted with a trumpet, clarinet, and trombone, these new smaller groups used a trumpet and saxophone, playing short unison riffs. As the musicians began to get more comfortable in the new performance format, the riffs lengthened and became more complex, leaving the middle sections of the tunes open for virtuosic solo improvisations.

One of the most impressive soloists at this time was trumpeter Jonah Jones. He joined the Stuff Smith band at the Onyx Club in 1936. Jonah made a reputation for himself and the club, with his long, Louis Armstrong-influenced solos that created drama and tension in the room. Jonah recalls, "With Stuff, I had all the solos I wanted. I'd be there blowing and Stuff would be playing riffs on his violin and muttering into my ear—'One more Jonah, blow one more.' " Blazing soloists weren't the only way these clubs created excitement. Many times, some of the hot big band "cats" would come and "sit in" with the house band. Musicians like Roy Eldridge (also known as "Li'l Jazz" because of his style and his stature) and Chu Berry, both working with the reformed Fletcher Henderson orchestra, would drop into a club after their main gig at a ballroom or theatre. They would be invited, or they would invite themselves, up on the stage to take furious solos, creating a cutthroat "cutting" competition between themselves and the soloists in the house band. These cutting contests would heat up the crowd and heat up the business, too. It didn't matter what great musician held the house gigs or what great musicians sat in; the 52nd street clubs quickly became the informal counterparts of big band swing. Rhythmically and harmonically the arrangements used in the big bands of Cab Calloway, Lunceford, Basie, and the white bands of Goodman and Dorsey were similar. But in the informal club setting, simple arrangements or "head charts" were used, leaving plenty of room for the soloists.

The small groups had enough room in their music to branch out, allowing tunes to expand with lengthier improvised solos. The big band solo space was typically only a few measures long, but in the smaller club bands, seemingly endless choruses of exploration were the norm. Noticing a large change in the music wasn't readily apparent to the standard listener, however, when saxophonist **Coleman Hawkins** returned from a five-year stint in Europe, he quickly noticed the pace of the music becoming frantic. Becoming one of the foundations of this new jazz style, Coleman Hawkins introduced new ideas in the 1940s.

Coleman Hawkins (1904–1969) and Lester Young (1909–1959)

Two saxophonists prompted many of the developments of this new style of music—**Coleman Hawkins** and another, cooler saxophonist named **Lester Young**. While in Europe, musicians in the states only mentioned Hawkins' name in their reminiscings. There was very little mention of his success in Europe in journals such as *Downbeat* or *Metronome*. Many European recordings Hawkins took part in were never released in the United States. In fact, only six of his fifty recordings had been re-issued in America.

Lester Young made a point to listen to Hawkins' "Paris" recordings, preparing for the day when Hawkins might return. Young followed Hawkins as the tenor saxophone soloist with the Fletcher Henderson Orchestra, and as Hawkins' replacement, he wasn't well received. Young, however, did build a successful career and following of his own with the Count Basie Orchestra, and he was widely regarded as New York's premier saxophonist. Coleman Hawkins returned to the United States in July of 1939, and within only a few weeks, took Lester Young on in a legendary "tenor battle." The opinions were divided on who triumphed. Billie Holiday defended Young, her on-again off-again lover; however, *Downbeat Magazine* claimed that Hawkins blazed into victory.

In Hawkins' famous version of **"Body and Soul,"** recorded on Oct. 11, 1939, there are numerous examples of the way he forced his virtuosity onto the harmonic structures of music, creating a new sound in jazz. His use of chromatic passing tones and his use of substitute harmonies, changing the original chords of the composer to delay the standard resolution of the harmonies, created a kind of dissonance that was incredibly new to the jazz language.

This new harmonic language, however, did not threaten Young; if anything, he embraced it. Lester Young became his own bandleader in 1941, and he had a short stint at Kelly's Stable. While serving in the Basie band, and serving as a sideman to other great musicians, such as **Teddy Wilson** and **Billie Holiday**, Young gained local and eventually national prominence for his alternative approach to the tenor saxophone. The *Downbeat Magazine* poll of 1940 voted

Lester Young as one of the best four tenor saxophonists. He topped that poll in 1944, just before he was inducted into the U.S. Army.

Young's following was equal to that of Hawkins', but his persona was much more remarkable than most jazz musicians. He dawned pin-striped suits, extremely fashioned shirts with the eccentric touches to compliment such garb, all the way down to his favorite decoration, the "pork-pie" hat. Young also caught the attention of most audiences in the way he held his saxophone—out away from his body and at a 45-degree angle. His appearance was even more accented by his own personal language, a fine mix of profanity, nicknames, and "jive-talk." All of these elements mixed together, suggesting that Young's approach to life, like his saxophone playing, was extremely original.

Although both players were incredible, there were definite differences. Hawkins would build his solos by moving away from the standard structure of the tune just as quickly as possible, introducing his own harmonic framework. Young employed the opposite technique, simplifying the harmonies and developing a single harmonic zone in which to create fluid melodies.

By focusing on the melodic direction of his playing, Young introduced dissonance in a way very different than did Hawkins. He accomplished this by constructing a melodic line using patterns. Sometimes, these melodic lines would not fit the underlying chord structure, and they created a positive dissonance against what was being played by the rhythm section. Nonetheless, the patterns created a logical illusion for the listener.

Both Young's and Hawkins' approach to melodic and harmonic improvisation provided great influence on younger generations of musicians who would absorb and master their techniques, adapting them into their own playing style. Many of the musicians who had worked with Hawkins and Young on 52nd street moved west to play on Central Avenue or went so far as Los Angeles for short residences, creating small swing groups that were similar to those in New York. Eighth Street, at the intersection with Central, was practically a parallel jazz world to that in Harlem, with pianists like Art Tatum and Nat King Cole working in its smaller number of clubs. **Benny Carter** also made the trek to the City of Angels and used many Central Avenue Alumni to create his new West Coast big band. There were frequent after hours jam sessions at the clubs on the avenues and also the old black musician's union building, local 767.

Lester Young co-led a band in Los Angeles from 1941 to 1942 with his brother Lee playing the drums. They worked at Billy Berg's club on Pico and La Cienega. Other acts previously mentioned made their way west, like the Spirits of Rhythm and Billie Holiday, establishing a small version of 52nd street. Overall, the Los Angeles scene mirrored New York's move to the small swing group, so that when be-bop truly began, it began almost simultaneously on opposite sides of the country.

New sounding harmonies were coming out of Coleman Hawkins, simplified melodic lines from Lester Young, and fast solos of Jonah Jones and "Li'l Jazz" Roy Eldridge. Melodically, fresh lines were not modeled on the simple riff patterns of the swing era, nor did the musicians intend to follow the general rules of lyric. Instead, the new melodies became jagged, full of dense rapid figures, going so far as to possess uneven phrases that could confuse the untrained listener. At the same time, improvised solos became harmonically intricate, achieving greater complexity in the music.

Harmony and rhythm developed in a new fashion. The "substitute" chord structure that was introduced by Coleman Hawkins worked its way into the standard language of many musicians. Chords that extended well beyond an octave became frequently employed. Art Tatum was one pianist that used this harmonic technique with ease, adding passing chords, replacing chords, and allowing him to create dissonant effects between two hands. Frequently, chord tones were altered up or down by half step. It became a common practice to replace entire harmonic passages with new ones.

The rhythmic elements became more complex. Instead of the standard 4/4 pattern of the swing music, the focus of the beat moved to the ride cymbal and bass drum accents, leaving the snare drum open for creative "chatter." Snare hits, or "rim shots," were not needed on beat two and four anymore. The accent on beats one and three traditionally provided by the bass drum was not often in use anymore; however, one thing that became popular was to "drop bombs" (named during the WWII time)—that is, creating a large accent on the last eighth note of the measure or two measure phrase.

With these new elements, a discernable new form of jazz was created. The principal musicians involved in this new movement were trumpeters **Dizzy Gillespie** and **Howard McGhee**; saxophonists **Don Byas**, **Budd Johnson**, and **Charlie "Bird" Parker**; pianists **Tadd Dameron**, **Thelonious Monk,** and **Bud Powell**; bassist **Oscar Pettiford**; and drummers **Kenny Clarke** and **Max Roach**. Many of these new ideas developed after hours in clubs in Harlem, mainly at Monroe's and Minton's. These were the places in the early 1940s where young African American musicians began playing in more informal jam sessions, gradually developing a completely new complex system of playing. This new style of playing was developed by these great musicians, according to legend, to keep the less adept musicians from being able to keep up with them.

Bebop was music developed by African Americans, rooted deeply in the uncomfortable interplays of racism in America. This innovative group of musicians wanted to put their own mark on jazz history, and they were willing to work, sometimes working at exhausting paces. Many were working two and three four-hour gigs per day, and then performing in the clubs all night. For these young musicians, it was an intense musical experience, allowing them to develop skills beyond normal musicianship. Dizzy Gillespie and his soon to be counterpart, Charlie "Bird" Parker, aimed to create a music they wanted to play, rather than provide just what the audience wanted to hear.

The Quintet

Bird and Dizzy fit just like a hand and a glove. They sounded like one horn. If somebody could put one mouthpiece on two horns and play it at the same time, that's what they sounded like. Bird used to play with Red Rodney and Miles, but it was never like when he played with Dizzy. (Alan Shipton, *A New History of Jazz*)

The epitome of bebop took the stage live at Massey Hall on May 15, 1953. Although bebop had been well established by this time, this was its defining concert. The musicians on the stage that night were its founding fathers—John Birks "Dizzy" Gillespie, trumpet; Charlie "Bird" Parker, alto saxophone; Bud Powell, piano; Charles Mingus, bass; and Max Roach, drums. Each musician had his own style. Dizzy, quite the showman, possessed a commanding presence. His brilliant stage personality was combined with his intense wardrobe of pin-stripe suits and horn-rimmed glasses, complimented by a goatee and topped off with a beret. All of this acting and garb gave the musical performance a visual dimension.

"Dizzy" was born **John Birks Gillespie,** in Cheraw, South Carolina, on October 21, 1917, a sibling to eight other children. His father, although a musician, was not the model father figure, often abusing his children after a hard day laying bricks. His father introduced Dizzy to music, but Dizzy was predominantly self-taught. At age fifteen, he attended the Laurinburg Institute where he played in the band. Although on scholarship, Gillespie supported himself by working on the school's farm. He studied agriculture, often discussing his love of farming in interviews throughout his life.

He was a very organized young musician, becoming a consummate professional. He was aware of appearance and promptness, and he was always well prepared. He was careful to be respectful to his sidemen off the stage; though a disciplinarian, he learned from bandleader Cab Calloway how to get the most from his sidemen during a performance and during a rehearsal. Gillespie was attentive to the value of organizing and writing down musical ideas. He also became a better-than-average pianist and was skilled with manuscript paper and pencil. Gillespie found a supportive woman that would be with him through many hardships, Lorraine Willis. They were together until Dizzy's death in 1993. No matter what troubles may have occurred because of the hard road life, she provided a stable home environment, laying the foundation for his career by keeping Gillespie from the dark temptations of drug and alcohol abuse that entered the lives of so many young bebop artists.

Charlie Parker was the antithesis of Dizzy, leading a chaotic lifestyle. Dizzy was a showman on stage, moving around easily as he soloed or heckled those that were improvising. Parker wouldn't move; in fact, he looked as if he were frozen, focusing all of his mental and physical energy into the saxophone. Off stage, he possessed a wide and varied intellect, a quick biting wit, and a graceful charm. Yet he had a dark side, one of addictions. His cravings for alcohol and heroine would plague him all of his adult life, causing him to become slave to their demands. Often, Parker was forced to pawn his horns in order to raise the cash necessary to buy his "smack." He could withstand large quantities of alcohol and narcotics, keeping his personal relationships in disarray. Although his personality was full of contradictions, light and dark, discipline and irresponsibility, master of the saxophone and slave to narcotics, Parker created a legendary musical figure.

The two musicians complimented each other on stage. Parker had his musical roots deeply ensconced in Kansas City blues. Gillespie, coming from the "Roy Eldridge School of trumpet," didn't have much of a background in the blues; instead, he spent an enormous amount of time acquiring a harmonic knowledge. Combining these two influences created a wonderful elixir on the musical stage. Gillespie described their meeting as "a meeting of the minds."

> *I know he had nothing to do with my playing the trumpet, and I think I was a little more advanced, harmonically, than he was. But rhythmically, he was quite advanced, with setting up the phrase and how you got from one note to another. Charlie Parker heard rhythms and rhythmic patterns differently, and after we started playing together, I began to play, rhythmically, more like him.* Dizzy Gillespie

Charlie Parker was born in Kansas City, Kansas, on August 29, 1920, just across the state line from the same namesake in Missouri. Gillespie and Parker had similar fathers in that one was abusive and the other, Parker's father, merely disappeared not long after the family moved to Kansas City, Missouri, in 1927. Parker's father, Charles Parker Sr., was also a musician. Like Gillespie's father, he was a singer and a dancer and quickly became familiar with the low-life drug and mob culture of Kansas City. Young Charlie's musical talent was not well developed when he started sitting in with local bands in the early 1930s. Although no future in music could be seen, he kept going to clubs, hearing the area's rich jazz music. During this time, Parker kept practicing his horn and listening to the music scene. He once told a fellow saxophonist, Buddy Collette, that he earned his nickname "Bird" from this time in his life, getting up as early as 4:00 a.m. to practice in a nearby park.

Gillespie and Parker traveled through various big bands, Gillespie performing with the Duke Ellington Orchestra and Parker taking a road gig with **Jay McShann,** but because of Parker's personality, he often found himself kicked out of the band and stranded in some town. It became more and more apparent that the front line soloists were the wave of the future. Earl "Fatha" Hines got Parker to consider performing in his band by telling him that Gillespie was already in the band. It was a double ploy—to get Parker in the band and to get Parker off the streets, drugs, and alcohol. When Hines' band came through Philadelphia in January 1943, he approached Gillespie and offered him a job, telling him that Parker had already agreed to be in his group. Gillespie accepted, marking the first time they would regularly play alongside each other.

"Fatha" Hines' band became known as the "incubator of bebop" because of the continuous contact between Parker and Gillespie. In August of 1943, they both left the Hines band—Gillespie to form his own band, and Parker to return home to Kansas City. Gillespie went through a number of musicians, Thelonious Monk, Billy Taylor, and "Doc" West, before he found the musicians he would use in the first real bebop quintet—Max Roach, drums; Budd Johnson, tenor sax; George Wallington, piano; and Oscar Pettiford, bass. These five musicians were the first group of this type to regularly appear at a nightclub, putting down roots on 52nd street as a regular club band, not an after-hours jam band.

In early March 1944, during two sextet recordings in which Parker participated, Gillespie formed what he thought would be the permanent quintet line up, himself and Parker as the front line horn players; Al Haig, piano; Curly Russell, bass; and Stan Levey, drums. Gillespie took this group to a club on 52nd street called **The Three Deuces**. The musical relationship between Gillespie and Parker during those four months at the Three Deuces was unmatched. Parker's musical persona was raw and primal, yet the more he played, the more refined it became. Gillespie's musical curiosity drove him toward experimentation with new ideas for a big band, the use of more dissonant harmonies in arrangements for that big band, and the incorporation of Cuban rhythms in those arrangements.

These two musicians exercised a great influence on the music and the musicians of the time. When asked about bebop, Gillespie frequently defined it as "an evolution, and not a revolution."

VOCABULARY

21 Club
52nd street
Art Tatum
Benny Carter
Billie Holiday
"Body and Soul"
Bud Powell
Budd Johnson
Café Society
Charles Mingus
Charlie "Bird" Parker
Coleman Hawkins

Don Byas
Downbeat Magazine
Jay McShann
John Birks "Dizzy"
    Gillespie
Kenny Clarke
Leon and Eddie's
Lester Young
Max Roach
Metronome Magazine
New Swing Street
Onyx Club

Oscar Pettiford
"Strange Fruit"
Tadd Dameron
Teddy Wilson
The Famous Door
The Hickory House
The Three Deuces
The Yacht Club
Thelonious Monk
Tony's

WEBSITE

Please refer to the *Music Through Time* site listed in the front of your book to investigate and complete more classroom activities and assignments.

CHAPTER

24

Country Music

Country music can be traced back to the era of European minstrelsy, which used stringed instruments performed by traveling musicians singing songs of love and everyday life. These story songs were reproduced in an aural tradition to each passing generation, changing slightly, then evolving into new tunes through constant adaptation and personalization. As people began to settle the Americas, this music migrated with them from Europe into the new world, mixing in this melting pot of cultural activity, constantly taking on additional flavors from the native artistic brew.

Before the industrial revolution, when the rural community was stable and typically isolated, change was slow; therefore, for over 100 years, the folk music created by Americans was still essentially European in origin and tradition. When the Industrial Revolution began in America and the development of communications emerged, the folk music of America's white rural working class began to change at an accelerated rate.

The Carter Family

Bristol, Tennessee, or Bristol, Virginia, no one is really sure since the state line runs right down the middle of main street, but this is the birthplace of recorded country music. In 1927, four people came from New York City to the Blue Ridge Mountains with a carload of recording equipment and a mission to capture the music of the hills. **Ralph Peer,** his wife, and two engineers rented an empty industrial warehouse right on Main Street (which side of the street is debated as one side of the street is in Tennessee with the other in Virginia). Bristol had a reputation for folk music activity, and it was well known that the musicians in the mountains still sang old English folk ballads from the eighteenth and even seventeenth centuries. Peer wandered the town and realized quickly that this quaint town of about 8,000 people showed great promise for his recordings. There were two newspapers, a Kiwanis club, a YMCA, an emerging middle class dabbling in the stock market, and even a new hotel that housed a hot jazz band. Peer took out an ad in the Sunday paper explaining his mission:

> Mountain Singers and entertainers will be the talent used for record making in Bristol. Several well-known native record makers will come to Bristol this week to record. Mr. Peer has spent some time selecting the best native talent. The mountain or "hillbilly" records of this type have become more popular and are in great demand all over the country at this time. They are practically all made in the South. In no section of the South have the prewar melodies and old mountaineer songs been better preserved than in the mountains of East Tennessee and South West Virginia, experts declare, and it was primarily for this reason that the Victor Company chose Bristol as its operating base.

Peer found many groups eager to sign a recording contract, including *Alvin P. Carter*, his wife *Sara Carter*, and his sister-in-law *Maybelle Carter*. The **Carter Family**, a vocal trio group from Maces Springs, Virginia, had been singing informal mountain gatherings for over ten years.

Peer was somewhat disarmed by the group that appeared in the recording studio, recalling, "They wandered in a little ahead of time, and they come about 25 miles through a lot of mud. He's dressed in overalls and the women are country women from way back there—calico clothes on—and the children are dressed very poorly." The Carter Family recorded six tracks, including "**The Wandering Boy**" and "**Single Girl, Married Girl**."

When the recording was released, the Carter family didn't even own a record player and first heard it being played on a floor-model Victrola at a store in Bristol. A. P. Carter didn't know the record had been released, but Ralph Peer reported that the recording had sold over 2,000 copies in the south alone. The Carter family soon received their first royalty check and, A. P. promptly split it three ways. It wasn't much money, but it was certainly enough to keep them interested in creating more records, and the Victor Record Company signed the Carter Family to a long-term recording contract.

The Carter Family would become the most influential group in country music history, shifting the emphasis from hillbilly instrumental performances to vocal performance styles and story songs, making many of their tunes standards in country music. Also, their style of guitar playing, known as "**Carter** picking," became the main guitar style in country music for many years. The Carter Family sang with a simple and pure harmony that influenced many others including, Woody Guthrie, the Kingston Trio, and even Bob Dylan.

It's unlikely that bluegrass music could have existed without the Carter Family's influence because A. P., the family patriarch, collected hundreds of British and Appalachian folk songs and arranged them for over 300 recording sessions. He modified and modernized the simple beauty of these older story songs, and in so doing, saved them for future generations. Hundreds of songs were adapted, arranged, and recorded by A. P., Sara, and Maybelle, and from then on they became known as "Carter songs," including, "**Wabash Cannonball**," "**Will the Circle Be Unbroken**," "**Wildwood Flower**," and "**Keep on the Sunny Side**."

The Carter Family's use and choice of instrumental accompaniment would also become influential. A Gibson L-5 guitar, played as a lead melodic accompaniment on the bass strings with the whole guitar tuned down from standard pitch became a main technique for future bluegrass guitarists because the Carter Family did it. Also, the use of autoharp or a second guitar became standard practice. Although the original Carter Family disbanded in 1943, their influence is evident in generations of musicians in all forms of popular music. In 1970, the Carter Family became the first group elected into the Country Music Hall of Fame in recognition of their immense influence and legacy.

Jimmie Rodgers (1897–1933)

"Jimmie Rodgers' name stands foremost in the country music field as the man who started it all."
Jimmie Rodgers' plaque at the Country Music Hall of Fame

The "Singing Brakeman" and the "Mississippi Blue Yodeler," whose six-year career was cut short by tuberculosis, **Jimmie Rodgers** became the first nationally known star of country music and the direct influence of many later performers, including Hank Snow, Ernest Tubb, Hank Williams, and Merle Haggard. Rodgers sang about gamblers and ramblers, a life he knew well. In an era when Rodgers' contemporaries were singing only mountain and folk music, he fused gospel, jazz, blues, hillbilly country, pop, cowboy, and folk music into a new style all his own. Many of his best songs were his own compositions, including "**TB Blues**," "**Waiting for a Train**," "**Travelin' Blues**," "**Train Whistle Blues**," and his thirteen blues yodels. Although Rodgers wasn't the first to yodel on records, his style was distinct from all the others. His yodel was not mere effect, but instead as important to the piece as the lyric.

The youngest son of a railroad man, Rodgers was born and raised in Meridian, Mississippi, and instead of school, he chose to join his father on the tracks working for the railroad. Eventually, Rodgers heard that Ralph Peer, a talent scout, was recording hillbilly and string bands in Bristol, Tennessee. He went to the audition as a solo artist, and Peer recorded two songs, "**The Soldier's Sweetheart**" and "**Sleep, Baby, Sleep**." Released in October of 1927, the record was not a hit, but **RCA Victor** did agree to record Rodgers again. In November of 1927, he cut four songs, including "T for Texas." Re-titled "**Blue Yodel**," the song became a huge hit and one of only a handful of early country records to sell a million copies.

Shortly after its release, Rodgers and his wife, Carrie, moved to Washington, where he began appearing on a weekly local radio show billed as the Singing Brakeman. By that time, Rodgers had recorded several more singles, including the hits "**Way Out on the Mountain,**" "**Blue Yodel No. 4,**" "**Waiting for a Train,**" and "**In the Jailhouse Now.**" Over the next two years, Peer and Rodgers tried out a number of different accompanying bands, including a jazz group featuring Louis Armstrong, orchestras, and a Hawaiian combo.

By 1929, Rodgers had become an official star, as his concerts became major attractions and his records consistently sold well. During 1929, he made a small film called *The Singing Brakeman.* Though his activity kept his star shining, his health began to decline under all the stress; nevertheless, he continued to record numerous songs and built a large home in Kerrville, Texas. By the middle of 1931, the Depression was beginning to affect Rodgers, as his concert bookings decreased dramatically and his records stopped selling. His health deteriorated as well, forcing him to cancel plans for several films. Despite his condition, he refused to stop performing, telling his wife that "I want to die with my shoes on."

Realizing that he was close to death, he convinced Peer to schedule a recording session that Rodgers used to provide needed financial support for his family. At that session, Rodgers was accompanied by a nurse and rested on a cot between songs. Two days after the sessions were completed, he died of a lung hemorrhage on May 26, 1933. Following his death, his body was taken to Meridian by train, riding in a converted baggage car. Hundreds of country fans awaited the body's arrival in Meridian, and the train blew its whistle consistently throughout its journey. For several days after the body arrived in Rodgers' hometown, it lay in state as hundreds, if not thousands, of people paid tribute to the departed musician.

In 1961, Rodgers became the first artist inducted into the Country Music Hall of Fame; twenty-five years later, he was inducted as a founding father at the Rock and Roll Hall of Fame. Country fans could have asked for no better hero than someone who thought what they thought, felt what they felt, and sang about the common person honestly and beautifully.

Hank Williams, Sr. (1923–1953)

One of its fastest rising stars hit country music totally by surprise. **Hank Williams, Sr.** was a raw talent but an inspired artist. His songwriting abilities grew ever better as he made his mark on country music. He became one of the finest performers and influential persons in country music. He left a mark on country music and is remembered with highest regards by many of country's greatest musicians.

The simplicity of his lyrics caught the attention of the normal culture. Williams has been classified along with Stephen Foster as one of the top American music composers. His music seems timeless and still touches hearts of faithful listeners to this day. Born just south of Montgomery, Alabama, in 1923, Hiram Hank Williams grew up in the heart of country music. He was greatly influenced by the Carter Family, as well as others who made their mark on country music around the same time. Williams intently listened to Roy Acuff as he strived to break into the professional music scene. Although Williams himself speaks of country music legends as his influence, his mother always made the claim that a man people called "Tee-Tot" was one of the biggest influences on Hank. "Tee-Tot" was a singer who would perform on the streets in Georgiana and Greenville, Alabama, where Hank spent his younger years. No one has yet been able to put down exactly how "Tee-Tot" influenced Williams, but it is said that this man taught Williams what he knew about the basics of blues and the limited guitar skills he possessed.

His lyrics were all his own, however. He seemed to have a natural feel for country music and a unique style. Williams' lyric sense is confirmed because he rarely performed songs by other writers, instead singing his own creations. Yet, Williams' songs are still recorded and performed by other artists today. Hank indeed became a tough country music star, surviving rough "blood-bucket" bars fights in southern Alabama. On more than one occasion, Williams ended up with broken bones because of altercations.

Williams never achieved a high level of musicianship on his instruments (guitar and fiddle); however, he consistently fronted a band from the time he was age thirteen. Although there were many musician changes over the years, the Drifting Cowboys, as Hank named the group, were successful due to Williams' leadership and charisma. Hank's mother, Lilly Williams, served as manager, bookkeeper, nurse, and sometimes cook for the band in their early years until Hank met a country beauty, Audrey Mae Sheppard, who took over the ranks. Eventually, the "limelight" seeking young lady married Williams, and their often torrent relationship served as creative inspiration for many of his songs. This turmoil led to their divorce and ultimately to some of Hank's best music.

After their separation in 1946, Hank left for Nashville, diving into the country music scene headfirst. He kept records of all of the songs he had written over the last ten years, calling them hymns, and since the only publishing companies of country music were in Nashville, Hank knew that was the place for him. Upon arriving at Nashville, Hank met female comedian **Minnie Pearl**, who remembers that, "his eyes were haunting, deep-set, with a very tragic emotion." Pearl helped Williams as much as she could, but she knew he wasn't prepared for the **Grand Ole Opry**. This wasn't necessarily Hank's intention; he was there to be a commercial songwriter. As it was, Williams knew of a company that had an outstanding reputation for honest dealings with songwriters, and it wasn't long before Williams was opening the door to **Acuff-Rose Publishing**. Williams lit up the studio and the producers couldn't believe what they were hearing. Not only was this music original, some of it was spontaneous. Hank awed them with his ability as a lyricist. Before Williams left that building, he had signed a contract.

In 1949, Williams was forced to deal with a drinking problem that kept him on a roller-coaster ride, yet he was able to keep many of his peers from knowing.

Some worried that Hank's premiere performance at the Grand Ole Opry on June 11 could be derailed if he were drinking. He entered the Ryman Auditorium that night, well composed, and took his place in front of the microphone to sing what was already a well-known hit, "**Lovesick Blues**." The record was already a hit, but no one expected what happened when he began the popular tune. The place erupted in a standing ovation. In fact, the frenzy was so great that there was a small riot when Hank tried to finish the song. Williams ended up singing the song six times, repeating the last line of the song over and over again before the auditorium finally calmed.

After such an astonishing first appearance at the Opry, no matter how bad his drinking became or how many shows he missed because of alcohol, his managers couldn't keep him from becoming a Grand Ole Opry fixture. Fred Rose, of the Acuff-Rose Company, never left Williams side, always believing in the talent of Williams even at his lowest points. Rose was focused on helping Williams grow as a songwriter. Rose took Williams' songs to top record executives, including **Mitch Miller** at Columbia Records. Miller listened to Williams' "**Cold, Cold Heart**" and knew exactly where it would fit perfectly—with an up-and-coming new vocalist named **Tony Bennett**. One of the most fateful strokes of luck in American pop music to that day, "Cold Cold Heart" sold millions of copies and immediately rose to number one on the pop charts. It shattered the barrier that seemingly separated country and pop music for many years. Williams continued writing for Acuff and Miller, his music and lyrics, overtime, becoming "American" music rather than merely country music.

Williams' creativity grew with his own life, with his songs of love and loneliness stemming from his own life experience. The many years of rough marriage supplied him with endless material, as did his long time bout with alcohol. In 1951, the Grand Ole Opry could no longer handle Williams' personality, and he was kicked off the show. Just prior to this event, Audrey was granted the finalized divorce and she received a large portion of his estate and royalties. Although Hank tried to do his best to clean up, he was a broken man. The experiences he suffered took their toll and sent him into a downward spiral of increasing alcoholism and even drug abuse. On New Years Eve 1952, Williams died quietly in the backseat of a car on the way to a show. Alcoholism had taken its final toll on his heart. Williams' funeral was the largest ever attended in the South until Dr. Martin Luther King's funeral fifteen years later. The effect Hank Williams had on country music is astounding; in fact, it changed the very perception of country music.

VOCABULARY

Acuff-Rose Publishing
Alvin P. Carter
"Blue Yodel"
"Blue Yodel No. 4"
Carter Family
Carter picking
"Cold, Cold Heart"
Grand Ole Opry
Hank Williams, Sr.
"In the Jailhouse Now"
Jimmie Rodgers
"Keep on the Sunny
    Side"

"Lovesick Blues"
Maybelle Carter
Minnie Pearl
Mitch Miller
Ralph Peer
RCA Victor
Sara Carter
"Single Girl, Married
    Girl"
"Sleep, Baby, Sleep"
"TB Blues"
"The Soldier's
    Sweetheart"

"The Wandering Boy"
Tony Bennett
"Train Whistle Blues"
"Travelin' Blues"
"Wabash Cannonball"
"Waiting for a Train"
"Way Out on the
    Mountain"
"Wildwood Flower"
"Will the Circle Be
    Unbroken"

WEBSITE

Please refer to the *Music Through Time* site listed in the front of your book to investigate and complete more classroom activities and assignments.

CHAPTER
25

Sam Phillips and Elvis Presley

Crossover music has become a familiar term in today's pop music world. Its meaning is simple; a crossover hit is one that receives airplay on a diverse group of radio stations. For example, one of the biggest crossover groups in history is The Temptations, a group of African American vocalists that were mass marketed by Berry Gordy to achieve popularity in both the African American and White culture. Country music has also seen its share of crossover acts, with Willie Nelson, Dolly Parton, "I Will Always Love You," performed by Whitney Houston, and recently Shania Twain's hit "From This Moment" which shattered the country and pop charts.

It's possible that no one person can be more responsible for the discovery of the crossover act than **Sam Phillips**. Phillips has been attributed with many discoveries of musical legends and to define him as only country or rhythm and blues would be both fact and fiction. Phillips' list of discoveries obliterates the definition of rhythm and blues as well as country music artists. He is responsible for both, and he is responsible for "The King." Indeed, Sam Phillips was the discoverer of one Elvis Presley, and he invented rock and roll.

©Bettmann/CORBIS

Sam Phillips *(1923–2003)*

Born in Florence, Alabama, in 1925 (home of blues legend W. C. Handy), Phillips began working as a radio announcer during the day after dropping out of high school in 1941. WLAY radio in Muscle Shoals, Alabama, hired Phillips as a D.J. in 1942. Sam quickly moved onto a larger station, WHSL, in Decatur, Alabama. In 1945, Phillips headed to Nashville to gain a radio spot on WLAC. However, his destiny would take him to Memphis, Tennessee, in 1946, where he worked on WREC radio until 1949. His radio show was promoted out of the famous **Peabody Hotel**.

While working as a D.J., Sam was able to stash enough money away to open his own recording studio in Memphis. Sam had a keen business mind. His studio at 706 Union Avenue was home to some of the best southern African American recordings that were ultimately leased (not sold) to independent record companies. Phillips recorded **Jackie Brenston**'s **"Rocket 88"** in 1951, and took a risk on the success of the record by adding some cutting-edge technology of the time. The harsher-sounding guitar was an accident; the amplifier fell from the car top and a tube broke, giving the recording the fuzzed-out sound. He added extra amplification to the guitar, which added a completely new dimension to the final recording. The risk paid off and the record had astounding sales figures. Many other artists signed on to record with Phillips, such legendary names as **"Howlin' Wolf," Bobby "Blue" Bland, Little Milton, James Cotton, Sleepy John Estes, Ike Turner**, and probably the most well-known bluesman, **B. B. King**. With the success of his studio, Phillips started his own record label.

July 5, 1954, Sam Phillips, **Scotty Moore, Bill Black,** and **Elvis Presley** entered the 30'x20' studio at **Sun Records**. What happened that day became an epic moment in the history of American music. The trio recorded a tune previously released by Bill Monroe and his Blue Grass Boys in 1945, a tune called **"Blue Moon of Kentucky."** What they were doing with the song wasn't traditional country, nor did it follow the rhythm and blues feel that had been recorded by Bill Haley and his Comets. Indeed, this was something new, and when this new sound made it to tape, on the playback Phillips states, "Hell, that's different. That's a pop song now, and that's good." The sound Phillips had been striving for had finally arrived. **Rock-a-billy** had just been invented.

Elvis Presley (1935–1977)

Growing up in Tupelo, Mississippi, Presley was surrounded by gospel music and exposed to jazz and blues. Born on January 8, 1935, **Elvis Aron Presley** was only thirteen when his family was uprooted from his Mississippi hometown to move to the western Tennessee city of Memphis. In the spring of 1953, Elvis graduated from Humes High School and began working for Precision Tool Company, then moved on to Crown Electric Company as a truck driver for $42.00 a week. He didn't realize (and neither did Sam Phillips) that stepping into Sam's **Memphis Recording Service** during the summer of 1953 would change his life forever. It didn't start that simple, however. Elvis first entered the studio merely to make a record for his mother's birthday. He paid his four dollars and entered the recording room with his guitar.

Marion Keisker, who was administrating the Memphis Recording Service at the time, heard this voice and as she later told Elvis' biographer Jerry Hopkins,

"The reason I paid particular attention to Elvis was this. Over and over again I could remember Sam saying, 'If I could find a white man who had the Negro feel, I could make a billion dollars.' This is what I heard in Elvis, what I guess is now called soul, this Negro sound, I heard and I wanted Sam to know about it." Phillips was only mildly impressed.

Several months later, in January 1954 (only months before Presley, Moore, and Black would have that new sound Phillips was looking for), Presley returned to the Memphis Recording Service, however, Marion was not in this time. Elvis ended up speaking directly with Sam Phillips. Elvis gave Sam his four dollars for the recording time for another cut. This time, Elvis recorded "I'll Never Stand in Your Way," a 1941 Clint Homer country song. Phillips also had Elvis learn a demo tune called "Casual Love Affair."

A few months later, a demo record of unknown origin arrived at Phillips' studio from Nashville. Sam was disturbed by the greatness of this demo, called "Without You," but even more disturbed to find out when he called Nashville that no one knew who it was or where it came from. In a panic to release this demo, Sam had to find someone to record it quickly. Marion, realizing his predicament, recommended, "That young kid that has come in to record a couple of times." Sam called Elvis, and he was there that afternoon learning the new tune. The session went poorly and Phillips became very frustrated. During a break for Sam to change tapes on the machine, Elvis and the band attempted to work off some frustration. Scotty Moore recalls, "Elvis started beating on this old guitar, beating the fire out of it, hard you know. He was trying to release some frustration, and he started singing this old blues tune, '**That's Alright Mama**.' Sam opened the door to the control room and shouted, 'Now that's what I want,' and he turned the tape on. 'That's Alright Mama' was cut just that way, by accident."

On July 19, 1954, Elvis' first record was released. Phillips personally took a copy to **Dewey Phillips**, who hosted the radio show "**Red Hot and Blue**" on WHBQ. He broadcast "That's All Right Mama." After extremely enthusiastic response to the single, disk jockeys began to play more of that record, including its flip side, "Blue Moon of Kentucky." It was only weeks before Memphis had a number one pop music record with "That's Alright Mama" and a number one country music record with "Blue Moon of Kentucky." This was indeed the time rock-a-billy was established, and Elvis would become the "King" of rock-a-billy.

In January 1956, after signing a contract with RCA Victor in Nashville, Elvis, accompanied by his band members Bill Black, Scotty Moore, and new drummer DJ Fontana, began recording the new music for his new label. Elvis wasn't alone with his band on this recording; RCA brought in some of Nashville's biggest guns to assist in the sessions. Chet Atkins, guitar; Floyd Cramer, piano; and the vocal group The Jordonaires also accompanied Elvis on his first recording "**Heartbreak Hotel**." It was truly a crossover hit, becoming number one on the country and pop charts, holding those spots for eight straight weeks. Presley and the crew were invited to perform on TV shows, the most famous being the "**Ed Sullivan Show**," where Presley impressed everyone with his charisma, performance, and hips, generating mass hysteria among the young women.

The momentum of Presley's career was interrupted when he enlisted in the armed service of the United States of America. In Germany for his country, he met his wife Priscilla while on his tour of duty. Upon his return, he devoted

much of his time to making movies and recording movie soundtracks. This was not his only focus, though; he returned to his roots to record an album of sacred songs. Toward the end of the 1960s, Elvis rekindled the rock-n-roll spirit with the broadcast of a TV special entitled, "Elvis." This set his career back in motion and in the direction of possibly some of his most influential work. He returned to recording in Memphis in 1969 and put on record some of his most classic music.

Elvis made his mark in history for his rigorous touring schedule that began in the early 1970s. He sold out over 95 percent of all venues he played, until his death from a heart attack in August 1977 at Graceland. Statistically, Elvis holds many industry records for his music. He has the most top 40 hits with 107, the most top 10 hits with thirty-eight, the most consecutive number one hits with ten and the most weeks at number one with eighty weeks in a row. No musical artist has come close to these numbers since. If there ever was a doubt, the numbers alone solidify Elvis as "The King of Rock-n-Roll."

VOCABULARY

B. B. King	Howlin' Wolf	"Red Hot and Blue"
Bill Black	Ike Turner	Rock-a-billy
"Blue Moon of Kentucky"	Jackie Brenston	"Rocket 88"
	James Cotton	Sam Phillips
Bobby "Blue" Bland	Little Milton	Scotty Moore
Dewey Phillips	Memphis Recording Service	Sleepy John Estes
Ed Sullivan Show		Sun Records
Elvis Presley	Peabody Hotel	"That's Alright Mama"
"Heartbreak Hotel"	RCA Victor	

WEBSITE

Please refer to the *Music Through Time* site listed in the front of your book to investigate and complete more classroom activities and assignments.

CHAPTER
26

The Beatles

The term "rock-n-roll" has been used since the mid 1950s and its original use was to define a new genre of music that involved smaller amplified ensembles. At the onset of rock-n-roll, there were no racial barriers. It was what is was and everyone wanted to be involved. Black, White, or European, it was new, and people wanted to hear it and musicians wanted to perform it. To say that rock-n-roll still encompasses American popular music in its entirety would be offensive to some; however, if traced back to the roots of rock-n-roll, it is a term that can be inclusive of rock-a-billy, rock, soul, R&B, heavy metal, alternative, and the "MTV Generation." One of the most important historical institutions, the **Rock-n-Roll Hall of Fame** in Cleveland, Ohio, does not discriminate against musical genre or race, it includes all genres that can be qualified as rock-n-roll and puts them under subcategories.

One attribute of rock-n-roll is that it stems from original American music. Rock-a-billy can be traced directly to the songs of Stephen Foster, who was an important source of Anglo-American folk music. Fusion and funk can be traced back to the rhythmic influences of African Americans. Every other genre becomes a mixture of those two streams of influence. Jazz emerged when the

©Bettmann/CORBIS

African American musicians of the late nineteenth century heard the military brass bands of Sousa and added their rhythmic heritage to this new European music they were hearing for the first time. Rock-n-roll has continuously developed since the mid-fifties, using a melting pot of past musical influences from traditional folk music, classical music, and spirituals, among others.

To say that rock-n-roll has been without controversy would be inaccurate. Driven harder for fame, greatness, and wealth, these seemingly golden prizes came with a high price, leading some great rock musicians down a self-destructive path of alcoholism and drug abuse. **Jim Morrison, Janis Joplin, Jimmy Hendrix,** and the King himself, **Elvis Presley,** all led hard lives on the road and ended up dying at a young age from one vice or another. The punk rock of the 1970s supposedly developed to battle the commercialism of rock-n-roll. Young bands of average talent but great passion created songs that bashed the "greedy rocker" and downplayed musical professionalism. Despite being grounded in commercialism, rock musicians chose this path to display their contempt for music's commercialization. This type of attitude has been maintained throughout the development of rock-n-roll and has helped it to prosper by giving it the rebellious, cutting edge that youthful generations can "sink their teeth into."

In the latter half of the 1960s, intellectualism entered the musical landscape of rock-and-roll. Classical era forms were beginning to be used, as well as classical or romantic compositions themselves. For example, the group *Emerson, Lake & Palmer* used some of romantic/twentieth century music's most popular pieces—"Pictures at an Exhibition" by Russian composer Modest Musorgsky and two pieces by Aaron Copland, "Fanfare for the Common Man" and "Hoedown" from Rodeo.

The Beatles

No one album in the history of rock-n-roll was more creatively produced with a crossover influence of classical, romantic, and rock-n-roll stylings than was the Beatles' album *Sergeant Pepper's Lonely Hearts Club Band*. The significance of this recording is so great to rock-n-roll because it is the first *art-rock* album. This recording impacted history because of its creative use of instruments, multi-time signatures, and song cycle concepts, all firmly embedded within the language of rock-n-roll.

The Beatles didn't start their career as "**The Beatles.**" Founder **John Lennon** invited the musicians to join on separate occasions and the band as a whole was formed in 1956 under the name "**Johnny and the Moondogs.**" They went through many names for the group until they finally ended up with "The Beatles," making the entire group the artistic focus rather than a single individual. When the Beatles first started in Great Britain, they spent the first few years honing their craft while performing in some of England's toughest clubs.

In 1961, under the new influence of manager **Brian Epstein,** they polished their image and performance, but it wasn't until **George Martin,** a classically trained musician/producer, signed them to a contract with **EMI Records** that they obtained a recording contract. He admitted later that he wasn't impressed with their originality or even their talent, but he was completely struck by the group's personalities. In fact, Martin remained unimpressed until he saw a live Beatles performance in Liverpool at the Cavern Club. The Beatles had learned all the major rock-n-roll hits covered from bands in the United States. Their sound was raucous, but if there was any one thing that caught the producer's ears, it was the fact that the listeners were going crazy for it. Martin realized almost immediately that the Beatles were the total package and no other British group would even come close to them in audience response.

Not long after signing with EMI, the Beatles recorded their first hits. In 1963, Lennon and McCartney began to develop original music, creating such a wave of popularity and fan hysteria that the term *Beatle-mania* was coined in the media to describe the frenzy. The group's success in the mid 1960s had no precedent, not even when compared to the fan frenzies of earlier ages with legendary performers Benny Goodman or Frank Sinatra.

The Beatles were a hit machine. From the time "**Please Please Me**" hit the radio, it was followed with eleven more consecutive number one hits—"**From Me to You**," "**She Loves You**," "**I Want to Hold Your Hand**," "**Can't Buy Me Love**," "**A Hard Days Night**," "**I Feel Fine**," "**Ticket to Ride**," "**Help!**," "**Day Tripper**," "**Paperback Writer**," and "**Yellow Submarine**." The curiosity of it all was not what record would hit, but how fast would it hit? The Beatles embedded themselves in American pop music history in early 1964 with their legendary appearance on the "Ed Sullivan Show" when the TV show received the highest Neilson rating yet recorded in television history.

A timeline of Beatles successes is as follows:

- 1964—The "Ed Sullivan Show" appearance
- 1965—The Beatles fill New York's Shea Stadium
- 1966—The last Beatles concert in San Francisco
- 1967—The Beatles release *Sergeant Pepper's Lonely Hearts Club Band* and *Magical Mystery Tour,* tying both into a movie with the same names
- 1968—Total record sales reach over 200 million worldwide
- 1970—Beatles release *Abbey Road* recording after which time Paul McCartney announces his separation from the group
- 1975—The Beatles peacefully dissolved their partnership.

Sergeant Pepper's… is one of the most magnificent creations of The Beatles. Because of the unity of the thirteen songs on the album, it has been called cyclical, or a *song cycle,* and a work of musical genius. **Paul McCartney** was responsible for the idea. The album idea was built around one song about a military band with a mythical leader named "Sergeant Pepper." McCartney said, "Why don't we make this album as though it were done by Sergeant Pepper and his band, dubbing in the necessary effects." And from that moment, *Sergeant Pepper* was brought to life. This idea would prove effective when the album not only became the best-selling Beatles album to date, but it also propelled the Beatles into genuine contributors to the development of artistic performance in the genre. *Sergeant Pepper* and *A Day in the Life* were both thought of as serious works of art, something literally unimaginable in rock-n-roll. Up to that point, only one other type of music had brought such a body of criticism, and that was jazz. The

creativity of writing, the controversial lyrics, and the uniqueness of production techniques all attracted young listeners who were intelligent and socially conscious—this music expressed their feelings well.

The album cover of *Sergeant Peppers* has become a cultural icon of a generation. During the time of the recording, it is apparent that the musicians (John Lennon, Paul McCartney, **George Harrison,** and **Ringo Starr**) were incorporating more classical and avant-garde sounds. The album used traditional European Classical sounds in such tunes as **"All We Need is Love"** and a highly uncommon instrument to the pop music world, the piccolo trumpet, in **"Penny Lane,"** without disorienting the audience with their new creations.

Because of their ingenuity, re-inventiveness, and progress, their fan base grew from young teenage girls to legions of fans, spreading across generation and gender gaps. Any group following them has rarely equaled their level of influence on popular music. Their catalog of music rivals that of Mozart and Duke Ellington in importance in their respective genres. Their financial success paved the road for future musicians as well. They, too, had their politically controversial music, although these recordings didn't appear until late in their career, reflecting the most intense periods of the Vietnam era political unrest in the United States. Because of their innovative techniques, they afforded other musicians the opportunity to be more creative, incorporating a variety of instruments, including winds and strings. Claiming that it added flash, fire, and something unique, rock-n-roll had added horns.

VOCABULARY

A Day in the Life	George Harrison	"Paperback Writer"
"A Hard Days Night"	George Martin	Paul McCartney
Abbey Road	"Help!"	"Penny Lane"
"All We Need is Love"	"I Feel Fine"	"Please Please Me"
Art-Rock	"I Want to Hold Your	Ringo Starr
Brian Epstein	Hand"	Rock-n-Roll Hall of Fame
"Can't Buy Me Love"	Janis Joplin	Sergeant Pepper's
"Day Tripper"	Jim Morrison	Lonely Hearts Club
Elvis Presley	Jimmy Hendrix	Band
Emerson, Lake &	John Lennon	"She Loves You"
Palmer	Johnny and the	The Beatles
EMI Records	Moondogs	"Ticket to Ride"
"From Me to You"	Magical Mystery Tour	"Yellow Submarine"

WEBSITE

Please refer to the *Music Through Time* site listed in the front of your book to investigate and complete more classroom activities and assignments.

27

Motown

*B*erry Gordy Jr. is the most influential African American man in the music scene of the early 1960s. His business knowledge afforded him the opportunity to promote the African-American culture in a way that had never been done before. Gordy's idea was to have a complete staff of producers, songwriters, artists, handlers, manufacturers, and business people, all working toward a focused goal. The founder of **Tamla-Motown** record labels, Gordy established **Motown Records** as one of the most important independent labels in history. Motown Records quickly built one of the most impressive rosters of artists in American popular music, and by 1964 had become the most successful independent record company in the United States.

His father, Berry Gordy Sr., who established his family in the farming and retail community in Georgia, instilled Gordy's business mind and discipline. In 1922, Gordy Sr. moved to Detroit with his first three children. There, he established a successful painting and construction business, affording him the

The Temptations
©Bettmann/CORBIS

opportunity to purchase commercial property on the corner of St. Antoine and Farnsworth streets in downtown Detroit. Gordy Sr. opened the "Booker T. Washington" grocery from which he tried to instill into the African-American community the values of discipline, family, and frugality, all which were so dear to Booker T. Washington. After studying business in college, Bertha co-founded the "Friendship Mutual Life Insurance Company." On November 28, 1929, the fourth child was born at Detroit's Harper Hospital; Berry Gordy Jr. was the newest addition to the family.

Gordy Jr. became a professional boxer after dropping out of the eleventh grade. He ended his featherweight career respectably in 1950, and then served in the Army in Korea from 1951–1953. Upon his return to the United States, his love for jazz prompted him to open the "*3-D Record Mart—House of Jazz.*" His first, and probably most important, business lesson came from this record store. Gordy's love of jazz made him too stubborn to stock the shelves with blues records that the neighborhood wanted so badly. Due to his hard-headedness, the store went bankrupt in 1955. While running the record store, Gordy married Thelma Coleman. After marriage, the couple quickly had three children. Shortly after the record store closed, Gordy found himself working at Ford's Lincoln-Mercury plant. By 1957, his heart led to him to quit the job and become a professional songwriter.

In 1949, on the corner of John R and Canfield, the Flame Show Bar opened. **The Flame** was the showplace for the top African-American talent in Detroit during the 1950s. Such great musicians as T-Bone Walker, Billie Holiday, Wynonie Harris and many others were among those that appeared at The Flame. The club asked sisters Gwen and Anna Gordy to handle the photo concessions at the club; their brothers George and Robert joined them. Al Green, the club's owner, invited Berry Gordy to be a songwriter for the artists that he managed, which included **Jackie Wilson**. Berry teamed up with Roquel "Billy" Davis and began songwriting in Green's office. Gwen would eventually be brought in for some assistance, and the three turned out several great hits, including "**To Be Loved**," "**Lonely Teardrops**," "**That's Why I Love You So**," and "**I'll Be Satisfied**," establishing their songwriting careers. By this time, Gordy Jr. began some producing of his own.

Raynoma Liles and her sister, Alice, entered Gordy's life for an audition. Raynoma not only became Gordy's next wife, but also his next business partner. Raynoma, or Miss Ray as she became known around the company, had perfect pitch and an uncanny ability to write out lead sheets. **The Rayber Music Writing Company** formed and for $100 would do whatever was necessary to help a young singer make a record, and find new talent they did. They also put together the "**Rayber Voices**," who provided background vocalists on many of the new talent's recordings. In 1957, Gordy had his first success with "**Reet Petite**," recorded by Jackie Wilson who was the lead singing replacement for Clyde McPhatter in the Dominoes. The next year, the previously written "Lonely Teardrops," became a hit for Wilson.

Gordy listened to an unsuccessful audition for the **Matadors** and Wilson's manager, Nat Tarnpool. This failure changed Gordy's life, sparking a long-time relationship between the Matadors' lead singer, **Smokey Robinson**, and Berry. The Matadors became the **Miracles**, involving Gordy as their manager. In 1958, he produced their single, "**Get a Job**," on The End Records label. After receiving a couple of small royalty checks for "Get a Job" and other songs he had either written or co-written, Gordy was finally convinced he needed to open his own label, **Tamla Records.**

Jobete Music Publishing was established in 1959 by Gordy, who named the company after his three children, Hazel Joy, Terry, and Berry. What made Jobete one of the most powerful publishers in the industry was, if Motown recorded you, Jobete subsequently published you.

Gordy scored a minor hit with Tamla's first release by R&B singer Marv Johnson with **"Come to Me."** As the success and demand for the album grew, Gordy realized he couldn't keep up with the production and leased the master recording to United Artists. Also in that first year, Gordy co-wrote and produced "Money" recorded by **Barrett Strong.** Gordy, who was not yet equipped to release a nationwide hit record let his sister's company, **Anna Records,** release the record. "Money" eventually reached the number two spot on the R&B charts. Gordy recorded *"Bad Girl"* in 1959, by his young friend William "Smokey" Robinson and the Miracles, reaching number 93 on the pop charts with the help of Chess Records' national distribution. Smokey, being a long time friend, convinced Gordy that the newly developed Motown Records should distribute its own material. Gordy co-wrote and distributed **"Shop Around"** by Smokey Robinson and the Miracles, which established Motown as an up-and-coming important independent company, giving them a number one hit. By this time, Gordy owned many complimentary businesses attached to his name—Motown Records Corporation, **Hitsville USA, Berry Gordy Enterprises**, and Jobete Music Publishing, and **International Talent Management, Inc.**, which was the management agency.

The "Girl Vocal Band" was becoming the big craze, and Gordy capitalized on the idea. **Mary Wells** approached Gordy with a song in mind for Jackie Wilson, but she couldn't write music. Instead, she sang the song to Berry. Impressed, he signed her to the record label and released her version of **"Bye Bye Baby,"** hitting the R&B top ten charts in 1960. Smokey Robinson got in on the act of co-writing with Wells and produced a string of hits with **"The One Who Really Loves You," "You Beat Me to the Punch,"** and **"Two Lovers."** Wells topped the charts again with the 1964 hit **"My Guy."**

Running in concurrence with Mary Wells, Gordy began producing the **Marvelettes** in 1961. Releasing their first hit "**Please Mr. Postman,"** after auditioning for Gordy. In 1962, the **Motortown Revue tour** started in the South. Gordy was encouraged by the success of these girl groups and signed yet another, **Martha and the Vandellas.** Martha Reeves was hired as a secretary to Gordy in 1961, and by 1962 she convinced him to give her and her friends an audition. This girl group sang back up on many Motown hits before venturing off on their own. Martha and The Vandellas, Mary Wells, and the Marvelettes established Motown as a reliable source for the girl group sound. Following his good business mind, Gordy's new sound was not complete without the look. If he were to introduce young African American ladies into mainstream America, they had to appear acceptable to white American record buyers. In 1964, Gordy hired **Maxine Powell**, who operated a finishing and modeling school, to prep his performers. Powell transformed Motown artists into polished professionals. Even after the success of adding Maxine, the total performance package was still missing something. A few months later, Gordy hired **Cholly Atkins**, a

dance choreographer who was well known for his work in the 1930s and 1940s at the Cotton Club and Savoy Ballroom, to teach these groups to move on stage during a performance.

Atkins began working with **Maurice King**, who was serving as the executive musical director for Motown. King arranged shows at Detroit's Flame Show Bar for years and had worked with numerous jazz artists. The two taught the Motown groups about stage patter.

Gordy assembled a Motown team by the mid 1960s that could take poor African American youths from Detroit and teach them to talk, walk, and dress as successful debutantes and suave gentlemen. Combining the new polished image with gospel-based music, Gordy made an effort to appeal to mainstream America. Gordy was aware that in order to win the hearts of supporters, he had to create a look that the mothers and fathers of the American record buying public could accept. Motown wanted to disassociate with the 1960s stereotypical image of drugs and booze that plagued R&B for so many years. With this in mind, the executives at Motown rejected anything that had a particularly strong blues influence. Gordy wanted a distinct sound of music grounded in a pulsating rhythm section that was accentuated by horns and featured the call and response in the vocals that had been ingrained into the older generations from the gospel music developed in the African American church. Building on the success of the girl bands, Gordy strived to produce a sound that was reminiscent yet an enhancement of Phil Specter's "Wall of Sound."

Setting his focus on the mass-market, Gordy called the music "The Sound of Young America" and placed a sign over the Motown studio that read, "Hitsville U.S.A." Gordy used his ever-expanding business knowledge to continue the success of such groups as the Supremes by assembling the parts of a hit-making machine. Those parts included standardized song writing, an in-house rhythm section, a quality control panel, a selective promotion committee, and a family atmosphere that was respectfully built around Henry Ford's assembly line concepts in use at the auto plants in the early twentieth century.

Brian Holland, Lamont Dozier, and **Eddie Holland** joined forces in 1962 and became a part of the songwriting team of Motown after perfecting the formula of success they had discovered in their hit composition "**Where Did Our Love Go**." All of the hits had a remarkably similar sound due to the fact that Motown employed a house rhythm section known as "**The Funk Brothers**," and in 1964 employed **Earl Van Dyke**, a former bebop jazz pianist who toured with R&B singer Lloyd Price. Van Dyke became the leader in the studio. Drummer **Benny Benjamin** and bassist **James Jamerson**, who backed Jackie Wilson and Smokey and the Miracles, joined the musical team, and that combination established the musical sound of Motown.

Gordy and company promoted everything they released through media that would keep the Motown image crisp and clean. Motown acts appeared regularly on "The Ed Sullivan Show," "The Dean Martin Show," "The Tonight Show," "The Hollywood Palace," and many others. He even employed other great stars like Carol Channing and Sammy Davis Jr. to write liner notes for newly released recordings.

In 1960, between sets at a local club, **Otis Williams** and **Melvin Franklin** met Mr. Gordy in a bathroom and introduced themselves. Otis and Melvin had been a part of many different vocal groups trying to succeed under different names—The Elegants, The Questions, and the Distants. Before giving them a shot at recording for Motown records, Gordy and the production crew insisted they come up with a new name. The group, Otis, Melvin, Paul, and Eddie (later adding David Ruffin) pondered all day outside of Hitsville U.S.A. until they came up with the name "**The Temptations**." Over the next forty years, The Temptations (not wanting to name any one member as the front man) would have top charting hits through the song-writing assistance of the Motown collection of writers. Smokey Robinson turned out some of the Temptations' great hits like "**Just My Imagination**" and "**My Girl**." The Temptations, unlike many other Motown groups, are still together and touring to this day, doing over 200 shows a year internationally. At the turn of this century, the Temptations enjoyed a monumental honor with "My Girl" being named the second "Most Important Song" of the twentieth century. (The number one song was Louis Armstrong's "What a Wonderful World.")

Gordy established a musical empire during the 1960s that included eight record labels, management services, and publishing companies and grossed millions of dollars from 1964 to 1967. Motown achieved fourteen number one pop singles, twenty number one singles on the R&B charts, forty-six more top fifteen singles, and seventy-five other top fifteen R&B singles. In 1966, three-fourths of everything Motown released was making the charts.

Gordy moved Motown's offices to Hollywood in an effort to expand the company into the realm of filmmaking. Berry produced the film, *Lady Sings The Blues* which starred *Diana Ross*. While successful, his concentration on business expansion actually hurt the record production part of the company, causing the record company's influence and success rate to decline. Many of the Motown artists were frustrated and left Motown for other labels. **The Four Tops** moved to ABC/Dunhill Label. **Gladys Knight and the Pips** began recording for Buddah in 1974. In 1975, the **Jackson Five** moved to Epic Records, as did **Michael Jackson** in 1978. The Miracles, needing new life after not having Smokey Robinson with them anymore, moved to Columbia Records. And in 1977, one of Motown's best-established male groups, The Temptations, signed with Atlantic Records. Motown however, still maintained the independent label status with recordings of Diana Ross, **Marvin Gaye**, **Stevie Wonder**, **The Commodores,** and **Rick James**.

More struggles hit Motown records in the 1980s. Diana Ross moved to RCA records and Marvin Gaye signed with Columbia. However, all was not lost, as the Temptations and the Four Tops returned to the Motown label. In 1988, on the heals of many lawsuits for allegedly not paying proper royalties, Berry Gordy could no longer handle the company that had once been his whole life. He sold Motown Records to MCA and Boston Ventures for $61 million. Boston Ventures later bought all of MCA's shares and sold Motown Records to Polygram for $325 million in 1993. Berry Gordy, for all of his achievements in the music business and for the African-American culture in his lifetime, was inducted into the Rock-n-Roll Hall of Fame in 1990.

VOCABULARY

3-D Record Mart—
    House of Jazz
Anna Records
"Bad Girl"
Barrett Strong
Benny Benjamin
Berry Gordy Enterprises
Berry Gordy Jr.
Brian Holland
"Bye Bye Baby"
Cholly Atkins
"Come to Me"
Diana Ross
Earl Van Dyke
Eddie Holland
"Get a Job"
Gladys Knight and the
    Pips
Hitsville U.S.A.
"I'll Be Satisfied"
International Talent
    Management, Inc
Jackie Wilson
Jackson Five
James Jamerson

Jobete Music Publishing
"Just My Imagination"
"Lady Sings The Blues"
Lamont Dozier
"Lonely Teardrops"
Martha and the
    Vandellas
Marvelettes
Marvin Gaye
Mary Wells
Matadors
Maurice King
Maxine Powell
Melvin Franklin
Michael Jackson
Miracles
"Money"
Motortown Revue Tour
Motown Records
"My Girl"
My Guy
Otis Williams
"Please Mr. Postman"
Rayber Voices
Raynoma Liles

Reet Petite
Rick James
"Shop Around"
Smokey Robinson
Stevie Wonder
Tamla Records
Tamla-Motown
The Temptations
"That's Why I Love You
    So"
The Commodores
The Flame
The Four Tops
The Funk Brothers
"The One Who Really
    Loves You"
The Rayber Music
    Writing Company
"To Be Loved"
"Two Lovers"
"Where Did Our Love
    Go"
"You Beat Me to the
    Punch"

WEBSITE

Please refer to the *Music Through Time* site listed in the front of your book to investigate and complete more classroom activities and assignments.

CHAPTER

28

The Horn Bands

It is not unusual to have live wind instruments in a musical group in American popular music. Orchestras used them for almost two hundred years, although in a much different setting. Classical and late Romantic composers sought to use more and more wind instruments in their music because of the projection, volume, and additional timbre choices. Hector Berlioz used double orchestras in order to accomplish his dynamic desires. In the late 1800s, military bands and the developing "Dixieland" bands used wind instruments as major figureheads in their ensembles. In the developmental years of the big band, the saxophone family of instruments, trumpet and trombone, all became staples in that ensemble configuration. As music developed in the early part of the 1900s in the clubs, it was easier and cheaper to use fewer horns with the standard rhythm section and still get the impact desired because of great horn soloists. The emphasis then was on improvisation during the development of bebop and cool jazz. Therefore, there was less of an emphasis on horn section members playing together as an ensemble and more individual attention given to the soloist.

The standard rock-n-roll ensemble had been around for years; one vocalist, drummer, bass player, and a harmony instrument—guitar or keyboard—before the term rock-n-roll was used. This type of ensemble developed in the jazz days

Tuscaloosa Horns ca 1979

with Billie Holiday, Ella Fitzgerald, Joe Williams, and many others. The ensemble configuration didn't change, but the music performed by the ensemble did. It would take many chapters to show the actual development of how all these types of bands came together to form rock-n-roll horn bands, but in brief, follow the timeline breakdown that follows.

As noted in the adjoining table, horns have been a vital part of the instrumentation of American pop music since the beginning of the twentieth century. The particular horns that have been predominantly used since the beginning are the trumpet, the saxophone family (alto, tenor, and baritone), and the trombone. There are four bands in American popular music that have forever marked the use of horns (combination of trumpet, saxophone, and trombone—typically four or five in a section) as an essential part of their sound rather than as an occasional inclusion. These four main bands are: **Blood Sweat & Tears, Chicago, Tower of Power,** and **Earth Wind & Fire.**

Chicago

A group highly responsible for the popularity of horn usage in rock-n-roll is named after a city. They didn't care what time it was, they spent their "**Saturdays in the Park**," and all of that was "**Only the Beginning**" to "**Make You Smile.**" Formed in 1967, these young musicians, **Walter Parazaider**, **Terry Kath**, **Danny Seraphine**, **Lee Loughnane**, **James Pankow**, **Robert Lamm**, and **Peter Cetera**, decided to get together and fulfill a dream of integrating the musical diversity of the city they grew up in, Chicago.

Walter Parazaider, a musician practically from birth, was exposed to music because of his father being a full-time musician. Walter became a clarinetist at a young age and developed a diligence regarding his practice. By his early teens, he was so musically advanced he became the protégé of the E^b clarinetist of the Chicago Symphony. Even for a young musician who was becoming classically trained and who's father worked in the big band music industry, the rebellious edge of rock-n-roll easily influenced him. Parazaider picked up the saxophone and began learning rock-n-roll tunes, like "Tequila" and any of the Ventures music that used sax; he also learned some of the Bill Haley and the Comets' tunes.

Pursuant to his career as a musician, Parazaider entered Chicago's DePaul University. While at DePaul, he noticed a disturbing trend in the newly arriving rock music. Even when the saxophone was heavily used in the mid 1950s, its popularity died off and other horns were only sporadically used by anyone else. It wasn't until 1966, when the Beatles put out the *Revolver* album, that horns would make a revival. On that album was a tune called "Got to get you into my life" (later covered by Earth Wind & Fire) that used two trumpets and two tenor saxes. After hearing it, Parazaider, who was now working with Jimmy Guercio and who would later become Chicago's producer, had the

Timeline	Jazz Develops	Blues/Rock Development	Horn Usage
Mid 1800s	Military Bands—Primarily Brass Instruments	Church Choir—Call and Response (Blues Form)—Primarily Vocals	
Late 1800s	Dixieland Bands—3 Wind Instruments: Trumpet, Clarinet, and Trombone. Rhythm Section: Drum set, String Bass, Piano/Banjo	Rhythm Section involved in Church. Use of Guitar, Piano, Drums, and Bass. Twelve-bar blues form based off of Call and Response.	
1900–1915	Dixieland Bands getting larger, incorporating more wind instruments. Written arrangements begin to enter the hot music scene.	Solo or duet blues musicians (typically guitar and harmonica). "Hillbilly" music becoming more popular in the Appalachian Mountains.	Saxophone enters into the blues scene because of the mournful sound it can achieve.
1915–1940	Dixieland Bands develop into the Swing Band Era—developing big bands with the use of 5 trumpets, 5 trombones, 5 saxophones, and rhythm section. Written arrangements become essential.	Rhythm Sections begin to entertain on their own, playing the blues in late nightclubs. First country music recordings in Bristol TN/VA, 1927.	One trumpet and 1 saxophone enter as a standard part of the blues band, playing horn parts to compliment the rhythm section and vocalist.
1935–1955	Economics and Bebop cut down on the size of ensembles playing in the nightclubs.	Sam Phillips adds distortion to Blues Guitarist Jackie Brenston. Hank Williams turns out more country pop music than anyone up to this point. Elvis was discovered.	Bill Haley & The Comets use the saxophone as a major part of their ensemble.
1956–1975	Hard Bop standardizes the use of horns in the small group (back to Dixieland ensemble size with much different groove). Hard Bop focuses on the use of the 12- or 16-bar blues form.	The Beatles record legendary album *Sergeant Pepper's Lonely Hearts Club Band.* Recording incorporates many various uses of wind instruments and orchestral sounds.	Four Rock Groups incorporate horns as an essential part of their ensemble. Chicago, Blood Sweat & Tears, Earth Wind & Fire and Tower of Power.
1975–Current	"Jazz" covers many various forms and ensembles. Some incorporating horns and vocals. Some are strictly rhythm sections.	Rock, rap, R&B, and country musicians all incorporate horns into their music. Horn sections become studio and locally contracted and organized.	"Horn Groups" still exist today with the primary focus being to accentuate live/recorded music with combinations of horns. Some include: The L.A. Horns, Sea Wind Horns, Memphis Horns, Muscle Shoals Horns, Heavy Metal Horns, TOP Horns, Harris Bros. Horns, and The Tuscaloosa Horns

thought of a rock-n-roll horn band. Parazaider was currently in a band called Missing Links with other band members, Danny Saraphine and Lee Loughnane (another DePaul music student).

With Parazaider, Saraphine, Loughnane, and Terry Kath all a part of Parazaider's emerging horn band, there was only one other horn player they needed to recruit. A new sophomore at DePaul, James Pankow, trombone player, was approached by Parazaider and Loughnane to discuss the idea of the band. Parazaider told Pankow, "I've been checkin' you out, and I like the way you play. You've got what it takes." Pankow's response was, "I don't know what the hell I've got, but he obviously likes the way I play."

With Parazaider, Loughnane, and Pankow all in the group, bringing the horn section count up to three, the group still needed a keyboard player and a bass player to be a complete group. On an evening out, the guys ended up in a bar in South Side Chicago checking out a group named "Bobby Charles and the Wanderers," with Bobby Charles on keyboards. Bobby Charles' real name was Robert Lamm.

It was shortly after they heard him play that they knew they could fill a void in their band with his talent. Parazaider called Lamm and talked over the idea of a rock-n-roll band that used horns. There was hardly any hesitation when Lamm agreed to be a part of the group. Finally, all the pieces were in place, with Lamm agreeing to play the bass parts on keyboard pedals to fill up that voice, and they began rehearsing in Parazaider's basement. This early group covered soul groups like Wilson Picket and James Brown because those were the only groups making any kind of music with horns. After much discussion about the group's name, they decided to use the name "The Big Thing" because the word *thing* was popular at the time. In 1967, The Big Thing had their first string of gigs lined up, starting off at the GiGi a-Go-Go in Lyons, Illinois.

On this string of gigs in the Midwest, the final piece of the puzzle was put into place and Lamm would no longer have to play pedal bass. Playing at a club called Barnaby's in Chicago and opening for the band called The Exceptions, The Big Thing had one of its most important gigs. After opening the concert that evening, all the guys stayed to hear The Exceptions because they were supposed to be the best band in the circuit. One of The Exceptions came early to check out The Big Thing, as well. Peter Cetera was greatly impressed by the new sounds coming from The Big Thing and told them later, "I don't know what you're doing, but I like it." Within two weeks of that night, Cetera left The Exceptions and joined The Big Thing. Cetera fulfilled all that was needed in the band. He provided the foundation with his bass, and Lamm would no longer have to play the pedals. Cetera's voice also added a higher register that was necessary.

In March of 1968, Parazaider's long time friend Jimmy Guercio, who was now working with CBS records, heard the group at Barnaby's and was so impressed that he told them to pack their things. They were moving to Los Angeles under a new name, the ***Chicago Transit Authority***. Arriving in L.A., things were not as smooth as they thought they would be. Guercio called Parazaider and told him that he had to record Blood Sweat & Tears' second album. The group felt betrayed because of BS&T's use of horns, and they felt that they were not getting the break they needed or were promised. Because BS&T were already established, even if it were only by a few months, Guercio had to do what he was instructed to do by his company, but he recorded a Chicago Transit Authority (CTA) demo recording that became popular with industry insiders. **Clive Davis**, CBS president, was so impressed by the sounds he heard on the demo, he reversed the lower executive's decision, and CTA entered the studio with a recording contract.

When the album *Chicago Transit Authority* was released in 1969, it reached number seventeen on the billboard charts and stayed there for 148 weeks, becoming the longest running jazz-rock album in chart history. Also during that first year, the name was shortened from Chicago Transit Authority to Chicago, as named by underground college students whose catch phrase was, "If you're not listening to Chicago, you're just not listening."

With the release of numerous recordings over a thirty-year period, Chicago is still touring with an unprecedented percentage of original band members, including the three original horns. They are a pillar in the four-corner foundation of horn band's development. People have always wondered how the name "Chicago" came about. A sentence from the inside liner notes of the very first album can answer that question. "If you must call them something, speak of the city where all save one were born, where all of them were schooled and bread. Call them Chicago."

Blood Sweat & Tears

The second pillar of the four-corner foundation of horn bands entered the music scene only months before Chicago. *Al Kooper* and *Bobby Colomby* put a band together in 1967 to do some gigs to make enough money for Al to travel to England. They believed in the use of horns immediately. This group consisted of classically- and jazz-trained musicians. Bobby and Al took their ensemble and combined it with The Blues Project headed up by guitarist *Steve Katz*. The sound was a blend of rock, jazz, big bands, and the newly developing sound of funk and fusion emerging in the late 1960s. This new group was Blood Sweat & Tears.

With the addition of vocalist *David Clayton-Thomas*, the success of the group grew exponentially, and it was a musical force to be reckoned with. Throughout the career of BS&T, as they were affectionately referred to by their many fans, the band has sold over 35 million albums and received several Grammy Awards. They never let up with their musical creativity, continuing to incorporate different aspects of jazz, blues, Latin, classical, and soul music into their already vast repertoire.

Many phenomenal musicians have entered and unfortunately exited the band. Some of these players have gone on to become some of the most influential musicians of today. **Randy Brecker, Lew Soloff, Jerry Fisher, Dave Bargeron**, and many others have passed through the BS&T fraternity. On the album *Blood Sweat & Tears 3*, Lew Soloff blew the trumpet onto the modern pop music map with his individual sound and improvisational skills. When recording the tune "*Spinning Wheel*," not only did the group put together a merry-go-round effect, the middle was left open for instrumental improvised solos. Soloff's trumpet solo in the middle of "Spinning Wheel" is an improvisation masterpiece. Continuing in the same vein, Dave Bargeron put, of all instruments, a tuba solo on "Go Down Gambling" that has also become a masterpiece of popular music. Because of a horn section's flexibility, the impact that they produce can be astounding, but the roots of jazz's influence in rock-n-roll is evidenced in the horn players' improvisational skills. Some of the greatest musical moments put on tape in the rock-n-roll genre have been spontaneous moments.

Earth Wind & Fire

Li'l Kim was the presenter of Earth Wind & Fire for induction into the Rock-n-Roll Hall of Fame. It was said after her presentation, "if the 'Negro media' actually cared about the majestic past, present and future culture, this young lady might have known enough about Earth Wind and Fire to recognize the song that was being played for them at their induction." Unfortunately, she didn't. Earth Wind & Fire knew the importance of the education of America to the African-American culture, and with showmanship and musicianship, they set out to do exactly that, becoming educators of and for that culture.

"None of this was planned. The universe played a part in the whole thing, obviously. We just took our cues from the universe and kept moving on."—Maurice White

Influenced by such musicians as John Coltrane, Miles Davis, J.S. Bach, W.A. Mozart, and Sly and the Family Stone, **Maurice White** had an idea of creating a band that would spread the message of love, peace, and harmony that would transcend all races and touch international audiences, hopefully for many years to follow. The name of that group would be Earth Wind & Fire. The world was introduced to this new group, after the personnel finally settled and the album ***Last Days and Time*** was released in 1972. Maurice White, determined to educate the public on the heritage of African Americans, introduced the sound of the Kalimba, also known as a thumb piano, on this recording. The album was a great success and shortly after its release the band began touring. In 1973, the second recording from Earth Wind & Fire, ***Head to the Sky***, was released. Two chart toppers came off of this recording, *"Evil"* and *"Keep Your Head to the Sky."*

EWF finally released their platinum album, ***Open Our Eyes***. Maurice states, "This music was a clear reflection of the vision I had for the group. From the onset of this project, I committed to have a different musical projection on stage. In a period of social confusion in the 1970s, I wanted Earth Wind & Fire to reflect the growing search for greater self-understanding, greater freedom from restrictions we placed on ourselves in terms of individual potential."

The only female of the group, Jessica Cleaves, departed the band before *Open Our Eyes* was released. She was never replaced, and the band consisted of eight members—*Maurice White*, **Phillip Bailey**, **Verdine White**, **Larry Dunn**, **Ralph Johnson**, **Johnny Graham**, **Andrew Woolfolk**, and **Al McKay**. *Open Our Eyes* yielded two hits, *"Mighty Mighty"* and the slow groove of *"Devotion."* EWF followed that album with the ever-popular ***That's the Way of The World***, becoming a double platinum selling album much on the success of the number one single release, *"Shining Star."*

Fred White, brother of Verdine and Maurice, joined the group around the same time CBS was calling for another album. EWF responded to the call immediately and gladly. Maurice explained to CBS records that their tour schedule wouldn't permit them to do a studio CD and asked if they could record some of their live concerts. CBS agreed and shortly after released EWF's first live recording, entitled ***Gratitude***, which became their second double platinum album. Two double platinum recordings was something no other African American group had come close to during that time. Earth Wind & Fire didn't stop with those two double platinum albums, they went on to have many more, including *Spirit* and another *All n All*, which held the hits *"I'll Write a Song for You," "Be Ever Wonderful," "Jupiter,"* and *"Fantasy."*

The group now performed in much larger venues such as Madison Square Garden, with a spectacular stage show that included magic tricks by Doug Henning as well as outrageous costumes. The costumes and magic brought in huge audiences, literally whipped into a frenzy by seeing band members disappear into a pyramid and Freddie White's drumsticks rise up into the air while he was still playing.

Over the next ten years, EWF released many new recordings, but Maurice White by this time had personally endured enough. After making records for twelve straight years, he called a meeting and announced that he was "burning out," and he took a four-year hiatus from 1983–1987. However, Maurice stayed in the business as a producer, producing Philip Bailey along with Phil Collins. In 1987, EWF re-entered the studio and released *Touch the World,* which yielded the hit *"System of Survival."* Since that time, EWF has been going strong with many more recordings and live tours. In 1999, they released their second live recording, this time recorded on a tour of Japan. It, too, did extremely well. Finally, in 2003, Earth Wind & Fire, after thirty years of recording, put out yet another CD, *Promises,* which is a musical marvel and has much of the sound that you would expect from Earth Wind & Fire.

Tower of Power

Based in Oakland, California, Tower of Power is less well-known nationally than the other three groups, yet they may have had more influence on the music industry as a whole. Tower of Power is the very definition of a "horn band." Boasting the largest horn section with two trumpets (sometimes trombone) and three saxophones, this west coast funk band has a fan base made up of fellow musicians, a cult of performers all over the world who admire the precision that the horns create and the rhythm section establishes in all of their tunes.

The primary arranger for the band's horn charts is **Gregg Adams**, and it is he that gives the band its unique horn sound and thus its following. While the other players in the horn section are impressive in their improvisational abilities and in

their mastery of their specific instruments, with this band, the whole is stronger than its individual parts.

The horn section, along with Adam's writing abilities, became so powerful and so impressive to the music industry in the late 1970s and 1980s, it was common for the horn section to record separately with other artists, even tour live with those same bands. The **Tower of Power Horns** became more famous than the entire band, establishing a huge discography of recordings. The overall effect the horns had on the music industry was to share the power, strength, energy, and timbre of horn sections to over two decades of the record-buying public. They created a demand from that audience, establishing an opportunity for other sections to fill, providing that same service to many bands that do not regularly include horns as permanent band members in their organizations.

Epilogue

These four groups laid the foundation for "Horn Bands" to continue in the pop music world. There are countless groups in American and the pop music world that incorporate horns as a part of their live shows and recordings. The sound of live horns is an irreplaceable sound, no matter how good of an imitation you have with a sequencer or keyboard patch. There is no musical feel like strong, confident horns. Today's artists such as Santana, Ricky Martin, Matchbox 20, Aerosmith, The Rolling Stones, Phil Collins, The Temptations, The O'Jays, The Four Tops, Stevie Wonder—and the list could continue for another chapter—all use horns in their live performances and recordings. There are a few "horn sections" that have been around, supplying this growth of horn use for the last thirty years. Many of them are contracted studio session sections, or are included as "sidemen" to the main acts. The most prominent horn sections in the United States today have done many performances with popular groups, and if you've caught any of those live acts listed previously, there is a good possibility you've seen some of these horn sections. The *L.A. Horns, The Memphis Horns, The Heavy Metal Horns,* and *The Tuscaloosa Horns* have a rich heritage. All of these horn sections, from Chicago on to some down home Alabama boys from Tuscaloosa, have made careers out of being musicians that literally "add the icing to the cake." Without them, the music could still be played, but it would never be the same. The musicians that carry those horns have to be very skilled, possessing abundant stylistic knowledge and abilities to meet the demands of pop music while combating the tyranny of technology that functions as a mere pretender of perfection using sequencers and keyboards. This entire chapter is dedicated to those musicians who have dedicated their lives to perfecting the art of "sweetening the tracks" and stirring our souls.

Vocabulary

Al Kooper
Al McKay
All n All
Andrew Woolfolk
"Be Ever Wonderful"
Blood Sweat & Tears
Bobby Colomby
Chicago
Chicago Transit
　Authority
Clive Davis
Danny Seraphine
Dave Bargeron
David Clayton-Thomas
"Devotion"
Earth Wind & Fire
"Evil"
"Fantasy"
Fred White
"Go Down Gambling"
Gratitude
Gregg Adams

Head to the Sky
"I'll Write a Song for
　You"
James Pankow
Jerry Fisher
Johnny Graham
"Jupiter"
"Keep Your Head to the
　Sky"
Larry Dunn
Last Days and Time
Lee Loughnane
Lew Soloff
"Make You Smile"
Maurice White
"Mighty Mighty"
"Only the Beginning"
Open Our Eyes
Peter Cetera
Phillip Bailey
Promises
Ralph Johnson

Randy Brecker
Robert Lamm
"Saturdays in the Park"
"Shining Star"
"Spinning Wheel"
Spirit
Steve Katz
"System of Survival"
Terry Kath
*That's the Way of The
　World*
The Heavy Metal Horns
The L.A. Horns
The Memphis Horns
The Tuscaloosa Horns
Touch the World
Tower of Power
Tower of Power Horns
Verdine White
Walter Parazaider

Website

Please refer to the *Music Through Time* site listed in the front of your book to investigate and complete more classroom activities and assignments.

APPENDIX FORMS

Rhythm

    1. Identify the meter.   _____

    2. Identify the tempo of the meter.   _____

    3. Are there tempo changes within one piece?   _____

Texture

    4. How many melodic ideas are sounding at the same time?   _____

    5. Does the texture change periodically?   _____

    6. If so, where and how often?   _____

Melody

    7. Is the melody easy to identify?   _____

    8. Can I remember it if I hear it again?   _____

    9. How many differing melodic ideas are there?   _____

   10. Are any repeated, recurring more than once?   _____

Harmony

   11. Is the rhythm of the chords fast or slow?   _____

   12. Does this change throughout the piece?   _____

   13. Does the key change at all in the music?   _____

   14. If so, where and how often?   _____

   15. Why do you think a key change was used?   _____

   16. Was a mode change used, major to minor, etc?   _____

   17. When and where did it occur?   _____

Timbre

   18. What instrument is producing the sound(s)?   _____

   19. Is there more than one timbre employed?   _____

   20. Are the timbre choices effective?   _____

   21. What families of instruments are represented?   _____

   22. Acoustic, electronic, or a combination?   _____

Texts

   23. Are there words in this piece?   _____

   24. What language is used?   _____

   25. Is there more than one layer of text?   _____

   26. Can you comprehend what is being sung/said?   _____

   27. Are you supposed to comprehend it?   _____

Form

28. Can you identify the formal structure? _____

29. Can you name it? _____

30. If there are melodic repetitions normally occurring in this formal shape, can you identify the melodies as they reappear? _____

31. What is the name of the form? _____

32. What is the name of the corresponding genre? _____

Musicianship

33. Was the performance clear and effective? _____

34. Were the rhythmic elements clear and precise? _____

35. Were the notes performed in tune? _____

36. Were the performers energetic and enthusiastic? _____

37. Were the performers skillful? _____

Personal Response

38. How do you feel during the performance? _____

39. How do you feel after the performance? _____

40. In your opinion, what were the composer's intended reactions? _____

41. Did you experience what the composer and performers intended? _____

42. Why or why not? _____

43. Do you need to hear this piece again in order to comprehend it more fully? _____

44. Will you invest your time and energy into the experience of this music again? _____

45. Why or why not? _____

NAME _____   DATE _____

NAME OF PIECE _____

Rhythm

    1. Identify the meter.   _____

    2. Identify the tempo of the meter.   _____

    3. Are there tempo changes within one piece?   _____

Texture

    4. How many melodic ideas are sounding at the same time?   _____

    5. Does the texture change periodically?   _____

    6. If so, where and how often?   _____

Melody

    7. Is the melody easy to identify?   _____

    8. Can I remember it if I hear it again?   _____

    9. How many differing melodic ideas are there?   _____

  10. Are any repeated, recurring more than once?   _____

Harmony

  11. Is the rhythm of the chords fast or slow?   _____

  12. Does this change throughout the piece?   _____

  13. Does the key change at all in the music?   _____

  14. If so, where and how often?   _____

  15. Why do you think a key change was used?   _____

  16. Was a mode change used, major to minor, etc?   _____

  17. When and where did it occur?   _____

Timbre

  18. What instrument is producing the sound(s)?   _____

  19. Is there more than one timbre employed?   _____

  20. Are the timbre choices effective?   _____

  21. What families of instruments are represented?   _____

  22. Acoustic, electronic, or a combination?   _____

Texts

  23. Are there words in this piece?   _____

  24. What language is used?   _____

  25. Is there more than one layer of text?   _____

  26. Can you comprehend what is being sung/said?   _____

  27. Are you supposed to comprehend it?   _____

Form

28. Can you identify the formal structure? _____
29. Can you name it? _____
30. If there are melodic repetitions normally occurring in this formal shape, can you identify the melodies as they reappear? _____
31. What is the name of the form? _____
32. What is the name of the corresponding genre? _____

Musicianship

33. Was the performance clear and effective? _____
34. Were the rhythmic elements clear and precise? _____
35. Were the notes performed in tune? _____
36. Were the performers energetic and enthusiastic? _____
37. Were the performers skillful? _____

Personal Response

38. How do you feel during the performance? _____
39. How do you feel after the performance? _____
40. In your opinion, what were the composer's intended reactions? _____
41. Did you experience what the composer and performers intended? _____
42. Why or why not? _____
43. Do you need to hear this piece again in order to comprehend it more fully? _____
44. Will you invest your time and energy into the experience of this music again? _____
45. Why or why not? _____

NAME _____   DATE _____

NAME OF PIECE _____

Rhythm

   1. Identify the meter.   _____

   2. Identify the tempo of the meter.   _____

   3. Are there tempo changes within one piece?   _____

Texture

   4. How many melodic ideas are sounding at the same time?   _____

   5. Does the texture change periodically?   _____

   6. If so, where and how often?   _____

Melody

   7. Is the melody easy to identify?   _____

   8. Can I remember it if I hear it again?   _____

   9. How many differing melodic ideas are there?   _____

  10. Are any repeated, recurring more than once?   _____

Harmony

  11. Is the rhythm of the chords fast or slow?   _____

  12. Does this change throughout the piece?   _____

  13. Does the key change at all in the music?   _____

  14. If so, where and how often?   _____

  15. Why do you think a key change was used?   _____

  16. Was a mode change used, major to minor, etc?   _____

  17. When and where did it occur?   _____

Timbre

  18. What instrument is producing the sound(s)?   _____

  19. Is there more than one timbre employed?   _____

  20. Are the timbre choices effective?   _____

  21. What families of instruments are represented?   _____

  22. Acoustic, electronic, or a combination?   _____

Texts

  23. Are there words in this piece?   _____

  24. What language is used?   _____

  25. Is there more than one layer of text?   _____

  26. Can you comprehend what is being sung/said?   _____

  27. Are you supposed to comprehend it?   _____

Form

28. Can you identify the formal structure? _____

29. Can you name it? _____

30. If there are melodic repetitions normally occurring in this formal shape, can you identify the melodies as they reappear? _____

31. What is the name of the form? _____

32. What is the name of the corresponding genre? _____

Musicianship

33. Was the performance clear and effective? _____

34. Were the rhythmic elements clear and precise? _____

35. Were the notes performed in tune? _____

36. Were the performers energetic and enthusiastic? _____

37. Were the performers skillful? _____

Personal Response

38. How do you feel during the performance? _____

39. How do you feel after the performance? _____

40. In your opinion, what were the composer's intended reactions? _____

41. Did you experience what the composer and performers intended? _____

42. Why or why not? _____

43. Do you need to hear this piece again in order to comprehend it more fully? _____

44. Will you invest your time and energy into the experience of this music again? _____

45. Why or why not? _____

NAME OF PIECE _____

Rhythm

1. Identify the meter.   _____
2. Identify the tempo of the meter.   _____
3. Are there tempo changes within one piece?   _____

Texture

4. How many melodic ideas are sounding at the same time?   _____
5. Does the texture change periodically?   _____
6. If so, where and how often?   _____

Melody

7. Is the melody easy to identify?   _____
8. Can I remember it if I hear it again?   _____
9. How many differing melodic ideas are there?   _____
10. Are any repeated, recurring more than once?   _____

Harmony

11. Is the rhythm of the chords fast or slow?   _____
12. Does this change throughout the piece?   _____
13. Does the key change at all in the music?   _____
14. If so, where and how often?   _____
15. Why do you think a key change was used?   _____
16. Was a mode change used, major to minor, etc?   _____
17. When and where did it occur?   _____

Timbre

18. What instrument is producing the sound(s)?   _____
19. Is there more than one timbre employed?   _____
20. Are the timbre choices effective?   _____
21. What families of instruments are represented?   _____
22. Acoustic, electronic, or a combination?   _____

Texts

23. Are there words in this piece?   _____
24. What language is used?   _____
25. Is there more than one layer of text?   _____
26. Can you comprehend what is being sung/said?   _____
27. Are you supposed to comprehend it?   _____

Form

28. Can you identify the formal structure? _____

29. Can you name it? _____

30. If there are melodic repetitions normally occurring in this formal shape, can you identify the melodies as they reappear? _____

31. What is the name of the form? _____

32. What is the name of the corresponding genre? _____

Musicianship

33. Was the performance clear and effective? _____

34. Were the rhythmic elements clear and precise? _____

35. Were the notes performed in tune? _____

36. Were the performers energetic and enthusiastic? _____

37. Were the performers skillful? _____

Personal Response

38. How do you feel during the performance? _____

39. How do you feel after the performance? _____

40. In your opinion, what were the composer's intended reactions? _____

41. Did you experience what the composer and performers intended? _____

42. Why or why not? _____

43. Do you need to hear this piece again in order to comprehend it more fully? _____

44. Will you invest your time and energy into the experience of this music again? _____

45. Why or why not? _____

NAME OF PIECE _____

Rhythm

1. Identify the meter.   _____
2. Identify the tempo of the meter.   _____
3. Are there tempo changes within one piece?   _____

Texture

4. How many melodic ideas are sounding at the same time? _____
5. Does the texture change periodically?   _____
6. If so, where and how often?   _____

Melody

7. Is the melody easy to identify?   _____
8. Can I remember it if I hear it again?   _____
9. How many differing melodic ideas are there? _____
10. Are any repeated, recurring more than once? _____

Harmony

11. Is the rhythm of the chords fast or slow?   _____
12. Does this change throughout the piece?   _____
13. Does the key change at all in the music?   _____
14. If so, where and how often?   _____
15. Why do you think a key change was used? _____
16. Was a mode change used, major to minor, etc? _____
17. When and where did it occur?   _____

Timbre

18. What instrument is producing the sound(s)? _____
19. Is there more than one timbre employed?   _____
20. Are the timbre choices effective?   _____
21. What families of instruments are represented? _____
22. Acoustic, electronic, or a combination?   _____

Texts

23. Are there words in this piece?   _____
24. What language is used?   _____
25. Is there more than one layer of text?   _____
26. Can you comprehend what is being sung/said? _____
27. Are you supposed to comprehend it?   _____

Form

28. Can you identify the formal structure? _____
29. Can you name it? _____
30. If there are melodic repetitions normally occurring in this formal shape, can you identify the melodies as they reappear? _____
31. What is the name of the form? _____
32. What is the name of the corresponding genre? _____

Musicianship

33. Was the performance clear and effective? _____
34. Were the rhythmic elements clear and precise? _____
35. Were the notes performed in tune? _____
36. Were the performers energetic and enthusiastic? _____
37. Were the performers skillful? _____

Personal Response

38. How do you feel during the performance? _____
39. How do you feel after the performance? _____
40. In your opinion, what were the composer's intended reactions? _____
41. Did you experience what the composer and performers intended? _____
42. Why or why not? _____
43. Do you need to hear this piece again in order to comprehend it more fully? _____
44. Will you invest your time and energy into the experience of this music again? _____
45. Why or why not? _____

NAME _____   DATE _____

NAME OF PIECE _____

Rhythm

    1. Identify the meter.   _____

    2. Identify the tempo of the meter.   _____

    3. Are there tempo changes within one piece?   _____

Texture

    4. How many melodic ideas are sounding at the same time?   _____

    5. Does the texture change periodically?   _____

    6. If so, where and how often?   _____

Melody

    7. Is the melody easy to identify?   _____

    8. Can I remember it if I hear it again?   _____

    9. How many differing melodic ideas are there?   _____

   10. Are any repeated, recurring more than once?   _____

Harmony

   11. Is the rhythm of the chords fast or slow?   _____

   12. Does this change throughout the piece?   _____

   13. Does the key change at all in the music?   _____

   14. If so, where and how often?   _____

   15. Why do you think a key change was used?   _____

   16. Was a mode change used, major to minor, etc?   _____

   17. When and where did it occur?   _____

Timbre

   18. What instrument is producing the sound(s)?   _____

   19. Is there more than one timbre employed?   _____

   20. Are the timbre choices effective?   _____

   21. What families of instruments are represented?   _____

   22. Acoustic, electronic, or a combination?   _____

Texts

   23. Are there words in this piece?   _____

   24. What language is used?   _____

   25. Is there more than one layer of text?   _____

   26. Can you comprehend what is being sung/said?   _____

   27. Are you supposed to comprehend it?   _____

Form

28. Can you identify the formal structure? _____

29. Can you name it? _____

30. If there are melodic repetitions normally occurring in this formal shape, can you identify the melodies as they reappear? _____

31. What is the name of the form? _____

32. What is the name of the corresponding genre? _____

Musicianship

33. Was the performance clear and effective? _____

34. Were the rhythmic elements clear and precise? _____

35. Were the notes performed in tune? _____

36. Were the performers energetic and enthusiastic? _____

37. Were the performers skillful? _____

Personal Response

38. How do you feel during the performance? _____

39. How do you feel after the performance? _____

40. In your opinion, what were the composer's intended reactions? _____

41. Did you experience what the composer and performers intended? _____

42. Why or why not? _____

43. Do you need to hear this piece again in order to comprehend it more fully? _____

44. Will you invest your time and energy into the experience of this music again? _____

45. Why or why not? _____

NAME _____   DATE _____

NAME OF PIECE _____

Rhythm

   1. Identify the meter.   _____

   2. Identify the tempo of the meter.   _____

   3. Are there tempo changes within one piece?   _____

Texture

   4. How many melodic ideas are sounding at the same time? _____

   5. Does the texture change periodically?   _____

   6. If so, where and how often?   _____

Melody

   7. Is the melody easy to identify?   _____

   8. Can I remember it if I hear it again?   _____

   9. How many differing melodic ideas are there?   _____

  10. Are any repeated, recurring more than once?   _____

Harmony

  11. Is the rhythm of the chords fast or slow?   _____

  12. Does this change throughout the piece?   _____

  13. Does the key change at all in the music?   _____

  14. If so, where and how often?   _____

  15. Why do you think a key change was used?   _____

  16. Was a mode change used, major to minor, etc?   _____

  17. When and where did it occur?   _____

Timbre

  18. What instrument is producing the sound(s)?   _____

  19. Is there more than one timbre employed?   _____

  20. Are the timbre choices effective?   _____

  21. What families of instruments are represented?   _____

  22. Acoustic, electronic, or a combination?   _____

Texts

  23. Are there words in this piece?   _____

  24. What language is used?   _____

  25. Is there more than one layer of text?   _____

  26. Can you comprehend what is being sung/said?   _____

  27. Are you supposed to comprehend it?   _____

Form

28. Can you identify the formal structure?   _____
29. Can you name it?   _____
30. If there are melodic repetitions normally occurring in this formal shape, can you identify the melodies as they reappear?   _____
31. What is the name of the form?   _____
32. What is the name of the corresponding genre?   _____

Musicianship

33. Was the performance clear and effective?   _____
34. Were the rhythmic elements clear and precise?   _____
35. Were the notes performed in tune?   _____
36. Were the performers energetic and enthusiastic?   _____
37. Were the performers skillful?   _____

Personal Response

38. How do you feel during the performance?   _____
39. How do you feel after the performance?   _____
40. In your opinion, what were the composer's intended reactions?   _____
41. Did you experience what the composer and performers intended?   _____
42. Why or why not?   _____
43. Do you need to hear this piece again in order to comprehend it more fully?   _____
44. Will you invest your time and energy into the experience of this music again?   _____
45. Why or why not?   _____

NAME _____   DATE _____

NAME OF PIECE _____

Rhythm

    1. Identify the meter.   _____

    2. Identify the tempo of the meter.   _____

    3. Are there tempo changes within one piece?   _____

Texture

    4. How many melodic ideas are sounding at the same time?   _____

    5. Does the texture change periodically?   _____

    6. If so, where and how often?   _____

Melody

    7. Is the melody easy to identify?   _____

    8. Can I remember it if I hear it again?   _____

    9. How many differing melodic ideas are there?   _____

    10. Are any repeated, recurring more than once?   _____

Harmony

    11. Is the rhythm of the chords fast or slow?   _____

    12. Does this change throughout the piece?   _____

    13. Does the key change at all in the music?   _____

    14. If so, where and how often?   _____

    15. Why do you think a key change was used?   _____

    16. Was a mode change used, major to minor, etc?   _____

    17. When and where did it occur?   _____

Timbre

    18. What instrument is producing the sound(s)?   _____

    19. Is there more than one timbre employed?   _____

    20. Are the timbre choices effective?   _____

    21. What families of instruments are represented?   _____

    22. Acoustic, electronic, or a combination?   _____

Texts

    23. Are there words in this piece?   _____

    24. What language is used?   _____

    25. Is there more than one layer of text?   _____

    26. Can you comprehend what is being sung/said?   _____

    27. Are you supposed to comprehend it?   _____

Form

28. Can you identify the formal structure? _____
29. Can you name it? _____
30. If there are melodic repetitions normally occurring in this formal shape, can you identify the melodies as they reappear? _____
31. What is the name of the form? _____
32. What is the name of the corresponding genre? _____

Musicianship

33. Was the performance clear and effective? _____
34. Were the rhythmic elements clear and precise? _____
35. Were the notes performed in tune? _____
36. Were the performers energetic and enthusiastic? _____
37. Were the performers skillful? _____

Personal Response

38. How do you feel during the performance? _____
39. How do you feel after the performance? _____
40. In your opinion, what were the composer's intended reactions? _____
41. Did you experience what the composer and performers intended? _____
42. Why or why not? _____
43. Do you need to hear this piece again in order to comprehend it more fully? _____
44. Will you invest your time and energy into the experience of this music again? _____
45. Why or why not? _____

Rhythm

   1. Identify the meter. _____

   2. Identify the tempo of the meter. _____

   3. Are there tempo changes within one piece? _____

Texture

   4. How many melodic ideas are sounding at the same time? _____

   5. Does the texture change periodically? _____

   6. If so, where and how often? _____

Melody

   7. Is the melody easy to identify? _____

   8. Can I remember it if I hear it again? _____

   9. How many differing melodic ideas are there? _____

   10. Are any repeated, recurring more than once? _____

Harmony

   11. Is the rhythm of the chords fast or slow? _____

   12. Does this change throughout the piece? _____

   13. Does the key change at all in the music? _____

   14. If so, where and how often? _____

   15. Why do you think a key change was used? _____

   16. Was a mode change used, major to minor, etc? _____

   17. When and where did it occur? _____

Timbre

   18. What instrument is producing the sound(s)? _____

   19. Is there more than one timbre employed? _____

   20. Are the timbre choices effective? _____

   21. What families of instruments are represented? _____

   22. Acoustic, electronic, or a combination? _____

Texts

   23. Are there words in this piece? _____

   24. What language is used? _____

   25. Is there more than one layer of text? _____

   26. Can you comprehend what is being sung/said? _____

   27. Are you supposed to comprehend it? _____

Form

28. Can you identify the formal structure? _____
29. Can you name it? _____
30. If there are melodic repetitions normally occurring in this formal shape, can you identify the melodies as they reappear? _____
31. What is the name of the form? _____
32. What is the name of the corresponding genre? _____

Musicianship

33. Was the performance clear and effective? _____
34. Were the rhythmic elements clear and precise? _____
35. Were the notes performed in tune? _____
36. Were the performers energetic and enthusiastic? _____
37. Were the performers skillful? _____

Personal Response

38. How do you feel during the performance? _____
39. How do you feel after the performance? _____
40. In your opinion, what were the composer's intended reactions? _____
41. Did you experience what the composer and performers intended? _____
42. Why or why not? _____
43. Do you need to hear this piece again in order to comprehend it more fully? _____
44. Will you invest your time and energy into the experience of this music again? _____
45. Why or why not? _____

Rhythm

   1. Identify the meter.   _____

   2. Identify the tempo of the meter.   _____

   3. Are there tempo changes within one piece?   _____

Texture

   4. How many melodic ideas are sounding at the same time?   _____

   5. Does the texture change periodically?   _____

   6. If so, where and how often?   _____

Melody

   7. Is the melody easy to identify?   _____

   8. Can I remember it if I hear it again?   _____

   9. How many differing melodic ideas are there?   _____

  10. Are any repeated, recurring more than once?   _____

Harmony

  11. Is the rhythm of the chords fast or slow?   _____

  12. Does this change throughout the piece?   _____

  13. Does the key change at all in the music?   _____

  14. If so, where and how often?   _____

  15. Why do you think a key change was used?   _____

  16. Was a mode change used, major to minor, etc?   _____

  17. When and where did it occur?   _____

Timbre

  18. What instrument is producing the sound(s)?   _____

  19. Is there more than one timbre employed?   _____

  20. Are the timbre choices effective?   _____

  21. What families of instruments are represented?   _____

  22. Acoustic, electronic, or a combination?   _____

Texts

  23. Are there words in this piece?   _____

  24. What language is used?   _____

  25. Is there more than one layer of text?   _____

  26. Can you comprehend what is being sung/said?   _____

  27. Are you supposed to comprehend it?   _____

Form

28. Can you identify the formal structure? _____
29. Can you name it? _____
30. If there are melodic repetitions normally occurring in this formal shape, can you identify the melodies as they reappear? _____
31. What is the name of the form? _____
32. What is the name of the corresponding genre? _____

Musicianship

33. Was the performance clear and effective? _____
34. Were the rhythmic elements clear and precise? _____
35. Were the notes performed in tune? _____
36. Were the performers energetic and enthusiastic? _____
37. Were the performers skillful? _____

Personal Response

38. How do you feel during the performance? _____
39. How do you feel after the performance? _____
40. In your opinion, what were the composer's intended reactions? _____
41. Did you experience what the composer and performers intended? _____
42. Why or why not? _____
43. Do you need to hear this piece again in order to comprehend it more fully? _____
44. Will you invest your time and energy into the experience of this music again? _____
45. Why or why not? _____

Rhythm

   1. Identify the meter.   _____

   2. Identify the tempo of the meter.   _____

   3. Are there tempo changes within one piece?   _____

Texture

   4. How many melodic ideas are sounding at the same time?   _____

   5. Does the texture change periodically?   _____

   6. If so, where and how often?   _____

Melody

   7. Is the melody easy to identify?   _____

   8. Can I remember it if I hear it again?   _____

   9. How many differing melodic ideas are there?   _____

  10. Are any repeated, recurring more than once?   _____

Harmony

  11. Is the rhythm of the chords fast or slow?   _____

  12. Does this change throughout the piece?   _____

  13. Does the key change at all in the music?   _____

  14. If so, where and how often?   _____

  15. Why do you think a key change was used?   _____

  16. Was a mode change used, major to minor, etc?   _____

  17. When and where did it occur?   _____

Timbre

  18. What instrument is producing the sound(s)?   _____

  19. Is there more than one timbre employed?   _____

  20. Are the timbre choices effective?   _____

  21. What families of instruments are represented?   _____

  22. Acoustic, electronic, or a combination?   _____

Texts

  23. Are there words in this piece?   _____

  24. What language is used?   _____

  25. Is there more than one layer of text?   _____

  26. Can you comprehend what is being sung/said?   _____

  27. Are you supposed to comprehend it?   _____

Form

28. Can you identify the formal structure? _____
29. Can you name it? _____
30. If there are melodic repetitions normally occurring in this formal shape, can you identify the melodies as they reappear? _____
31. What is the name of the form? _____
32. What is the name of the corresponding genre? _____

Musicianship

33. Was the performance clear and effective? _____
34. Were the rhythmic elements clear and precise? _____
35. Were the notes performed in tune? _____
36. Were the performers energetic and enthusiastic? _____
37. Were the performers skillful? _____

Personal Response

38. How do you feel during the performance? _____
39. How do you feel after the performance? _____
40. In your opinion, what were the composer's intended reactions? _____
41. Did you experience what the composer and performers intended? _____
42. Why or why not? _____
43. Do you need to hear this piece again in order to comprehend it more fully? _____
44. Will you invest your time and energy into the experience of this music again? _____
45. Why or why not? _____

NAME _____ DATE _____

NAME OF PIECE _____

Rhythm

    1. Identify the meter. _____

    2. Identify the tempo of the meter. _____

    3. Are there tempo changes within one piece? _____

Texture

    4. How many melodic ideas are sounding at the same time? _____

    5. Does the texture change periodically? _____

    6. If so, where and how often? _____

Melody

    7. Is the melody easy to identify? _____

    8. Can I remember it if I hear it again? _____

    9. How many differing melodic ideas are there? _____

    10. Are any repeated, recurring more than once? _____

Harmony

    11. Is the rhythm of the chords fast or slow? _____

    12. Does this change throughout the piece? _____

    13. Does the key change at all in the music? _____

    14. If so, where and how often? _____

    15. Why do you think a key change was used? _____

    16. Was a mode change used, major to minor, etc? _____

    17. When and where did it occur? _____

Timbre

    18. What instrument is producing the sound(s)? _____

    19. Is there more than one timbre employed? _____

    20. Are the timbre choices effective? _____

    21. What families of instruments are represented? _____

    22. Acoustic, electronic, or a combination? _____

Texts

    23. Are there words in this piece? _____

    24. What language is used? _____

    25. Is there more than one layer of text? _____

    26. Can you comprehend what is being sung/said? _____

    27. Are you supposed to comprehend it? _____

Form

28. Can you identify the formal structure? _____
29. Can you name it? _____
30. If there are melodic repetitions normally occurring in this formal shape, can you identify the melodies as they reappear? _____
31. What is the name of the form? _____
32. What is the name of the corresponding genre? _____

Musicianship

33. Was the performance clear and effective? _____
34. Were the rhythmic elements clear and precise? _____
35. Were the notes performed in tune? _____
36. Were the performers energetic and enthusiastic? _____
37. Were the performers skillful? _____

Personal Response

38. How do you feel during the performance? _____
39. How do you feel after the performance? _____
40. In your opinion, what were the composer's intended reactions? _____
41. Did you experience what the composer and performers intended? _____
42. Why or why not? _____
43. Do you need to hear this piece again in order to comprehend it more fully? _____
44. Will you invest your time and energy into the experience of this music again? _____
45. Why or why not? _____

NAME _____   DATE _____

NAME OF PIECE _____

Rhythm

    1. Identify the meter.   _____

    2. Identify the tempo of the meter.   _____

    3. Are there tempo changes within one piece?   _____

Texture

    4. How many melodic ideas are sounding at the same time?   _____

    5. Does the texture change periodically?   _____

    6. If so, where and how often?   _____

Melody

    7. Is the melody easy to identify?   _____

    8. Can I remember it if I hear it again?   _____

    9. How many differing melodic ideas are there?   _____

  10. Are any repeated, recurring more than once?   _____

Harmony

  11. Is the rhythm of the chords fast or slow?   _____

  12. Does this change throughout the piece?   _____

  13. Does the key change at all in the music?   _____

  14. If so, where and how often?   _____

  15. Why do you think a key change was used?   _____

  16. Was a mode change used, major to minor, etc?   _____

  17. When and where did it occur?   _____

Timbre

  18. What instrument is producing the sound(s)?   _____

  19. Is there more than one timbre employed?   _____

  20. Are the timbre choices effective?   _____

  21. What families of instruments are represented?   _____

  22. Acoustic, electronic, or a combination?   _____

Texts

  23. Are there words in this piece?   _____

  24. What language is used?   _____

  25. Is there more than one layer of text?   _____

  26. Can you comprehend what is being sung/said?   _____

  27. Are you supposed to comprehend it?   _____

Form

28. Can you identify the formal structure? _____

29. Can you name it? _____

30. If there are melodic repetitions normally occurring in this formal shape, can you identify the melodies as they reappear? _____

31. What is the name of the form? _____

32. What is the name of the corresponding genre? _____

Musicianship

33. Was the performance clear and effective? _____

34. Were the rhythmic elements clear and precise? _____

35. Were the notes performed in tune? _____

36. Were the performers energetic and enthusiastic? _____

37. Were the performers skillful? _____

Personal Response

38. How do you feel during the performance? _____

39. How do you feel after the performance? _____

40. In your opinion, what were the composer's intended reactions? _____

41. Did you experience what the composer and performers intended? _____

42. Why or why not? _____

43. Do you need to hear this piece again in order to comprehend it more fully? _____

44. Will you invest your time and energy into the experience of this music again? _____

45. Why or why not? _____

Rhythm

    1. Identify the meter.   _____

    2. Identify the tempo of the meter.   _____

    3. Are there tempo changes within one piece?   _____

Texture

    4. How many melodic ideas are sounding at the same time?   _____

    5. Does the texture change periodically?   _____

    6. If so, where and how often?   _____

Melody

    7. Is the melody easy to identify?   _____

    8. Can I remember it if I hear it again?   _____

    9. How many differing melodic ideas are there?   _____

  10. Are any repeated, recurring more than once?   _____

Harmony

  11. Is the rhythm of the chords fast or slow?   _____

  12. Does this change throughout the piece?   _____

  13. Does the key change at all in the music?   _____

  14. If so, where and how often?   _____

  15. Why do you think a key change was used?   _____

  16. Was a mode change used, major to minor, etc?   _____

  17. When and where did it occur?   _____

Timbre

  18. What instrument is producing the sound(s)?   _____

  19. Is there more than one timbre employed?   _____

  20. Are the timbre choices effective?   _____

  21. What families of instruments are represented?   _____

  22. Acoustic, electronic, or a combination?   _____

Texts

  23. Are there words in this piece?   _____

  24. What language is used?   _____

  25. Is there more than one layer of text?   _____

  26. Can you comprehend what is being sung/said?   _____

  27. Are you supposed to comprehend it?   _____

Form

28. Can you identify the formal structure? _____

29. Can you name it? _____

30. If there are melodic repetitions normally occurring in this formal shape, can you identify the melodies as they reappear? _____

31. What is the name of the form? _____

32. What is the name of the corresponding genre? _____

Musicianship

33. Was the performance clear and effective? _____

34. Were the rhythmic elements clear and precise? _____

35. Were the notes performed in tune? _____

36. Were the performers energetic and enthusiastic? _____

37. Were the performers skillful? _____

Personal Response

38. How do you feel during the performance? _____

39. How do you feel after the performance? _____

40. In your opinion, what were the composer's intended reactions? _____

41. Did you experience what the composer and performers intended? _____

42. Why or why not? _____

43. Do you need to hear this piece again in order to comprehend it more fully? _____

44. Will you invest your time and energy into the experience of this music again? _____

45. Why or why not? _____

Rhythm

   1. Identify the meter.   _____

   2. Identify the tempo of the meter.   _____

   3. Are there tempo changes within one piece? _____

Texture

   4. How many melodic ideas are sounding at the same time? _____

   5. Does the texture change periodically? _____

   6. If so, where and how often? _____

Melody

   7. Is the melody easy to identify? _____

   8. Can I remember it if I hear it again? _____

   9. How many differing melodic ideas are there? _____

  10. Are any repeated, recurring more than once? _____

Harmony

  11. Is the rhythm of the chords fast or slow? _____

  12. Does this change throughout the piece? _____

  13. Does the key change at all in the music? _____

  14. If so, where and how often? _____

  15. Why do you think a key change was used? _____

  16. Was a mode change used, major to minor, etc? _____

  17. When and where did it occur? _____

Timbre

  18. What instrument is producing the sound(s)? _____

  19. Is there more than one timbre employed? _____

  20. Are the timbre choices effective? _____

  21. What families of instruments are represented? _____

  22. Acoustic, electronic, or a combination? _____

Texts

  23. Are there words in this piece? _____

  24. What language is used? _____

  25. Is there more than one layer of text? _____

  26. Can you comprehend what is being sung/said? _____

  27. Are you supposed to comprehend it? _____

Form

28. Can you identify the formal structure? _____

29. Can you name it? _____

30. If there are melodic repetitions normally occurring in this formal shape, can you identify the melodies as they reappear? _____

31. What is the name of the form? _____

32. What is the name of the corresponding genre? _____

Musicianship

33. Was the performance clear and effective? _____

34. Were the rhythmic elements clear and precise? _____

35. Were the notes performed in tune? _____

36. Were the performers energetic and enthusiastic? _____

37. Were the performers skillful? _____

Personal Response

38. How do you feel during the performance? _____

39. How do you feel after the performance? _____

40. In your opinion, what were the composer's intended reactions? _____

41. Did you experience what the composer and performers intended? _____

42. Why or why not? _____

43. Do you need to hear this piece again in order to comprehend it more fully? _____

44. Will you invest your time and energy into the experience of this music again? _____

45. Why or why not? _____

GLOSSARY

21 Club—One of seven segregated jazz clubs on 52nd Street, New York City, in 1935.

3-D Record Mart—House of Jazz—Berry Gordy Jr.'s first business was opened in 1953 after his return to the US from a tour of Korea with the Army. His love of jazz prompted him to open the record store.

52nd Street—The "Jazz Club" district in New York City housing many bands and famous band leaders.

A Cappella (in the manner of a chapel)—Vocal music performed without instrumental accompaniment, as opposed to Cathedral performances which doubled the voice parts with instruments.

A Day in the Life—Hailed as the best British song of all time and recorded in 1967 on the classic Beatles album "Sergeant Pepper's Lonely Hearts Club Band," this song topped surveys of music experts by Q magazine.

A Lincoln Portrait—An important work for orchestra by Aaron Copland.

A Tale of Two Cities—A novel by Charles Dickens.

Aaron Copland—The first American-born composer of international importance in the twentieth century.

Abbess Hildegard von Bingen—(1098–1179) a poet, musician, composer, and religious writer known for her melismatic chants.

Academic Festival—An important Romantic period instrumental piece composed by Johannes Brahms.

Accent—A stress placed on the first beat of the grouping within a measure, singling it out and making it more recognizable.

Accompanied Recitative—A type of Baroque opera recitative which includes more elaborate orchestral accompaniment, establishing a more specific rhythm than that found with the secco recitative.

Acuff-Rose Publishing—Formed by country music performer Roy Acuff and Fred Rose, it was a major Nashville music-industry icon, having a respected track-record as a country music song publishing company. Acuff-Rose headquarters was on 8th Avenue South in the Melrose district of Nashville and was a landmark to those knowledgeable of the music industry. It was at those headquarters that Hank Williams Sr. proved to Rose his ability, writing the hit song,

"I Can't Help It If I'm Still in Love with You." Rose immediately befriended Williams, as he did with many other successful country music stars.

Adam Smith—He is considered to be the father of modern economics and author of the text The Wealth of Nations, which introduced the concept of the capitalist free enterprise system.

Advent—Forty days of preparation before Christmas.

Aesthetic—The knowledge and recognition of beauty in life, in nature and in reality.

Agnus Dei—"Lamb of God," one of the five texts of the Mass Ordinary.

Aida—An important Romantic period opera composed by Giuseppi Verdi.

Air—A metered dance rhythm and form found in dance suites of the Baroque period.

Al Kooper—Co-founder of Blood Sweat & Tears along with Bobby Colomby, who decided to put the band together in 1967 to do some gigs. Immediately both agreed on the use of horns.

Al McKay—One of eight original members and guitarist for Earth Wind & Fire.

Alban Berg—An Expressionistic composer and member of the "Second Viennese School" of composition.

Albert A. Michelson—An American physicist who experimentally established the speed of light as a fundamental constant and the first American to win the Nobel Prize for science.

Albert Einstein—An important 20th century scientist.

Alessandro Volta—A scientist who developed the forerunner to the electric battery that produced a steady stream of electricity.

Alexander Fleming—An important 20th century scientist.

Alexander Graham Bell—A Professor of Vocal Physiology, he invented the telephone and founded the Bell Telephone Company and established the Volta Laboratory.

Alfred B. Nobel—A Swedish chemist and industrialist who invented dynamite and founded the Nobel prizes.

Allegro Barbaro—A popular piano piece composed by Bela Bartok.

Allemande—A metered dance rhythm and form found in dance suites of the Baroque period.

Alvin P. Carter—A founding member of the Carter Family group, the only male member and husband to Sara Carter. In 1927 the group was signed to a recording contract by Ralph Peer and Victor recording.

Andrea Gabrielli—The Uncle, teacher, and predecessor of Giovanni Gabrielli.

Andre-Marie Ampere—A French physicist and mathematician who founded the science of electrodynamics. The ampere, a unit used to measure the rate of flow of an electric current, is named for him.

Andrew Woolfolk—One of eight original members and saxophonist for Earth Wind & Fire.

Anna Records—Berry Gordy co-wrote and produced "Money" recorded by Barrett Strong. Gordy, who was not yet equipped to release a nationwide hit record let his sister's company Anna Records (owned by Anna Gordy) release the record. "Money" eventually reached the number two spot on the R&B Charts.

Anton Webern—An Expressionistic composer and member of the "Second Viennese School" of composition.

Antonio Vivaldi—(1678–1741) A celebrated violinist and prolific composer of concerto grossi during the Baroque period. Nicknamed the "Red Priest" because of his red hair, he spent the majority of his life as teacher of violin at the Pio Ospedale della Pieta, one of four orphanages for girls in Venice.

Appalachian Spring—An important ballet by Aaron Copland.

Arcangelo Corelli—(1653–1713) A virtuoso violinist in the Baroque period and composer of early instrumental works which aided in the development of the trio sonata and early solo sonatas. He held court positions and as a composer influenced J.S. Bach's style and that of Handel.

Architecture—The discipline of design as applied to constructing living spaces or buildings.

Aria—In opera, a piece for solo voice and orchestra accompaniment that reflects on the actions within a dramatic scene that requires an emotional comment. The opportunity within an opera for the beautiful reflective song.

Arnold Schoenberg—Expressionist composer and leader of the "Second Viennese School" of composition.

Ars Antiqua—"Antique Art", referring to art and music from the 13th century.

Ars Nova—"New Art", referring to art and music from the late Gothic Period, 14th–15th centuries.

Art—The manipulation of component parts of nature through useful technique to create an artifact or action.

Art of Fugue, The—A treatise written by J.S. Bach exploring every conceivable way that a fugue could be composed.

Art of Fugue, The—Bach's definitive work in the art of fugal counterpoint which is based on notes in a theme which spell out his last name, personalizing it forever. Written in Bach's last years while slowly going blind, The Art of Fugue trails off unfinished in the climactic four-part fugue.

Art Tatum—Born Arthur Tatum, Jr. on October 13, 1909 in Toledo, Ohio, he lost most of his sight by the age of four. Considered one of the greatest improvisers in jazz history, Art Tatum also set the standard for technical dexterity. He led "Spirits of Rhythm" as his main act at the Onyx club on 52nd street.

Art-Rock—A term coined to describe the Beatles recording Sergeant Pepper's Lonely Hearts Club Band. This recording impacted history because of its creative use of compositional techniques involving instruments, multi-time signatures, and song cycle concepts, yet all firmly embedded in the language of rock-n-roll.

Ascension Day—Forty days following Easter, celebrated the sixth Sunday after Easter and marks the day of Christ's ascension into heaven.

Ash Wednesday—Church holy day that begins the season of Lent.

Auguste Rodin—A famous sculptor and creator of "Gates of Hell," inspired by Dante's Inferno.

Authentic cadence—The final punctuation, or period, in a musical phrase which brings closure to the melody, usually occurring at the end of the second melody of a two-phrase period.

B.B. King—"King of the Blues," B.B. King was born Riley B. King in 1925 in Indianola, Mississippi. He has had one of the most enduring music careers in existence. He is respected as a blues diplomat and deserves most of the credit for the blues genre entering the mainstream.

Back Water Blues—A popular blues record composed and performed by Bessie Smith.

Ballet—Artistic dance with its own set of disciplined body motions and visually stunning steps, ballet music is composed to accompany this type of dance and serves primarily as background to the dancers on the stage.

Banjo—An instrument belonging to the plucked string category of instruments.

Banjo, The—One of Louis Moreau Gottschalk's most popular piano compositions.

Barcarolle—An important Romantic period piano piece composed by Frederic Chopin.

Baritone—One of the standard range categorizations of the human voice, the fifth highest vocal range. Also, a brass instrument, variance of the Euphonium.

Barons of Rhythm—A group of musicians put together by William Basie which eventually became the "Count Basie Orchestra" and went onto become one of the greatest big bands of the swing era.

Barrett Strong—Recorded "Money" which was produced by Berry Gordy and nationally released on Anna Records. The tune eventually reached number two on the R&B charts.

Bass—One of the standard range categorizations of the human voice, the lowest vocal range. Also, a string instrument, the lowest pitch range of the string family.

Bass clef—One of the most common clef indications, indicating notation spaces for pitches sounding in the lower register of human hearing, those below "Middle C."

Bassoon—The bass instrument (or the fourth highest pitch range) of the woodwind family of instruments belonging to the double reed group.

Beale Street Blues Boy—Moniker given to Riley B. King as a disc jockey in Memphis. This was eventually shortened to B.B. King.

Beat—In music, a consistently ordered event, where events follow one another, possessing a consistent amount of time between each event.

Beatles, The—British-invasion rock-n-roll group from Liverpool, England held in very high regard for both their artistic achievements and their huge commercial success, and have amassed an enormous worldwide fan base that continues to exist to this day. Comprising John Lennon, Paul McCartney, George Harrison and Ringo Starr, the group shattered many sales records and charted more than fifty top 40 hit singles. They were the first British pop act to achieve major ongoing success in the United States, scoring twenty #1 hits in the USA alone, becoming the biggest musical act of the twentieth century. EMI estimated in 1985 that the band had sold over a billion records worldwide.

Beatrice et Benedict—An important Romantic period opera composed by Hector Berlioz.

Bela Bartok—A Hungarian composer and pianist who drew inspiration from Hungarian folk music to form his new musical works.

Benjamin Franklin—An important Enlightenment thinker and American Statesman and the only man to sign the Declaration of Independence, the Peace treaty of Paris in 1783, and the Constitution of the United States of America.

Bennie Moten's Kansas City Orchestra—One of the most successful big bands of the Midwest. Moten's orchestra toured all over the country and had a top selling recording for Victor records in 1927, entitled "South."

Benny Benjamin—Original drummer for "The Funk Brothers," the house rhythm section for all Motown Records.

Benny Carter—Saxophonist, trumpeter, composer, arranger, and band leader, Carter was a major figure in jazz from the 1930s to the 1990s. Often recognized by other jazz musicians as "King," he was among a small group to leave New York City and move toward Los Angeles to create his new "West Coast" big band.

Benny Goodman—A young man who would accept nothing from his band except perfection provided the drive needed to divert America's attention to the new style of swing music. Benny Goodman was a clarinetist and bandleader who demanded countless hours of rehearsal to obtain the perfection he was seeking and who first brought the sound of swing to a white teenage audience.

Berceuse—An important Romantic period piano piece composed by Frederic Chopin.

Berry Gordy Enterprises—One of many owned complimentary businesses of Berry Gordy. Others attached to his name were: Motown Records Corporation, Hitsville USA, Jobete Music Publishing and International Talent Management, Inc.

Berry Gordy Jr.—The most influential African-American man in the music scene of the early '60's. His business knowledge afforded him the opportunity to promote the African-American culture in a way that had never been done before. Gordy's idea was to have a complete staff of producers, songwriters, artists, handlers, manufacturers, and business people, all working toward a focused goal.

Bessie Smith—A performer and composer from the Chattanooga, Tennessee area, she influenced generations of vocalists, including Billie Holiday and Janice Joplin. Her life was lived with confidence and self-assurance. Her rich and expressive vocals often leaned on these two traits.

Bessie's Blues—A popular blues record composed and performed by Bessie Smith.

Bill Black—A member of the rhythm section that backed Elvis Presley and one third of the trio that was responsible for coining the sound and term "Rock-a-Billy." The sound was conceived by Sam Phillips and recorded into history at Sun Records Studio.

Billie Holiday—Also called "Lady Day" and generally considered one of the greatest jazz voices of all time (alongside Sarah Vaughan and Ella Fitzgerald), she settled in Harlem. Holiday began singing informally in numerous clubs. In 1939, at Café Society in Greenwich Village, Holiday performed the land mark "Strange Fruit," Abel Meeropol's politically strong poem and song about the brutality of racism in the south.

Billy the Kid—An important ballet by Aaron Copland.

Binary—A form or shape of music with a two part melodic sectional design, A–B.

Black, Brown, & Beige—A famed artistic achievement by "Duke" Ellington, this work was composed and premiered for the beginning of an annual concert series at Carnegie Hall.

Blood Sweat & Tears—Founded by Bobby Colomby and Al Kooper, this band was put together in 1967 for the purpose of doing gigs to raise money for Al to travel to England. The group consisted of classically and jazz trained musicians. By adding musicians Steve Katz and David Clayton-Thomas the sound became a blend of jazz, rock, big-bands and a newly developing sound of funk and fusion emerging from the 60s.

Blue Devils—Walter Page's legendary Midwestern group which employed William "Count" Basie also included Jimmy Rushing. Both Page and Rushing would be a vital part of Count Basie's own band.

Blue Yodel—A famous country music song recorded by Jimmie Rodgers, also known as the "Mississippi Yodeler." Originally titled "T for Texas" and re-titled to "Blue Yodel" as the song became a huge hit, it was one of few country records to sell a million copies.

Blues—Blues is defined as a melancholy or sad feeling; however, to the people that sing or play "the blues," it is not limited to one particular feeling. In fact it encompasses all emotion and is expressionistic by nature.

Bobby "Blue" Bland—Born Robert Calvin Bland in January, 1930. He was an original member of "The Beale Streeters." After a couple of unsuccessful singles and a short stint in the Army, leaving with an honorable discharge, Sam Phillips became a major influence in Bland's eventual success.

Bobby Colomby—Co-founder of Blood Sweat & Tears along with Al Kooper who decided to put the band together in 1967 to do some gigs. Immediately both agreed on the use of horns.

Body And Soul—Coleman Hawkins's famous version of Body and Soul, recorded on October 11th, 1939, displayed many examples of his virtuosity on the harmonic structures of the music.

Bolero—A famous orchestra piece by Maurice Ravel.

Bourree—A metered dance rhythm and form found in dance suites of the Baroque period.

Brass—A family of instruments made from brass alloy, producing a sound through the buzzing of the lips into a mouthpiece. Includes the Trumpet, French horn, Trombone, and Tuba groups.

Brian Epstein—A Jewish-English businessman and the manager of The Beatles, Epstein first noticed the Beatles name on a concert bill and thought that is was "silly." Although he had no prior experience in artist management, Epstein became a major force behind the band's early appearances and successes.

Brian Holland—Part of a three member team that joined forces in 1962 and became a part of the songwriting team of Motown.

Bud Powell—Born in 1924, Powell is considered to be the most important pianist in jazz history. In 1944, at age 20, he made his first recordings with the Cootie Williams Band.

Budd Johnson—Tenor saxophonist who was among the principal musicians involved in the Bebop movement.

Cadence—equivalent to a punctuation point in language. The closing of a music thought.

Café Society—A landmark club in Greenwich Village, opened by Barney Josephson, was the first to try integration. This was the club that Billie Holiday took completely by surprise when she performed Abel Meeropol's, "Strange Fruit."

Call and Response—A technique that assisted in creating the early "Delta Blues." The process of one person stating a musical phrase with a group of people responding to the first statement with a repetition of the first statement or a closing statement and often done in the 12 bar blues form.

Camerata—society of intellectuals in Florence, Italy, around 1600 which included poets, amateur musicians, and scholars, whose objective was to recreate the emotional impact of the fabled Greek tragedies. Jacopo Peri, the composer of the first opera was a Camerata member.

Canon—The strictest form of imitative polyphony where one voice begins a melody and is precisely imitated by a voice or voices.

Cantata—A form or shape of music emerging from the late seventeenth and early eighteenth century Lutheran church service. It is a musical sermon, using Biblical text appropriate to the liturgical calendar, employing choral, vocal solo, instruments (especially pipe organ) and continuo as its primary performance force with melodies derived from chorales or hymn tunes.

Cantata—A genre form that is the musical equivalent of the sermon in a Lutheran church service with text taken from the church calendar lectionary and themes taken from chorales as source material for choruses. Often employs recitative and aria, as well as choruses and orchestral and organ accompaniments.

Capitalism—The economic notion that an entity can produce a product or commodity and sell, exchange, or trade that product or commodity on an open free market to those willing to trade or pay for that product.

Carnival—A set of famous character pieces for solo piano by Robert Schumann.

Carolus Linnaeus—A Swedish botanist who developed a universal system for the naming of plants and animals according to genus and species.

Carter Family, The—A country music group that began its public performance and recording careers in 1927, when Ralph Peer and Victor signed them to a record deal. This group, from Maces Springs, Virginia, consisting of Alvin P. Carter, Sara Dougherty-Carter and Maybelle Carter, was well versed in tight mountain harmonies and gospel music. They made the trek to Bristol, Tennessee to audition for a record contract and received $50.00 for each song that was recorded.

Carter Picking—Maybelle Carter would use her thumb to pick up the bass lines that were missing in the ensemble and a new form of guitar style was born in country music and dubbed with the name "Carter Picking."

Celeste—A melodic percussion instrument.

Cello—The tenor instrument (or the instrument with the third highest pitch range) of the string family of instruments.

Chant—(Plainsong) Monophonic liturgical chant in free rhythm, not measured. Melodies were intoned using free rhythm and derived from medieval modes, making the text audible to many.

Character Piece—A short programmatic work for solo piano that is descriptive of an emotion or feeling made popular by Robert Schumann.

Charles "Buddy" Bolden—Considered "King" of the cornet. Bolden was the first band leader to employ improvisation as a technique in the creation of music.

Charles Babbage—An English mathematician and inventor who invented the principle of the analytical engine, the forerunner of the computer. Also, he invented the calculator that could tabulate mathematical computations to eight decimals.

Charles Darwin—Author of On the Origin of Species by Means of Natural Selection that promoted the idea of evolution in animals through genetic mutation.

Charles Dickens—The most widely read Victorian novelist who appealed to social consciousness to overcome social misery. His works include, A Tale of Two Cities, Great Expectations, Oliver Twist, and David Copperfield.

Charles Mingus—Bassist and member of "The Quintet," he was part of the founding members of the Bebop movement. Born on a military base in Nogales, Arizona in 1922 and raised in Watts, California, his earliest musical influences came from the church and Duke Ellington. He studied double bass and composition formally while absorbing vernacular music from the great jazz masters.

Charley Patton—Born in Edwards, Mississippi, in 1891, Patton is the uncontested "Father of the Delta Blues." Patton's fiery and energetic renditions stirred crowds on a regular basis. His raw vocal style and the ability to be a one-man percussion section with his guitar, combined with his ability to create innovative flows of rhythm, keeping his listeners tuned into the music.

Charlie "Bird" Parker—One of the most influential alto saxophonists and improvising soloists in jazz history. Parker was a monumental figure in the development of Bebop in the 1940s. "Bird," nick-named for his affinity for chicken, was legendary in his own time and was an idolized musician.

Chicago—Founded by Walter Paraziader, Terry Kath, Danny Seraphine, Lee Loughnane, James Pankow, Robert Lamm, and Peter Cetera, this group is highly responsible for the popularity of horn usage in rock-n-roll and is named after the city in which they all grew up, Chicago.

Chicago Electric Blues—This sound was created by bandleader Muddy Waters. Putting together a sizeable blues band and using electric instruments with amplification, the Chicago Electric Blues became the model for the rock-n-roll bands of the following generations.

Chicago Transit Authority—Jimmy Guercio, producer at CBS Records, upon hearing Chicago at Barnaby's told Parazaider to pack the bags, they're moving to Los Angeles under a new name, Chicago Transit Authority.

Cholly Atkins—A dance choreographer who was well known for his work in the '30's and '40's at the Cotton Club and Savoy Ballroom was hired by Gordy to teach his new stars staged dance moves, ultimately becoming a long standing tradition for Motown performing artists.

Chorale—German word for hymn, or hymn tune. The congregational song or hymn from the German Lutheran Church.

Chorale prelude—A solo piece for organ built from the theme of a chorale.

Chord—A chord is created when three or more notes sound at the same time.

Chorus—A musical tool used in the creation of opera, oratorio, passion, and cantata genres. Involves choral forces with orchestral and or organ accompaniments designed as the musical tool of maximum dramatic emotional effect.

Christmas—Birth of Christ in the liturgical calendar.

Chromatic scale—A scale that contains only half-steps.

Civil Rights Movement—A deliberate social struggle to bring racial inequities, common in America since the Civil War, to the forefront of public consciousness for the purpose of permanent legislative relief and equality of opportunity for citizens of any race.

Clara Schumann—The wife of Robert Schumann and an important Romantic period concert pianist who promoted her husband's compositions and those of other friends such as Johannes Brahms through her many concert events. She was also a significant early female composer in her own right.

Clarinet—the tenor instrument (or the third highest pitch range) of the woodwind family of instruments belonging to the single reed group.

Claude Debussy—He established the impressionistic technique in the musical world through tonally extended harmonies, exotic scales, and freer flowing rhythms, thus breaking from the tyranny of the sonata allegro form.

Claude Monet—A painter in the Impressionist school known for his renderings of outdoor sunlight with a direct, sketch-like application of bright color. He is known for his paintings of his lily pond with a Japanese bridge overhung with willows and clumps of bamboo.

Claudio Monteverdi—(1567–1643) An important figure in two musical periods, the Renaissance and the Baroque, he is an important madrigal composer in the Renaissance style and he composed the first masterpiece of opera, Orfeo, in 1607, which expanded the orchestra, gave each character a distinctive accompaniment, and expanded the concept of monody to one of recitative, while including an overture. He held the position of "Head of Choral Music" at St. Mark's Cathedral in Venice.

Clef—A graphic symbol specifying a range of high versus low notes that is to be placed on a staff. Most commonly used clef signs are the treble and bass.

Clive Davis—CBS President, responsible for overturning lower executives' decision to turn down CTA (Chicago Transit Authority) for a recording contract and requested they enter the studio and a recording contract with CBS records.

Cold, Cold Heart—A popular country music song written by Hank Williams Sr. and placed in the hands of an "up and coming" vocal artist Tony Bennett, by Mitch Miller at Columbia Records, the match of tune and vocalist was a huge success. Cold, Cold Heart sold millions of copies and soared to number 1 on the pop charts immediately, creating country music's first "cross-over" hit.

Cold War, The—The longest unofficial war of the century, fought between the Soviet Union and the United States, a standoff of nuclear powers that ended only because the arms race it created bankrupted the economy of the Soviet Union.

Coleman Hawkins—One of two extremely influential tenor saxophonists of the time. Spending time in Europe with great success before moving back to the USA, Hawkins' famous recording of Body & Soul introduced a new harmonic sound. His use of chromatic passing tones and different harmonies in a "standard" piece helped coin the use of the "substitute" chord.

The Commodores—Highly successful Soul/R&B band in the 1970s. They met as freshmen at Tuskegee Institute and signed to Motown records and caught the attention of the national public while supporting the Jackson 5 on tour.

Communism—A social and economic model of governance that theoretically creates a classless society through the abolishment of private ownership of land and property, graduated income tax, and inheritance, while controlling the production and transportation of goods, assigning these to the "state," through the idea "...from each according to his ability, to each according to his need."

Communist Manifesto—A social, political, and economic model of government that formed the basis of Communism and ultimately the Cold War.

Concert Overture—Orchestral incidental music by composers for use with dramatic plays in the Romantic period, found at the beginning of the play.

Concertino—A term given to the group of instrumental soloists in a Baroque concerto grosso form.

Concerto—A Classical period genre of music for one instrumental soloist with orchestral accompaniment composed in modified sonata form performed in a large concert setting.

Concerto for Orchestra—A popular orchestral piece composed by Bela Bartok.

Concerto for Piano and Winds—An important work by Igor Stravinsky.

Concerto Grosso—A multiple movement form with a standardized three-movement design, fast, slow, fast, which uses a group of soloists pitted against an accompanying orchestra group for the purpose of virtuosic display for a group of instrumental soloists. Popular with the public in the Baroque period.

Consonance—Pitches possessed of vibrations that are in accord with each other, or at rest.

Continuo—The unit in the Baroque orchestra that is comprised of a polyphonic instrument, most often a keyboard instrument or lute, and a bass voice instrument, most often a cello or bassoon. The continuo is responsible for the chordal harmony, generating rhythm, and the bass line.

Contralto—One of the standard range categorizations of the human voice, the third highest vocal range.

Cosi fan tutti—A Mozart opera with libretto by Lorenzo da Ponte commissioned for the Royal Theater of Emperor Joseph II of Austria.

Cotton Club— In 1930, The Cotton Club became the mainstay for the Duke Ellington Orchestra. After many appearances in movies and on radio broadcasts, Duke's group became the house band for the Cotton Club in Harlem.

Count Leo Nikolaevich Tolstoy—An important Russian writer, moral thinker and reformer, and author of War and Peace, Anna Karenina, A Confession, and What I Believe.

Countertenor—A male voice with an unusually high range.

Courante—A metered dance rhythm and form found in dance suites of the Baroque period.

Crazy Blues—In 1920, Mamie Smith recorded the first blues tune ever.

Creation, The—An oratorio composed by Joseph Haydn.

Credo—"Creed," one of the five texts of the Mass Ordinary.

Creole—A racial mixture of French and African American.

Creole Jazz Band—Headed up by Band Leader "King Oliver," this Dixieland group employed such great musicians as Clarinetist Johnny Dodds, Trombonist Honore Dutry, Pianist, Lil Hardin, Drummer Baby Dodds, and Bassist/Banjo player, Bill Johnson. The group began its recording career in 1923.

Critique of Judgment—A philosophical treatise by Immanuel Kant.

Critique of Practical Reason—A philosophical treatise by Immanuel Kant.

Critique of Pure Reason—A philosophical treatise by Immanuel Kant.

Crossroads Blues—A legendary blues record composed and originally recorded by Robert Johnson.

Cyclic Mass—All movements are based upon the same tenor melody or begin with identical opening phrases.

Cymbal—A non-melodic percussion instrument group.

Da Capo Aria—An aria designed to showcase the individual singer's performance skill through opportunities to improvise and ornament the aria melody in a repeat of the initial theme now played by the orchestra alone.

Dafne—First true opera, composed in 1598 by Jacopo Peri.

Damnation of Faust, The—An important Romantic period choral piece composed by Hector Berlioz.

Dance—Kinesthetic movement designed to be a vehicle of emotion for the dancer through the body's motions, while also designed to invoke emotion in the consuming observer.

Dance suite—A popular Baroque genre of instrumental music for orchestra with multiple movements of dances of varying number, using differing rhythmic patterns and meters, often preceded by a preparatory piece called a French Overture.

Danny Seraphine—Co-founder and drummer for Chicago.

Das Lied von der Erde—A famous symphony by Gustav Mahler.

Dave Bargeron—Original trombonist and tuba player for the group Blood Sweat & Tears.

David Clayton-Thomas—Lead singer for Blood Sweat & Tears who helped produce three gold singles and three Grammy Awards, including "Album of the Year" in 1969. This album included Clayton-Thomas's own composition "Spinning Wheel" which was an international hit.

David Copperfield—A novel by Charles Dickens.

Declaration of Independence—A document authored by Thomas Jefferson which declared a breaking away from English rule by the people of what would become the United States of America, putting Enlightenment philosophies into experimental practice for the first time.

Denis Diderot—A philosopher and chief editor of the French Encyclopedie, who became a prolific writer, publishing novels, plays, satires, essays and letters.

Development—term referring to the middle section in the sonata allegro movement where the composer takes elements from the melodies found in the exposition and creatively manipulates them causing as much density and tension as desired for the movement prior to its melodic and tonal resolution found in the recapitulation section that follows.

Dewey Phillips—Radio show host of "Red, Hot and Blue" on WHBQ Radio in Memphis. Dewey broadcast Elvis's "That's All Right Mama" after the hand delivery of the recording from Sam Phillips. After an extremely enthusiastic response to the single, disk jockeys began to play more of that record and the flip side as well, "Blue Moon of Kentucky."

Dexter Avenue Baptist Church—A church in Montgomery, Alabama, where Dr. Martin Luther King, Jr. was pastor and a central facility for gathering and planning social responses in the Montgomery Bus Boycott.

Diana Ross—Vocalist for the female vocal trio of The Supremes. She was also a solo recording artist for Motown Records and star of "Lady Sings the Blues."

Diatonic scale—Any one of the major or minor scales that possesses seven notes.

Dido and Aeneas—Important short Baroque opera in English composed by Henry Purcell for the English Royals.

Die Neue Zeitschrift fur Musik—A professional music journal founded by Robert Schumann which is devoted to the promotion of new music and concert artists of merit.

Dimitri Shostokovitch—A Russian-born composer of importance in the twentieth century.

Discourse on the Origin and Foundations of Inequality Amongst Men—A social commentary by Jean Jaques Rousseau.

Dissonance—Pitches whose waves conflict with each other, or are in motion.

Diva—An audience favorite in the world of female opera singers. One who has great skill and great fame.

Don Byas—Tenor saxophonist born October 21, 1912 in Muskogee, Oklahoma, had a long residence in Europe, keeping him out of the public eye in the USA. His career started with Lionel Hampton, the progressed to performances with Don Redman, Lucky Millinder, and Count Basie. He was a major influence in the Bebop era with other saxophonists such as Charlie Parker and Budd Johnson.

Don Giovanni—A Mozart opera with libretto by Lorenzo da Ponte commissioned for the Royal Theater of Emperor Joseph II of Austria.

Double bass—The bass instrument (or the instrument with the lowest pitch range) of the string family of instruments.

Double reed instrument—A term referring to the oboe and bassoon families of instruments which use two cane reeds fixed together to produce their sound.

Downbeat Magazine—An American magazine devoted to jazz. First established in 1935 in Chicago, Illinois, it is named after the "downbeat" in music which is also the first beat of a measure.

Dr. Martin Luther King, Jr.—A pastor of the Dexter Avenue Baptist Church in Montgomery, Alabama who led the Montgomery Bus Boycott and the strategist in national civil rights movement who advocated social change through non-violent social protest.

Drum—A non-melodic percussion instrument group.

Dying Poet, The—One of Louis Moreau Gottschalk's most popular piano compositions.

Earl Van Dyke—Keyboardist for "The Funk Brothers" and was the rhythm section leader in the studio.

Earth Wind & Fire—Among the most influential African American funk groups in history. The line-up consisted of Maurice White, Phillip Bailey, Verdine White, Larry Dunn, Ralph Johnson, Johnny Graham, Andrew Woolfolk, and Al McKay and turned out brilliant vocal harmonies, magnificent horn-lines, all backed up with an incredible rhythm section.

Easter Sunday—The day of Christ's resurrection in the liturgical calendar.

Ebony Concerto—An important work by Igor Stravinsky.

Ed Sullivan Show—A TV variety show that ran for more than 20 years on CBS, every Sunday night at 8:00 p.m. The Ed Sullivan Show hosted virtually every type of entertainment and ultimately some of the biggest names in music history, including Elvis Presley, The Beatles, and Motown's the Temptations and the Supremes.

Eddie Holland—Part of a three member team that joined forces in 1962 and became a part of the songwriting team of Motown.

Edgar Allan Poe—An American poet, editor, and writer of macabre stories such as The Fall of the House of Usher and Murders in the Rue Morgue. He is considered the father of the detective story and stepfather of science fiction.

Edgar Degas—A French painter who was a master craftsman of the human figure and primarily concerned with depicting movement through pastels.

Edouard Manet—The first modern painter to inspire the French Impressionist movement.

Edward Kennedy "Duke" Ellington—Edward Kennedy Ellington was born in Washington, DC on April 29th, 1899. He began studying piano at age seven and was greatly influenced by stride piano greats like James P. Johnson, Fats Waller, and Willie "the Lion" Smith. Edward Kennedy "Duke" Ellington is one the most productive and creative composers of the 20th century. His outstanding number of compositions and variety of musical forms, from big band to orchestral, have been unmatched by any other composer in the century.

Edwin Powell Hubble—An important 20th century scientist.

Elijah—An important Romantic period oratorio composed by Felix Mendelssohn.

Elvis Presley—Growing up in Tupelo, Mississippi, Presley was surrounded by gospel music and exposed to jazz and blues. Born on January 8th, 1935, Elvis Aron Presley was only 13 when his family was uprooted from his Mississippi hometown to move to the western Tennessee city of Memphis. After the discovery of Presley by Sam Phillips and his recording of "Blue Moon of Kentucky," Presley was destined to be the "King" of Rock-n-roll.

Emerson, Lake & Palmer—One of the groups influenced by the Beatles avid display of contemporary compositional techniques. E.L.P. used Classical and Romantic compositional forms for their own albums. They also incorporated music by Romantic and 20th century composers such as; Pictures at an Exhibition by Russian composer Modest Mussorgsky and two pieces by Aaron Copland, Fanfare for the Common Man and Hoedown.

EMI Records—Earlier Beatles albums had been released on Parlophone in the United Kingdom, and Capitol Records or United Artists Records in the United States. In a new recording deal, EMI and Capitol agreed to distribute Apple Records until 1975; Apple owned the rights to records by artists they signed, while EMI retained ownership of the Beatles' records, though issuing them under the Apple label.

Emma—A novel by Jane Austen.

Emperor Joseph II of Austria—An enlightened Emperor of Austria who established a haven for enlightened politics and artistic creation in Vienna during the Classical period in music.

Encyclopedie—The favorite literary work of the Enlightenment thinkers, edited by philosopher Denis Diderot.

Ensemble—An opera innovation made popular by Mozart which effectively replaced the older recitative design for the delivery of dialogue within a dramatic scene. Now, multiple characters could have spontaneous dialogue exchanges during the same musical passage, pushing the scenes dramatic elements to a higher level than was allowed with the recitative.

Epiphany—Season of celebration immediately after Christmas in the liturgical calendar.

Episode—Referring to a section within a fugue where statements and transpositions of the initial melodic subjects are introduced in the various voices and cadenced before entering a subsequent section where similar melodic events occur in the various voices.

Erlkonig—A short vocal composition for a male soloist with piano accompaniment based on a dramatic tale of crisis and superstition by Schubert.

Ernest Rutherford—An important 20th century scientist.

Eroica Symphony—The name given to Beethoven's Third Symphony, originally dedicated to Napoleon, but at the last minute the composer scratched out the dedication on the title page and renamed it in honor of heroic men.

Estampie—An instrumental composition of the 13th and 14th centuries.

Euridice—An opera composed by Jacopo Peri in 1600 for a royal wedding celebration in that established opera as an important artistic form and introduced it to the early Baroque nobility.

Experiment in Modern Music—A 1924 concert by the Paul Whiteman Orchestra that present Gershwin's "Rhapsody in Blue" which received rousing applause from the critics for its great artistic success.

Exposition—A term referring to the first section within the sonata allegro form where two themes are presented, contrasting in tempo, key, and potentially meter, introducing the necessary melodic material used for creative activity found later within the movement.

Expressionism—A visual art style created by artists Kandinsky and Munch, capturing a distorted reality, drawing attention to the artist's inner emotions; often dark and conflicted, music composed by Arnold Schoenberg, Anton Webern, and Alan Berg musically attempts similar emotional qualities through the blurring or elimination of tonality, creating distorted sonic environments.

F. V. Eugene Delacroix—The greatest French Romantic painter whose art is centered on a revolutionary idea born with the Romantics—that art should be created out of sincerity and express the artist's truest conviction's.

Fairy Queen, The—An opera in English by Henry Purcell.

Falstaff—An important Romantic period opera composed by Giuseppi Verdi.

Famous Door, The—One of seven segregated jazz clubs on 52nd street, New York City, 1935.

Fanfare for the Common Man—An important work for orchestra by Aaron Copland.

Fantasy in F minor—An important Romantic period piano piece composed by Frederic Chopin.

Fats Waller—Among the greatest ragtime, stride and early jazz pianists, Waller was a teacher of William "Count" Basie and a great influence for Duke Ellington.

Faux-bourdon—A 15th century French technique where two voices are written and sung, and a third voice is not written but sung parallel to the upper part.

Felix Mendelssohn—An important Romantic period composer, conductor, educator, and historian, who composed numerous instrumental and choral works, became a premier conductor or orchestras, founded the Leipzig Conservatory, and brought J. S. Bach from the brink of historical obscurity through the first presentation of the St. Matthew Passion in its first modern performance.

Ferdinand "Jelly Roll" Morton—Self-proclaimed "inventor" of jazz, the New Orleans pianist was not responsible for the invention of jazz, however was the first musician to show that jazz can be put into written form. Morton was the first to write arrangements that would fit on one side of a 78-rpm record.

Field Hollers—The musical leaders of slaves, the field hollers would begin work songs and/or spirituals and favored the "call and response" technique while laboring, making back breaking work pass quicker.

Figured Bass—A time-saving device of composers in the Baroque period or code of symbols and numbers above a bass voice that the keyboard or lute players would "realize" or interpret, adding the appropriate intervals of chords suggested for the given bass melody.

Final Tone (Resting Tone)—The pitch upon which a chant comes to its closing cadence.

Fine Art—An ornamentation to life which makes it beautiful and meaningful for individuals.

Fingal's Cave—A famous concert overture by Felix Mendelssohn.

Firebird—An important work of ballet by Igor Stravinsky.

Five Pieces for Orchestra—A significant work of Arnold Schoenberg.

Fletcher Henderson—A big band leader and one of the first arrangers for such an ensemble configuration. Henderson is considered the father of big band jazz.

Fletcher Henderson's Orchestra—Among the most commercially successful groups of the 1920s. The smooth sound of his orchestra essentially prepared the way for the swing style. Henderson employed some of New Orleans's greatest musicians including the great Louis Armstrong.

Florid Organum—A form of Medieval polyphony where the upper voice moves independent of the chant voice.

Flute—The soprano instrument (or the highest pitch range) of the woodwind family of instruments.

Flying Dutchman, The—An important Romantic period opera composed by Richard Wagner.

Form—A term describing the design or shape in music through logically related sections of melody and/or harmony, centered in certain tonal areas.

Four Seasons—A set of four concerto grossi composed by Antonio Vivaldi separately entitled, Spring, Summer, Autumn, and Winter, Vivaldi's most famous pieces.

Four Tops, The—Among a number of groups who helped define the Motown Sound of the 1960s, including The Miracles, The Marvelettes, The Temptations, and The Supremes, The Four Tops were notable for having Stubbs, a baritone, as their lead singer; most groups of the time were fronted by a tenor. The group was the main male vocal group for the songwriting and production team of Holland-Dozier-Holland, who crafted for the group a stream of popular hit singles, including two #1 hits: "I Can't Help Myself (Sugar Pie, Honey Bunch)" and "Reach Out I'll Be There."

Francesco Guardi—A painter who's work "The Concert" portrays a scene of Venetian artistic life in the Classical period.

Francios Marie Arouet—A French author of political pamphlets, plays, and articles under the pen name Voltaire during the Enlightenment.

Francis Crick—An important 20th century scientist.

Francisco Goya—A painter who's work "The Shooting" portrays a social protest depicting man's inhumanity to man in the brutality of Napoleon's campaign with Spain.

Frans Hals—Dutch painter born in 1581, considered one of the greatest portrait artists of the seventeenth century. He influenced future artists Manet and van Gogh through his works.

Franz Joseph Haydn—Classical period composer who excelled in the traditional musician servant role in his employment to Prince Esterhazy as his chief musician and personal composer. Haydn helped to solidify the sonata form, making it the popular genre of instrumental music it would become through his many symphonies and string quartets. He would influence both Mozart and Beethoven who followed.

Franz Liszt—A Romantic composer who is important in the development of the symphonic poem and in the concert performance practices of pianists.

Franz Peter Schubert—A Romantic composer who is important in the development of the lied. He composed over 600 songs or lieder, including his most famous—Erlkonig.

Fred White—Brother of Verdine and Maurice White, founders of Earth Wind & Fire, who joined the group when CBS records was calling for a third recording.

Frederic Chopin—A Romantic composer who is important in the development of piano music. He is also known as the "poet of the piano."

French horn—The alto instrument (or the second highest pitch range) of the brass family of instruments.

French Overture—The preparatory piece which begins a dance suite in the Baroque period.

Friedrich Engels—A co-author of the Communist Manifesto, published in 1848.

From Spirituals to Swing—A legendary John Hammond Concert that took place in New York's Carnegie Hall. Bessie Smith was scheduled for the premier performance when a fatal car accident pre-empted the performance. The concert was instead dedicated to the Bessie Smith.

Fugue—The most complex and purely absolute music genre of the Baroque period, a multi-voiced imitative polyphonic melodic texture based on a single motive called the subject.

The Funk Brothers—All of the Motown hits had a remarkably similar sound due to the fact that Motown employed a house rhythm section known as "The Funk Brothers" and in 1964 employed Earl Van Dyke, a former be-bop jazz pianist. Van Dyke became the leader in the studio. Drummer Benny Benjamin and bassist James Jamerson, who backed Jackie Wilson and Smokey and the Miracles, joined the musical team and that combination established the musical sound of Motown.

Fyodor Dostojevski—A Russian novelist who wrote Crime and Punishment, The Idiot, and The Brothers Karamazov.

Galilei Galileo—Born in Pisa, Italy, he is regarded as the founder of modern science when he developed the notion that the planets revolved around the sun rather than the Earth. His science was considered religious heresy.

Galliard—A metered dance rhythm and form found in dance suites of the Baroque period.

Gavotte—A metered dance rhythm and form found in dance suites of the Baroque period.

Genre—A name given a piece of music specified with regards to formal shape, instrumentation, and intended performance space.

Georg Friedrich Handel—(1685–1759) a famous German organist and composer of opera seria, oratorio, and other instrumental music. He held the position of "Music Director at the Court of Hanover prior to moving to London and becoming a naturalized English citizen. His most famous composition is the oratorio Messiah.

George Gordon, Lord Byron—A famous English poet and author of Child Harold, Manfred, and Don Juan.

George Harrison—Best known as the lead guitarist for The Beatles, he was a popular British guitarist, singer, songwriter, and record and film producer.

George Martin—Classically trained musician and producer responsible for signing The Beatles to a record contract with EMI records.

George Sand—The pen name for female author Amandine—Aurore—Lucille Dudevant who wrote over 100 books, including, Indiana, a passionate protest against the social conventions that bind a wife to her husband against her will. For a time, she was Chopin's lover.

German Requiem—An important Romantic period requiem composed by Johannes Brahms.

Gigue—A metered dance rhythm and form found in dance suites of the Baroque period.

Giovanni Bernini—A key architect, sculptor, and painter in the Baroque period who designed the colonnade in the piazza outside St. Peters in Rome.

Giovanni Gabrielli—(1577–1612/13) a Venetian composer known for polychoral works created for St. Mark's Cathedral.

Giovanni Pierluigi da Palestrina—(1525–1594) a prolific composer of works in the Franco-Flemish style. Palestrina became the most valued Catholic composer of his day.

Giuseppi Verdi—An important Romantic period composer of opera.

Gladys Knight and the Pips—One of the original female vocalists with back-up group to be signed to Motown Records.

Glockenspiel—A melodic percussion instrument.

Gloria—"Glory," one of the five texts of the Mass Ordinary.

Goetz von Berlichingen—A drama which captured the spirit of German Nationalism written by Johann Wolfgang von Goethe.

Good Friday—The day of Christ's crucifixion in the liturgical calendar.

Gospel Lesson—A seasonal text of the Mass Proper.

Gothic Period—The last three decades of the Medieval Age (1100–1430).

Grand Ole Opry—An icon in country music, it started as the WSM Barn Dance in the new 5th floor radio studio of the National Life & Accident Insurance Company in Nashville. It was (and still is) a weekly Saturday night country music radio program, typically broadcast live. It is the oldest continuous radio program in the United States having broadcast since November 28th, 1925.

Grand staff—the connecting of the treble clef and bass clef staffs produces a grand staff, widening the range available on which to write musical pitches.

Great Expectations—A novel by Charles Dickens.

Gregg Adams—Primary horn arranger for Tower of Power and member of the T.O.P. horn section performing on trumpets and flugel horns.

Guillaume de Machaut—(1300–1377) a French composer, theologian, and canon highly regarded for intellectual and technical advances in music.

Guillaume Dufay—(1400–1474) a French composer who wrote more than 130 works in the Burgundian style.

Guitar—An instrument belonging to the plucked string category of instruments.

Gustav Mahler—An important Late Romantic period composer of symphonies as well as orchestral song cycles.

Half cadence—An incomplete phrase point, requiring a second melodic phrase to complete the melodic idea.

Half step—the smallest distance that is musically recognized in Western music.

Hank Williams Sr.—Born Hiram "Hank" Williams on September 17th, 1923. As a singer/songwriter he has become an icon of country music and one of the most influential musicians of the 20th century. The Hank Williams's songbook is one of the backbones of country music and has been covered in a range of pop and rock styles. After his premature death at age 29, his legend reached mythic proportions.

Hans Christian Andersen—A Danish writer and storyteller or children's fairy tales such as The Tin Soldier, The Tinderbox, and The Ugly Duckling.

Harmony—More than one pitch sounding simultaneously.

Harold in Italy—An important Romantic period program symphony composed by Hector Berlioz.

Harpsichord—A seventeenth century keyboard instrument possessing a high degree of aural clarity and dexterity due to its plucked string construction.

Healer, The—The monumental blues recording by John Lee Hooker using many blues musicians influenced by Hooker over the last half-century.

Heavy Metal Horns, The—Contemporary horn group that follows in the steps of the predecessors. Original compositions and horn charts prevail in this group.

Hebrides, The—A famous concert overture by Felix Mendelssohn.

Hector Berlioz—An important Romantic period composer important in the development of the program symphony, opera, and in the craft of orchestration.

Hello Dolly—Recorded in 1963 by Louis Armstrong & the All-Stars, this recording knocked the Beatles off of the number one spot at the top of the pop charts.

Henry Purcell—(1659–1695) an important English composer and keyboardist in the Baroque period, he was appointed composer to the King of England and was organist at Westminster Abbey where he composed famous dramatic music, both sacred and secular vocal music, and much instrumental music.

Hickory House, The—One of seven segregated jazz clubs on 52nd street, New York City, 1935.

Hitsville USA—One of many owned complimentary businesses of Berry Gordy. Others attached to his name were: Motown Records Corporation, Berry Gordy Enterprises, Jobete Music Publishing, and International Talent Management, Inc.

Hocket—A 13th century technique that divides a melody between two voices, one is silent while the other is sounding.

Homily—A short sermon designated as part of the Mass Proper.

Homophonic texture—Music having one main melody accompanied by other supporting musical material that does not distract the listener from the focus of the primary melody.

Homophony—A musical texture that is dominated by one melody, all voices and accompaniments move together.

Hot Five & Seven, The—Louis Armstrong's venture into "Band Leader." His creation of the Hot Five & Hot Seven was the first time Armstrong recorded using his own name as band leader. The recording of the Hot Five & Hot Seven show evidence of Armstrong's powerful creativity which made these recordings easily considered jazz classics.

Howlin' Wolf—Born Chester Arthur Burnett on June 10th, 1910, he was an influential blues singer, songwriter, guitarist and harmonica player. His first recordings came in 1951 when he was signed to four record labels simultaneously.

Human voice—The musical instrument possessed by all humans.

Hungarian Rhapsodies—An important Romantic period piano piece composed by Franz Liszt.

Hymns—Seasonal music of the Mass Proper.

I've Got a Woman—A popular record composed and performed by Ray Charles.

Idée fixee—The name given to a single melody which is transformed to mirror programmatic elements within each movement of Hector Berlioz's program symphony, Symphony Fantastique.

Igor Stravinsky—The most significant Neoclassical composer of the twentieth century.

Ike Turner—Born Izear Luster Turner Jr. in November 1931. He is best known for his work with wife Tina Turner; however he was also a bandleader, pianist, guitarist, talent scout and record producer by the end of his career. In 1951, Turner's recording of "Rocket 88" is considered one of the earliest examples of rock-n-roll.

Il trovatore—An important Romantic period opera composed by Giuseppi Verdi.

Images—A popular Impressionistic orchestra piece by Claude Debussy.

Imitative Polyphony—A musical texture of two or more voices, one voice repeats or simulates the melody of another voice.

Immanuel Kant—One of the greatest philosophers of all time whose works offer an analysis of speculative and moral reason, including Critique of Pure Reason, Critique of Practical Reason, and Critique of Judgment.

Impressionism—A technique in painting initiated by Claude Monet whose objective was to capture the natural outdoors, focusing on how light reflected within the scene through techniques that softened edges and blurred details. Also, a name given to music composed by Claude Debussy, Maurice Ravel and others who tried to do similar things as the Impressionistic painters through music.

Instrument—Anything that has the ability to produce a pitch.

International Talent Management, Inc—One of many owned complimentary businesses of Berry Gordy. Others attached to his name were: Motown Records

Corporation, Berry Gordy Enterprises, Jobete Music Publishing, and Hitsville USA.

Interval—The distance between any two pitches.

Intone—To sing words on a single pitch without rhythmic or melodic structure.

Isorhythm—A 14th and 15th century technique that repeats a rhythmic pattern throughout a voice part, regardless of melodic shape or textual content. It is costumed and acted with scenic set constructs and in the early days included dance as well.

J. Robert Oppenheimer—An important 20th century scientist.

J. W. Goethe—The greatest of all German poets and contributor to German nationalism. He is the author of Faust, The Sorrows of Younger Werther, and Goetz von Berlichingen.

Jackie Brenston—Recorded "Rocket 88" for Sam Phillips in 1951. Phillips and Brenston took a chance at success by adding a harsher guitar sound, caused by an accident that broke a tube in the amplifier. Adding extra amplification to a broken "fuzzed out" guitar created a new dimension to the recording and ultimately paid off with astounding sales figures.

Jackie Wilson—Recording artist managed by Al Green and performed songs written by Berry Gordy. Wilson was the lead singing replacement for Clyde McPhatter in the Dominoes and recorded "Lonely Teardrops" which ultimately became one of his biggest hits.

Jackson Five—Vocal group from Gary, Indiana, and active from 1962 to 1990. They are considered one of the biggest phenomena in pop music. The members were Jackie, Tito, Jermaine, Marlon, Michael, and Randy Jackson. The Jackson 5 was signed to the Motown label from 1969 to 1975.

Jacopo Peri—Composer of the first true opera, Dafne, in 1598; also, composed Euridice in 1600 for a royal wedding celebration.

James Clerk Maxwell—One of the great physicists the world has ever seen, who united electricity and magnetism into the concept of the electromagnetic field which paved the way for Einstein's special theory of relativity.

James Cotton—Born in Tunica, Mississippi on July 1st, 1935, Cotton was a blues harmonica player, singer, songwriter and ultimately bandleader for the James Cotton Blues Band. In 1967, under the direction of Sam Phillips, the James Cotton Blues Band recorded two live CDs in which all of Cotton's classics were performed.

James Jamerson—Original bassist for "The Funk Brothers," the house rhythm section for all Motown Records.

James Marshall "Jimi" Hendrix—An African-American musician, singer, songwriter, guitarist and cultural icon. Widely lauded by music fans and critics alike, he is regarded by many as the greatest and most influential electric guitarist in rock-n-roll history.

James P. Johnson—An important transitional figure between ragtime and jazz piano styles. His style became known as "stride." As a boy, Johnson studied classical music and ragtime. He started playing professionally in a sporting house, and then progressed to rent parties, bars, and vaudeville. He was highly influential to young greats such as Count Basie and Duke Ellington.

James Pankow—Co-founder and trombonist for Chicago.

James Watson—An important 20th century scientist.

James Watt—A Scotsman who started as an instrument maker and ultimately went on to make improvements to the new steam engine that helped the Industrial Revolution get off the ground.

Jan Vermeer—Dutch painter of the people in the middle-class using slightly blurred outlines and his favorite colors blue and yellow.

Jane Austen—An important English novelist and author of the first novel, opening the door to the world of fiction through her works including, Sense and Sensibility, Mansfield Park, Emma, and Persuasion.

Janice Joplin—A prominent female vocalist of the 1960s and 70s, Joplin was greatly influenced by blues woman Bessie Smith.

Jay McShann—He was born James Columbus McShann in Muskogee, Oklahoma in 1916. Despite his parent's disapproval of his musical interest, he taught himself the piano and began his professional career with Don Byan in 1931. In 1939, McShann assembled a big band which ultimately recorded for the Decca Label in 1941 and toured extensively. His band's recording of modern compositions assisted in bridging the gap between the traditional Kansas City jazz sound and bebop.

Jean Baptiste Racine—Born 1639 in France, a playwright regarded as the master of tragic pathos, he is the author of Andromaque, Berenice, and Phedre among others.

Jean de LaFontaine—Born in 1621, he is a great French writer of many fables and tales.

Jean Jaques Rousseau—A French author who wrote Discourse on the Origin and Foundations of Inequality Amongst Men and The Social Contract which introduced the slogan, "Liberty, Equality, Fraternity."

Jean-Baptiste Colbert—Economist for Louis XIV of France who over saw the enrichment of the French treasury through the colonization of the "New World" which sent its goods and service back home to the "Motherland."

Jean-Baptiste Lamarck—A French biologist who published Zoological Philosophy in 1809 that advocated similar thoughts to those of Charles Darwin.

Jeux—A popular Impressionistic ballet by Claude Debussy.

Jim Morrison—Lead singer/songwriter for The Doors. Morrison, a poet, born in Melbourne, Florida became the lyricist of one of the most popular American rock bands in history and is considered to be one of the most charismatic front men in the history of rock-n-roll.

Jimmie Rodgers—The youngest son of a railroad man, Rodgers was born and raised in Meridian, MS. Jimmie Rodgers' name stands foremost in the country music field as the man who "started it all," being the first country music star to have a million selling record.

Jobete Music Publishing—One of many owned complimentary businesses of Berry Gordy. Others attached to his name were: Motown Records Corporation, Berry Gordy Enterprises, International Talent Management Inc., and Hitsville USA.

Joe "King" Oliver—Cornetist converted from trombone while playing in brass bands of New Orleans around 1907, "King" Oliver became a bandleader after moving to Chicago in 1920. In June of 1922, Oliver's Creole Jazz Band began working at the Lincoln Gardens and employed the new rising star Louis Armstrong.

Johann Christoph Friederich von Schiller—Poet and German author of "Ode To Joy" a poem highlighted in Beethoven's 9th Symphony, who's writings strive for human freedom and served as inspiration to German liberals in their fight for liberty during the early 1800s.

Johann Sebastian Bach—(1685–1759) a composer and organist of the highest order active in the Baroque period; Bach is perhaps the greatest composer of polyphony in Western music. Active in all genres except opera, he is influential in cantatas and other scared vocal music in the Protestant church, prolific composer of keyboard and other instrumental music, and he wrote The Art of Fugue, the definitive set of pieces representing imitative polyphonic compositional technique. His most famous works include the Mass in B minor, St. Matthew Passion, The Well-Tempered Clavier, and The Art of Fugue.

Johann Wolfgang von Goethe—A writer considered the greatest of all German poets who wrote the drama, Goetz von Berlichingen, which captured the spirit of German Nationalism in the Classical period.

Johannes Brahms—An important Late Romantic period composer of symphonies, other instrumental and choral music as well as lieder.

Johannes Ockeghem—(1410–1497) a Franco-Flemish composer known for imitative polyphony and credited with extending the bass voice into its lower register.

John Birks "Dizzy" Gillespie—Born John Birks Gillespie, in Cheraw, South Carolina, on October 21st, 1917, he was a sibling to 8 other children. His father introduced Dizzy to music but Dizzy was predominantly self-taught. At age 15, he attended the Laurinburg Institute where he played in the band. Dizzy is one of the five members of "The Quintet" that performed live at Massey Hall and is considered to be one of the Fathers of "Bebop."

John Bunyan—An English religious writer born in 1628 and author of "Pilgrim's Progress" a famous religious tract.

John Dalton—An English chemist and physicist who determined the relative weights of atoms and formulated the atomic theory that all elements are composed of tiny, identical, and indestructible particles.

John Hammond—Born Dec. 15th, 1910 in New York City, he was one of swing music's greatest propagandists and he was responsible for the partial discovery of such musicians as Billie Holiday, Count Basie and Charlie Christian. As talent scout, producer, promoter, and early force against racism, Hammond was dominant and forceful in his viewpoints.

John Lee Hooker—The master of "Boogie" with a sensuous and haunting vocal style, John Lee Hooker had the ability to create a groove on just one repetitive chord. Born in Clarksdale, Mississippi in 1917, his style paved the way for the blues and rock-n-roll jam bands, riffing tirelessly over only a few chords.

John Milton—English author of Paradise Lost and many other pamphlets addressing the idea of personal liberties during the Commonwealth period.

John Winston Lennon—Best known as a singer, songwriter, poet, and guitarist for the Beatles. His creativity found him in roles as a solo musician, political activist, artist, actor and author. As half of the legendary Lennon-McCartney songwriting team, he heavily influenced the development of rock-n-roll, leading it toward the more advanced and multi-layered arrangements, mature lyrical sentiments and musical eclecticism. Lennon is recognized as one of the greatest musical icons of the 20th century.

Johnny and the Moondogs—One of the first names of "The Beatles" before the name was agreed upon.

Johnny Graham—One of eight original members and guitarist/percussionist for Earth Wind & Fire.

Jonathan Swift—Regarded as the greatest satirist of English literature and author of Gulliver's Travels.

Joseph Priestly—Discoverer of oxygen.

Josquin Desprez—(1445–1521) A Franco-Flemish composer who published more than 200 works.

Justus Liebig—A chemist and author of two books, Organic Chemistry and its Application to Agriculture and Physiology and Organic Chemistry in its Application to Physiology and Pathology which revolutionized food production.

Karl Friederich Benz—A German engineer who built the first practical automobile powered by an internal combustion engine.

Karl Marx—A co-author of the Communist Manifesto, published in 1848.

Kenny Clarke—Also known as Kenneth Spearman, Klook, Klook-mop, Salaam, and Liaquat Ali, born in 1914, he was a drummer and a bandleader. He began his professional drumming career with Leroy's Bradley's band in Pittsburgh when he was still a teenager. He later joined Roy Eldridge and began performing in the Midwest as well as the East during the beginning of the Bebop era.

Key—The melodic and harmonic pitch material based on a scale creating a specific tonal area.

King Porter Stomp—Composed by Jelly Roll Morton, the Benny Goodman Orchestra performance gave the tune great popularity and was performed at practically every Goodman Orchestra performance.

Kitty Hawk—Kitty Hawk, NC is the place where the Wright Brothers made history with their first manned flight in a plane.

Korean War—A mid-century conflict between capitalistic and communistic governments.

Kyrie—"Lord, have mercy," one of the five texts of the Mass Ordinary.

La forza del destino—An important Romantic period opera composed by Giuseppi Verdi.

La Mer—A popular Impressionistic orchestra piece by Claude Debussy.

La traviata—An important Romantic period opera composed by Giuseppi Verdi.

Lady Macbeth of the Mtsensk District, The—An important opera composed by Dimitri Shostokovitch.

Lady Sings The Blues—Berry Gordy moved Motown's offices to Hollywood in an effort to expand the company into the realm of filmmaking. Berry produced the film, "Lady Sings The Blues" which starred Diana Ross in the lead roll.

Lamont Dozier—Part of a three member team that joined forces in 1962 and became a part of the songwriting team of Motown.

Larry Dunn—One of eight original members and keyboardist for Earth Wind & Fire.

Le Nozze di Figaro—A Mozart opera with libretto by Lorenzo da Ponte commissioned for the Royal Theater of Emperor Joseph II of Austria.

Ledger line—A flexible extension of the lines and spaces of the staff at the top or bottom of a staff.

Lee Loughnane—Original trumpet player for the group Chicago.

Leipzig Conservatory—The first conservatory or school for the training of musicians founded by Felix Mendelssohn.

Leitmotiv—A melody that is associated with an operatic character's emotion, branding the melody in the ears of the audience with a character or emotion. Richard Wagner was able to tell aspects of the story in his music dramas without the use of dialogue, employing purely musical devices and speeding the story along or adding insight to the character's mental state.

Lent—Forty days, not counting Sundays, of preparation before Easter in the liturgical calendar.

Leon & Eddie's—One of seven segregated jazz clubs on 52nd Street, New York City, 1935.

Leonard Bernstein—The first great American-born and exclusively American-trained composer and conductor of international importance in the twentieth century.

Leonhard Euler—The most prolific mathematician of all time who contributed new ideas in calculus, geometry, algebra, probability and number theory. Through his work, many areas of applied mathematics, such as acoustics, optics, mechanics, astronomy, artillery, and navigation were expanded.

Leopold Mozart—The father of Wolfgang Amadeus Mozart, he was the vice-Kapellmeister to the Archbishop at Salzburg who showcased his children's unusual talent to the courts and palaces of Europe.

Les Preludes—A set of six symphonic poems by Franz Liszt.

Lester Young—One of two extremely influential tenor saxophonists of the time in counterpart with Coleman Hawkins, Young is also known as "The Prez." Born in 1909, he was the oldest of three children and grew up in the vicinity of New Orleans. In November of 1936, Young used members of the Count Basie Orchestra to make his first recordings. The solos on Lady Be Good and Shoe Shine Boy were highly regarded by musicians; many musicians transcribed the solos verbatim. Young became a prominent soloing figure in Basie's orchestra as a result of his own recordings.

Letter sur les aveugles—"Essay on Blindness" written by philosopher Denis Diderot.

Lew Soloff—Original trumpet player for the group Blood Sweat & Tears.

Librettist—The person who creates the libretto for an opera, either through an original work or through the adaptation of an existing tale.

Libretto—"The book" or story in an opera production, inclusive of the layout in acts, scenes, and dialogue that the composer sets to music to create an opera.

Lied—German word for song and a short usually descriptive piece for solo singer and piano accompaniment.

Little Milton—Was the stage name for Milton Campbell, Jr., blues guitarist and vocalist best known for the hits "Grits Ain't Groceries" and "We're Going to Make It." While a teenager performing in local bars, he caught the attention of Ike Turner, who was a talent scout for Sam Phillips at Sun Records. He signed a contract with the label and recorded a number of singles.

Liturgical Year—A calendar highlighting all meaningful passages of the Bible, important events in the life of Christ, and the essential doctrines of the Catholic Church.

Lohengrin—An important Romantic period opera composed by Richard Wagner.

Louis Armstrong—Considered the greatest jazz musician by many, he defined what it is to play jazz. Born on August 4, 1901 and referred to as "Satchmo" or "Satchelmouth" (because of the size of his mouth and smiling teeth,) his influence of technical ability, happiness and spontaneity, and an inventive, musical mind still dominate jazz music even to this day.

Louis Armstrong Jazz All-Stars—Formed from the Armstrong Orchestra, the Jazz All-Stars became one of the most popular bands in jazz history. This band's popularity and international touring schedule dubbed Armstrong with the moniker "America's Jazz Ambassador."

Louis Moreau Gottschalk—America's first great native-born pianist and composer in the Romantic period and style.

Louis Pasteur—He proved that microorganisms cause fermentation and disease. He showed that microbes can be killed by chemical and physical means and that the spread of disease can be controlled.

Louis XIV—King of France in 1643 who enjoyed a seventy-two year reign and brought France to its peak of political power.

Ludwig van Beethoven—A great transition composer between the Classical period and the Romantic period and important piano virtuoso, he is significant for his strong will and since of self which reflected the revolutionary political ideas of his time and brought on the age of the artist as important to society for his/her ideas and valued for their creations rather than for their utilitarianism to the employer. He is especially important in the development of the sonata form genres and for his strength in overcoming his physical limitations to compose much of his best work.

Ma Rainey—One of the great female vocalists that significantly influenced the sound of the delta blues around the turn of the last century was Gertrude Pridgett. Born in Columbus, Georgia in 1886, she became known as "The Mother of the Blues." At age 14 she began touring and performing in the vaudeville circuit and is considered to be among the first women to perform blues in that circuit.

Macbeth—An important Romantic period opera composed by Giuseppi Verdi.

Madrigal—A 14th century vocal setting of poetic verse. An early Renaissance secular court vocal genre, similar to a sacred motet but rather with serious or amorous text, often employing "fa-la-la" choruses and using "text painting" techniques.

Magic Flute, The—A Mozart opera which would be his last opera, premiered not in the Royal Theater of Austria, but rather in the public theater where it was a financial success.

Major scale—A scale that has the intervallic construction of W-W-H-W-W-W-H.

Mamie Smith—Born May 26th, 1883, in Cincinnati, Ohio, she was a vaudeville circuit singer that made blues history by being the first woman and singer to record a blues tune. In 1920, "Crazy Blues" became a huge hit, selling more than a million copies within the first year of its release.

Mandolin—An instrument belonging to the plucked string category of instruments.

Mansfield Park—A novel by Jane Austen.

Marie Lafayette—Born in 1634, she wrote some of the earliest novels from Paris including La Princess de Cleves.

Marimba—A melodic percussion instrument.

Mark Twain—An American writer, famous humorist lecturer, and author of the American classics The Adventures of Tom Sawyer and The Adventures of Huckleberry Finn.

Marriage of Figaro—The first Mozart opera to break the tradition of opera seria type plots through its use of more realistic characters, plots, and human intrigue as was espoused by the philosopher Rousseau.

Martha and the Vandellas—Martha Reeves was hired as a secretary to Gordy in 1961 and by 1962 she convinced him to give her and her friends an audition. This girl group sang back up on many Motown hits before venturing off on their own. Martha & The Vandellas, Mary Wells, and the Marvelettes established Motown as a reliable source for the girl group sound.

Marvelettes—Martha and The Vandellas, Mary Wells, and the Marvelettes established Motown as a reliable source for the girl group sound. The Marvelettes had one of their largest hits with "Please Mr. Postman."

Marvin Gaye—R&B singer/songwriter, arranger, and record producer. Gaye gained international fame during the '60s as an artist on the Motown Label. After joining Motown records, he became the top solo male artist. He also recorded several duets with Tammi Terrell before moving on to his solo career and his own form of musical self-expression.

Mary Wells—Approached Gordy with a song in mind for Jackie Wilson, but she couldn't write music. Instead she sang the song to Berry. Impressed, Berry signed her to the record label and released her version of "Bye Bye Baby," hitting the R&B top ten charts in 1960. Smokey Robinson got in on the act of co-writing with Wells and produced a string of hits with "The One Who Really Loves You," "You Beat Me to the Punch," and "Two Lovers." Wells topped the charts again with the 1964 hit "My Guy."

Mass—Refers to the systematic method of worship in the Catholic church as well as describing a medieval vocal genre of church music employing the Latin text in the Ordinary of the Mass, including the Kyrie, Gloria, Credo, Sanctus, and Agnus Dei.

Mass in B Minor—An epic mass composed by J. S. Bach toward the end of his life which represents a summation of his life's work in the are of sacred vocal literature in the Baroque period.

Maundy Thursday—The Thursday before Good Friday in the liturgical calendar. In the afternoon, Christ shares the "Last Supper" with the apostles. Christ then goes to the garden to pray and is arrested.

Maurice King—Served as the executive musical director for Motown. King arranged shows at Detroit's Flame Show Bar for years and had worked with numerous jazz artists.

Maurice Ravel—A composer often linked with Debussy as a fellow musical Impressionist composer and outstanding orchestrator.

Maurice White—One of eight original members, vocalist and percussionist for Earth Wind & Fire.

Maxine Powell—Operated a finishing and modeling school, to prep his performers. Powell transformed Motown artists into polished professionals.

Maxwell Lemuel Roach—A New York City native, Max grew up in a musical family and began playing on the bugle, but he switched to drums by age 10. He finished the Manhattan School of Music in 1942 with a degree in Percussion. He was the counterpart to Kenny Clarke. Max was the drummer of "The Quintet" and is also a major figure in the development of Bebop.

Maybelle Carter—A founding member of the Carter family group and sister of Alvin and sister-in-law to Sara Carter. In 1927 the group was signed to a recording contract by Ralph Peer and Victor Recording. Maybelle Carter is responsible for the well known country style of guitar picking called "Carter Style."

Measure—A regular pattern of beats grouped together in similar and recognizable units.

Meistersingers of Nuremberg, The—An important Romantic period opera composed by Richard Wagner.

Melismatic Chant—Singing groups of more than five or six notes for each syllable of text.

Melodic percussion—A grouping of percussion instruments that produce a pitch and may be used to play melody, including the marimba, xylophone, celeste, vibraphone, glockenspiel, chimes, bells, and others.

Melody—Musical material of interest that is the most important and memorable, involving the succession of pitches that fall into units, one after another, of completeness and can contain emotion and meaning for the listener.

Melvin Franklin—Bass vocalist best known for his role as a member of Motown super-singing group "The Temptations" from 1961 to 1994. Franklin's nephew was Rick James, later a Motown star in his own right during the late 1970s and early 1980s.

Memphis Blues—The first song to be published with "Blues" in the title.

Memphis Horns, The—Memphis Horns, Andrew Love, tenor sax, and Wayne Jackson, trumpet, have provided back-up for a vast array of entertainers from Elvis to the Doobie Brothers.

Memphis Recording Service—A studio owned by Sam Phillips where Elvis would ultimately get his break in the summer of 1953 when he made a record for his mother's birthday. Elvis paid the four dollars and entered the recording room with his guitar. Sam Phillips heard Elvis and consequentially began using him for other recordings in the studio.

Messiah—An oratorio composed by G. F. Handel based on the story of Jesus' life in the scriptures. Handel's most famous composition and most frequently performed piece of choral literature ever composed in English in the Western world.

Meter—A consistent pattern of stressed and unstressed beats within a measure.

Metronome—An instrument that allows a musician to accurately establish the speed of a beat by grouping them in units of beats per minute.

Mezzo soprano—One of the standard range categorizations of the human voice, the second highest vocal range.

Michael Jackson—Lead singer for the Jackson 5, signed by the Motown label, soon became national stars with their first four singles charting at number one. Young Michael released four solo albums in the '60's and '70's and charted many hit singles as part of the Jackson 5 franchise before leaving the band to go solo.

Mikrokosmos—A popular piano work composed by Bela Bartok.

Minnesingers—12th and 13th century poet/musicians from Germany, including Bavaria and Austria.

Minnie Pearl—Female comedian in Nashville that befriended Hank Williams and assisted in preparing him for the country music market. Born Sarah Ophelia Colley Cannon on October 25th, 1912, she was a mainstay comedienne on the Grand Ole Opry and on the television show Hee Haw from 1970 to 1991.

Minor scale—A scale that has the intervallic construction of W-H-W-W-H-W-W.

Minuet—A very popular social dance rhythm in triple meter that was originally found in the Baroque period's dance suite but survived in the Classical period as the third movement in the sonata form, also possessing an additional component, the trio.

Miracles—Previously named "The Matadors," Smokey Robinson and Berry Gordy managed the group and Robinson maintained his position as the lead singer of the Miracles.

Missa solemnis—A "Solemn Mass" composed by Beethoven in his later years.

Mitch Miller—Top record executive with Columbia Records, responsible for launching Hank Williams' crossover songwriting potential by placing "Cold, Cold Heart" in the capable hands of artist Tony Bennett.

Mode—A form of scale used for melodic material by the ancient Greeks.

Modulation—The process of changing keys, higher or lower, major or minor.

Monody—A technique of solo singing with free rhythm and simple accompaniment created by Jacopo Peri to replace recitation of text in his attempt to recreate the fabled pathos of Greek tragedies in his early Baroque operas.

Monophonic Plainchant—(Plainsong, chant) Monophonic liturgical chant in free rhythm.

Monophonic texture—Music that contains one melody sounding alone, without any supporting material.

Montgomery, Alabama—the birthplace of the Civil Rights Movement.

Motet—(1200–1450) A brief composition for multiple voices, in which the tenor voice is a chant, serving as the foundation for the upper voices. Also,

1450–1600—A polyphonic setting of a sacred Latin text. Also, 1600–present, a serious, imitative style of church music.

Motive—A short, incomplete melodic building block.

Motortown Revue Tour—A Tour of major Motown artists performing to spread the name of Motown and the groups on the label, including Martha Reeves & the Vandellas, Mary Wells, The Marvelettes, The Temptations and others.

Motown Records—Established by Berry Gordy and is one of the most important independent labels in history. Motown Records quickly built one of the most impressive rosters of artists in American popular music, and by 1964, had become the most successful independent record company and black owned business in the United States.

Movement—A complete piece functioning as a chapter within a larger musical work which contains several movements necessary to achieve it overall design.

Muddy Waters—Creator of the "electric blues" sound, McKinley Morganfield, better known in the blues world as Muddy Waters, took his nickname from one of his favorite Mississippi creeks. Although not readily skilled in performing, he worked hard and was influenced by passionate performances of both House and Johnson.

Music—The greatest form of fine art. An abstraction of performed symbols through instruments creating organized waves of sound that house meaning for individuals.

Music for Strings, Percussion, and Celesta—A popular orchestral piece composed by Bela Bartok.

Musical Offering—A sequence of complex contrapuntal movements for keyboard, including a sonata for violin and flute, dedicated to King Frederick the Great of Prussia in Potsdam and based on a theme provided to J. S. Bach by the King himself, ingratitude for the warm reception Bach received on a visit to he Palace in Bach's final years.

NAACP—The National Association for the Advancement of Colored People, an organization formed to aid and guide African Americans in their struggle for civil rights through legal, financial, and social advice and counsel at the local, regional and national levels.

Nabucco—An important Romantic period opera composed by Giuseppi Verdi.

Nadia Boulanger—A French composer, conductor, and teacher of composition and theory who taught a generation of American composers how to sound American.

NASA—National Aeronautics and Space Administration

Nationalism—A musical movement using native folk elements to inspire new musical works.

Neoclassicism—A term applying to visual arts, literature, and music of the mid-twentieth century. It was spawned as a reaction to the overpowering Romanticism of the nineteenth century, choosing instead to employ emotional restraint and return to the forms and genres of the Baroque and Classical eras, yet infusing them with modern developments in craftsmanship.

Neumatic Chant—Singing groups of five or six notes for each syllable of text.

New Orleans—Considered the "Birthplace of Jazz." The music market in New Orleans is responsible for many of the greatest jazz musicians in history.

New Swing Street—By 1935 in New York City, many of the swing clubs had moved from 48th street to 52nd street. This, in turn, dubbed 52nd street with the nickname "New Swing Street."

New Testament Lesson—A seasonal text of the Mass Proper.

Nick LaRocca—Leader of "The Original Dixieland Jazz Band" claims to have played a vital role in the invention of jazz. Through much criticism, LaRocca maintained that white men created jazz and the African-American culture merely imitated the creation originated by white men.

Nocturnes—A popular Impressionistic orchestra piece by Claude Debussy.

Non-melodic percussion—A grouping of percussion instruments that do not produce a pitch; rather, they produce musically useful timbres, including drums, cymbals and others.

Nutcracker, The—A famous ballet score composed by Peter Tchaikovsky.

Oboe—The alto instrument (or the second highest pitch range) of the woodwind family of instruments belonging to the double reed group.

Octave—The mathematical doubling of the number of vibrations in one cycle of a vibrating source per second.

Octet for Strings—An important Romantic period piece composed by Felix Mendelssohn.

Ode to Joy—Poem authored by Johann Christoph Friederich von Schiller was set to music by Beethoven in his famous 9th Symphony.

Oedipus Rex—An important opera by Igor Stravinsky.

Old Testament Lesson—A seasonal text of the Mass Proper.

Oliver Twist—A novel by Charles Dickens.

On the Origin of Species by Means of Natural Selection—A book promoting the idea of evolution in animals through genetic mutation by Charles Darwin.

One O'clock Jump—Originally entitled "Blue Balls" by the Count Basie Orchestra band members, when Basie was asked the title of the last tune they would be performing on the radio, the name dubbed by the band members would not be received well by the public, so at 1:00 a.m. at the closing of the radio show Basie said, "Call this one—One O'Clock Jump." Since that time this tune has become the nightly closing to any performance by the Count Basie Orchestra.

The Onyx Club—One of seven segregated jazz clubs on 52nd Street, New York City, 1935.

Opera—The greatest musical form of the Baroque era, employing solo and choral vocal forces with orchestral accompaniment and continuo in the forms of recitative, aria, and chorus in multiple scenes and acts similar to a play with sung dialog rather than spoken.

Opera Buffa—A term meaning comic Italian opera.

Opera Seria—The most popular form of opera in the late Baroque period which includes libretto derived from myths and legends portraying lofty emotions and virtuous characters involved in plots demonstrating moral choices.

Oratorio—Similar to opera seria in form, using the tools of recitative, aria, and chorus with orchestra accompaniment, the oratorio uses epic tales and Biblical narratives as its libretto sources. Oratorios are generally not staged, costumed, or acted out, but rather, performed in a concert environment.

Orchestral Song Cycle—A development of Gustav Mahler similar to a song cycle, but with orchestral accompaniment to a solo singer rather than piano accompaniment and singer.

Ordinary of the Mass—The chants and prayers within the Mass that remain the same throughout.

Orfeo—The first masterpiece of Baroque opera composed by Claudio Monteverdi in 1607.

Organ chorale—Synonym for chorale prelude, a composition for organ based on a chorale melody.

Organic Chemistry and its Application to Agriculture and Physiology—A text which helped to revolutionize food production in the 18th century written by Justus Liebig.

Organic Chemistry in its Application to Physiology and Pathology—A text which helped to revolutionize food production in the 18th century written by Justus Liebig.

Organum—Gothic period church vocal genre first initiating polyphony as a texture through parallel organum, where an additional melodic line is added above the original chant voice in parallel intervals and similar rhythm, and later through florid organum, which allows for a newly composed upper voice to move independently of the original chant melody.

Original Dixieland Jazz Band, The—Under the leadership of Nick LaRocca became the first group to record "Dixieland" for Victor Talking Machine label on February 26th, 1917. This first recording of "jazz" sold over a million copies.

Orlando di Lasso—(1532–1594) a Franco-Flemish composer who held positions throughout Europe and wrote published many sacred and secular works.

Oscar Pettiford—Born in Okmulgee, Oklahoma on September 30th, 1922. He was a bassist and one of the first to use the Cello as a solo instrument in jazz. He has performed with an all-star line up of jazz greats including: Coleman Hawkins, Earl "Fatha" Hines, Ben Webster, Dizzy Gillespie, Duke Ellington, Woody Herman, and he was responsible as a bandleader for the discovery of Cannonball Adderly.

Otello—An important Romantic period opera composed by Giuseppi Verdi.

Otis Williams—Second tenor/baritone singer/songwriter and founder of the Motown recording group "The Temptations." Williams continues to perform as the sole surviving original member.

Overture—An instrumental genre of orchestral music usually seen as a preparatory piece associated with another genre such as ballet, theatrical music, or suite.

Overture to a Midsummer Night's Dream—A famous concert overture by Felix Mendelssohn.

Painting—A part of the visual arts using the mediums that may be perceived with eye, along with the disciplines of photography and sculpture and others. Painting usually involves the manipulations of pigment on canvas or paper.

Palm Sunday—The Sunday before Easter Sunday marks the day Christ entered Jerusalem in the liturgical calendar.

Parallel Organum—A form of Medieval polyphony where the upper voice moves with the chant pin a parallel rhythm and interval before resolving to the chant final tone.

Parsifal—An important Romantic period opera composed by Richard Wagner.

Passion—A genre similar to oratorio but differing in the limitation of its libretto to the story of the life of Jesus beginning with his return to Jerusalem, through the crucifixion and resurrection.

Pastoral Symphony—The name of Beethoven's Sixth Symphony which contains early elements of program music.

Paul Cezanne—A French painter who laid the groundwork for the modern styles like Cubism.

Paul Gauguin—A French artist and pioneer of Post-Impressionism.

Paul McCartney—(Now Sir James Paul McCartney) A British musicians who first came to prominence as a member of the Beatles. Recognized as a top musical icon of the 20th century along with his counterpart John Lennon, McCartney is listed in the Guinness Book of World Records as the most successful composer in popular music history. He has a record 29 US number one singles. McCartney has been an influential bassist as well as an accomplished singer, guitarist, pianist, songwriter and drummer.

Paul Whiteman—With a background in classical music, this bandleader was filled with many ideas about jazz. Orchestrator Ferde Grofe was a master musician who could translate Whiteman's ideas into notes. The result was the sensational "Paul Whiteman Orchestra."

Pavan—A metered dance rhythm and form found in dance suites of the Baroque period.

Peabody Hotel—Sam Phillips worked as a disc jockey in Memphis from 1946 to 1949. His show was broadcast on WREC Radio which was promoted out of the famous Peabody Hotel.

Pelleas et Melisande—A popular Impressionistic opera by Claude Debussy.

Pensees Philosophiques—"Philosophical Thoughts" a philosophical work by Denis Diderot which caused the Parliament of Paris to burn it because of its "anti-Christian" ideas.

Pentatonic scale—A scale having five notes.

Pentecost Day—The Sunday after Ascension marks the day the Holy Spirit descended on the apostles in the liturgical calendar.

Percussion—A family of instruments that produce their sound by means of striking usually with the hand, stick, or mallet creating a musically useful timbre. There are two main divisions of percussion instruments, melodic and non-melodic.

Persuasion—A novel by Jane Austen.

Peter Cetera—Original bassist, vocalist, and songwriter for Chicago/Chicago Transit Authority.

Peter Tchaikovsky—An important Romantic period composer of symphonies, symphonic poems, and ballets.

Petrushka—An important work of ballet by Igor Stravinsky.

Phillip Bailey—One of eight original members, vocalist and percussionist for Earth Wind & Fire.

Photography—A part of the visual arts using the mediums that may be perceived with eye, along with the disciplines of photography and sculpture and others. Photography usually involves the capture of light creating images.

Phrase—A musical thought, constructing a musical sentence.

Piano-forte—The popular eighteenth and nineteenth century keyboard possessed of a felt hammer striking the string instead of the plucking action of the harpsichord, allowing for a wider range of dynamic contrast by the performer. An immediate predecessor to the modern piano.

Pierre Auguste Renoir—A French painter who developed the broken color technique of Impressionism and one of history's most prolific artists, with nearly 6000 paintings.

Pierrot lunaire—A significant work of Arnold Schoenberg.

Pio Ospedale della Pieta—One of four orphanages for girls in Venice during the Baroque period, Antonio Vivaldi taught violin and conducted an influential orchestra there and composed much of his instrumental music for the girls' technical development.

Pipe organ—The first great keyboard instrument designed for use in European cathedrals and the Christian church, uses moving air through a series of pipes as its sound source.

Pitch—Sound that is musically useful.

Polychoral—A composition for two or more choirs, often separating the choirs.

Polyphonic (Polyphony)—A musical texture of two or more voices, each voice moves independently.

Polyphonic texture—Music that contains more than one melody, of equal importance, sounding at the same time.

Prayers—A seasonal text of the Mass Proper

Prelude—A short often lyrical introductory piece to a fugue in the Baroque period.

Prelude a L'apres-midi d'un faune—A popular Impressionistic orchestra piece by Claude Debussy.

Prima Donna—An audience favorite in the world of opera singers. One who has great skill and great fame. Also, refers to the lead female role in an opera.

Program Music—Music that brings to mind images or associations other than purely musical notions.

Program symphony—An extension of the symphonic poem, program music composed for orchestra, but in multiple descriptive movements.

Proper—The chants, prayers, and readings within the Mass that vary according to the liturgical occasion.

Psalm—A seasonal text of the Mass Proper

Public subscription concerts—The emergence of concerts of primarily instrumental music where tickets were sold to the public, thus providing a stream of income for composers and instrumentalists other than the church or opera house.

Quadrivium—The curricular aspects of a liberal education in the Middle Ages that included the subjects of arithmetic, geometry, music, and astronomy.

Rake's Progress, The—An important opera by Igor Stravinsky.

Ralph Johnson—One of eight original members and drummer for Earth Wind & Fire.

Ralph Peer—Born Ralph Sylvester Peer in Independence, Missouri, he was a talent scout, recording engineer, and record producer. He is responsible for recording and signing many musicians from Mamie Smith to the Carter Family.

Randy Brecker—One of the original trumpet players for the group Blood Sweat & Tears.

Rapsodie Espagnole—A famous orchestra piece by Maurice Ravel.

Ray Charles—Born in Albany, Georgia in 1923, Charles is well known for his innovation in blending popular music into his rhythm and blues performances and recordings. His work reflects inspiration from gospel, blues, jazz, pop, rock, R&B, soul and country musics. As a vocalist, he was originally inspired by pianist/songwriter Nat King Cole and his early recordings reflect that influence.

Rayber Music Writing Company, The—Was formed and for $100 would do whatever necessary to assist young artists make records. They also put together the "Rayber Voices" who would provide background vocals on many of the new talent recordings.

Rayber Voices—The Rayber Music Writing Company formed and for $100 would do whatever necessary to assist young artists to make records. They also put together the "Rayber Voices" who would provide background vocals on many of the new talent recordings.

Raynoma Liles—She and her sister Alice entered Berry Gordy's life for an audition. Raynoma not only became Gordy's next wife, but also his business partner.

RCA Victor—RCA (Radio Corporation or America) purchased the Victor Talking Machine Company in 1929, becoming RCA-Victor, and is responsible for recording some of America's most historic records.

Recapitulation—Term referring to the third and final section in the sonata allegro movement where the composer restates melodic elements found in the exposition and presents them again in the same key, effectively bringing the tonal tension of the exposition and the development to tonal resolution.

Recitative—A storytelling musical device in Baroque opera which portrays action and dialogue between characters in a dramatic scene through the use of a solo singer intoning pitches in a ration of one pitch per syllable of text.

Reciting Tone—The pitch upon which most syllables of a chant are sung, generally located above the final.

Red Hot Peppers, The—Created in Chicago, Jelly Roll Morton and the Red Hot Peppers became a staple in the Victor recording studio, recording an entire series of jazz works for the label in 1930.

Requiem Mass—A funeral mass, Mozart composed one of these to fulfill a secret commission, but died before he could complete the work. Also Romantic composers Berlioz, Verdi, and others have composed these.

Resting Tone (Final)—The pitch upon which a chant comes to its closing cadence.

Rhine Gold, The—One of the four music dramas that Richard Wagner composed to create the famous Ring of the Nibelung.

Rhythm—The progression of logically and exactly ordered events through time.

Richard Starkey or Richard Parkin—Ringo Starr (a stage name), a British musician most popular as the drummer for The Beatles. He is known for reliable, steady drumming and innovation as applied to fills. He was the oldest member of The Beatles and the last one to join the "Fab Four."

Richard Wagner—An important Romantic period composer important in the development of the opera and subsequent music dramas. Also, he developed the leitmotif as an important melodic component of his music dramas.

Rick James—Nephew of Melvin Franklin and Motown recording artists in the mid '70s.

Rienzi—An important Romantic period opera composed by Richard Wagner.

Rigoletto—An important Romantic period opera composed by Giuseppi Verdi.

Ring of the Nibelung, The—A set of four operas connected together by Richard Wagner, created to demonstrate his "music drama" philosophy they include The Rhine Gold, The Valkyrie, Siegfried, and The Twilight of the Gods.

Ripieno—A term given to the group of instruments serving as the accompaniment force to the concertino in a Baroque concerto grosso form.

Rite of Spring, The—An important work of ballet by Igor Stravinsky.

Ritornello—A sectionalized design shape associated with the Baroque concerto grosso, usually found in the first movement, alternating between the concertino and the ripieno.

Robert Johnson—Born in Hazlehurst, Mississippi on May 8th, 1911, Johnson was the illegitimate son of Julia Dodd and Noah Johnson, ultimately never meeting his father. Because of dire work situations, Johnson and his mother moved quite frequently from Memphis to various parts of the Delta. Johnson, as a young boy, began working in the cotton fields of a Robinsonville plantation.

Robert Lamm—From the group Bobby Charles and the Wanderers, Bobby Charles was a keyboard player who's real name was Robert Lamm. He joined Chicago as a keyboardist.

Robert Schumann—A Romantic period composer who is important in the development of the lied and the character piece for solo piano. He also founded the professional music journal, Die Neue Zeitschrift Musik, which was the first attempt in music journalism.

Rock-A-Billy—The "sound" created by the trio of Elvis Presley, Scotty Moore, and Bill Black when they recorded Bill Monroe's "Blue Moon of Kentucky." The recording was a combination of bluegrass and blues in one record, creating its own sound.

Rock-n-Roll Hall of Fame—Museum that contains equally remarkable interactive exhibits, films, videos and priceless and poignant artifacts, and serves as host of the permanent Hall of Fame exhibits. In addition to its permanent exhibits, the Museum stages a number of temporary exhibits throughout the year, including large-scale exhibits that occupy the top two levels of the building. The Museum also produces programs for the public that include concerts, lectures, panel discussions, film series, teacher education and other events.

Romanesque Period—The first seven centuries of the Medieval Age (400–1100).

Romeo and Juliet—A famous symphonic poem by Peter Tchaikovsky.

Romeo et Juliette—An important Romantic period program symphony composed by Hector Berlioz.

Rondo—A formal design for composition which is a sectionalized scheme that shows a recurring "A" section, alternating with other contrasting melodic material, ABABACA, or some other paradigm. The tempo in the first "A" section is usually fast and the meter is most often duple or quadruple.

Rosa Parks—An African American seamstress who took a bus ride home from work and was arrested for not giving up her seat to a white man in accordance with local law and social custom. Her arrest and defiance was the catalyst for the Civil Rights Movement.

Rounded binary—A form or shape of music with a two part melodic sectional design, A-B, repeated.

Rousseau—A French philosopher who advocated the creation of music with real emotion and real plots by natural people in natural environments in his articles in the French Encyclopedie.

Saltarello—A metered dance rhythm and form found in dance suites of the Baroque period.

Sam Phillips—Born in Florence, Alabama in 1925, Sam began his career as a radio announcer after dropping out of high school in 1941. He worked as a DJ from 1942 through 1949. During this time, Sam was able to put away enough money to open his own recording studio. Sam was responsible for signing many artists including Howlin' Wolf, Bobby "Blue" Bland, Little Milton, James Cotton, Ike Turner, B.B. King and Elvis Presley. With the success of his recording studio, Phillips started his own record label.

Samuel B. Morse—An American painter and inventor of the electric telegraph, conceived in 1832.

Sanctus—"Holy," one of the five texts of the Mass Ordinary.

Sara Carter—A founding member of the Carter Family group and wife to Alvin P. Carter. She played the autoharp and guitar. In 1993, her image appeared on a US Postage stamp honoring the Carter Family.

Sarabande—A metered dance rhythm and form found in dance suites of the Baroque period.

Saxophone—A single reed woodwind instrument group. The newest of the woodwind family of instruments.

Scale—A set of pitches that have certain interval relationships.

Scenes from Childhood—A famous set of character pieces for piano by Robert Schumann.

Scherzo—A replacement compositional design for the minuet and trio in the sonatas of Ludwig von Beethoven. He saw the minuet as homage to the aristocracy of an older age who first supported the orchestra's development but reflected the musician's servant status.

Science—The mental process of dissecting nature's whole forms into component parts, observing and labeling these parts, for the purpose of knowing and predicting the functions of the whole.

Scotty Moore—A member of the rhythm section that backed Elvis Presley and one third of the trio that was responsible for coining the sound and term "Rock-a-Billy." The sound was conceived by Sam Phillips and recorded into history at Sun Records Studio.

Sculpture—A part of the visual arts using the mediums that may be perceived with eye, along with the disciplines of photography and sculpture and others. Sculpture usually involves the creation of a three dimensional creation in stone, metal or other material.

Secco Recitative—Meaning "dry," a type of recitative in which a harpsichord alone provides rhythmic freedom and flexibility to the singer in a dramatic scene in Baroque operas.

Second Viennese School—A name given to the Expressionistic composers of Arnold Schoenberg, Anton Webern, and Alban Berg.

Sense and Sensibility—A novel by Jane Austen.

Sharecropping—Working to grow, maintain, and produce crops on someone else's land for a "share" of the profit when the crop was sold, many bluesman maintained jobs as sharecroppers in order to survive.

Siciliana—A metered dance rhythm and form found in dance suites of the Baroque period.

Sidney Bechet—Considered to be a child prodigy, by his teenage years, Bechet was a featured performer with Buddy Bolden and many other great bands of New Orleans. His style of playing clarinet and soprano saxophone dominated groups, ultimately seeing Bechet play the lead lines typically reserved for the more powerful trumpet.

Siegfried—One of the four music dramas that Richard Wagner composed to create the famous Ring of the Nibelung.

Sigfried Idyll—An important Romantic period orchestral piece composed by Richard Wagner.

Single reed instrument—— A term referring to the clarinet and saxophone families of instruments which use a cane reed fixed to a mouthpiece to produce their sound.

Sir Christopher Wren—English architect and scientist born in 1632 who spent most of his career rebuilding St. Paul's Cathedral and other churches after the Great Fire of 1666. He also made contributions to anatomy, mechanics, and mathematics.

Sir Isaac Newton—Professor of Mathematics at Cambridge in England who wrote Philosophiae naturalis principia which supplied a complete proof of gravitational laws. He also developed calculus and invented the reflecting telescope.

Sleeping Beauty, The—A famous ballet score composed by Peter Tchaikovsky.

Social Contract, The—A social commentary by Jean Jaques Rousseau.

Soldier's Tale, The—An important dramatic work by Igor Stravinsky.

Son House—Originally a preacher and greatly influenced by the black Baptist church, House incorporated intense passion in his Delta blues performances. With his ability to move the listener in such a powerful and musical way, his stage presence was intriguing and sometimes even frightening.

Sonata—A large-scale multi-movement work serving as the primary genre for instrumental music in the Classical period; also, a term for a genre employing a solo instrument with keyboard accompaniment.

Sonata allegro form—A term referring to the first movement in the sonata form paradigm and possessing three main sections including the exposition, the development, and the recapitulation.

Song—Term for the 20th century solo vocal music, usually associated with folk music in America, it is similar to German lieder but with English text and may involve more than one vocal performer with varying instrumental accompaniment forces.

Song cycle—Romantic solo vocal genre employing a grouping of textually related lieder.

Song of the Earth, The—A famous orchestral song cycle by Gustav Mahler.

Songs of a Wayfarer—A famous orchestral song cycle by Gustav Mahler.

Songs on the Death of Children—A famous orchestral song cycle by Gustav Mahler.

Songs Without Words—An important Romantic period piano piece composed by Felix Mendelssohn.

Soprano—One of the standard range categorizations of the human voice, the highest vocal range.

Soul—A style of African American music created from the combining of gospel music and rhythm and blues.

Spirituals—Church songs created by slaves which were used as a means of expression and communication among themselves. Instruments were not allowed on plantations, therefore, voices and body percussion were the only means of the creation of music.

St. Mark's Cathedral—The most famous church in Venice, Italy. Important site of musical development in the late Renaissance and early Baroque period.

St. Paul—An important Romantic period oratorio composed by Felix Mendelssohn.

Staff—A visual graph where specific pitches, high versus low, can be specified on a series of five lines and four spaces.

Steve Katz—Guitarist which headed up "The Blues Project" and was contacted by Bobby Colomby and Al Kooper to become part of the group Blood Sweat & Tears.

Stevie Wonder—Born Steveland Judkins and later changed to Steveland Morris, Stevie Wonder recorded more than 30 top 10 hits, won 24 Grammys, a lifetime achievement award, and he has been inducted into both the Rock-n-Roll and Songwriters Hall of Fame. Blind from infancy, Wonder has become one of the most successful and well-known artists on the Motown label, with nine US #1 hits to his name and album sales totaling more than 70 million units.

Stormy Monday—A popular blues record composed and performed by B.B. King.

Storyville—The famous "Red-Light" district of New Orleans. This district employed many great musicians and comedians in the brothels.

Strange Fruit—A political poem by Jewish immigrant Abel Meeropol performed in song by Billie Holiday about the brutality of racism in the South. Holiday performed Strange Fruit to an astonished crowd in 1939 at Café Society.

Strict Imitation—Imitative polyphony where one voice begins a melody and is precisely imitated by a voice or voices. Also known as "canon."

String quartet—A genre of music for two violins, viola, and cello, composed in sonata form performed in a small or intimate concert setting.

Strings—A family of instruments which produces its sounds primarily through the vibration of a length of gut or metal string set in motion through the use of a bow affixed to a wooden body, includes the violin, viola, violoncello, and double bass instruments.

Strophic form—A form or shape of music with a single melodic sectional repetition, A-A-A-A-, etc.

Subject—the primary thematic material in a fugue.

Sun Records—There were four record labels with the moniker Sun Records, the most famous to bear the name was indeed the fourth label & it was based out of Memphis Tennessee, started in operations by Sam Phillips on March 27th, 1952. Sun Records was known for giving notable musicians such as Elvis Presley, Carl Perkins, Roy Orbison, Johnny Cash and many others their first recording contracts and helping to launch their careers. Phillips, founder of Sun Records, loved rhythm and blues music and wanted to get the "black" music recorded for a white audience.

Swan Lake—A famous ballet score composed by Peter Tchaikovsky.

Symphonic Poem—A genre of program music for orchestra in one movement similar to the character piece for solo piano, but now for full orchestra, first created by Franz Liszt in his Les Preludes.

Symphony—A genre of music for instrumental orchestral composed in sonata form performed in a large concert setting.

Symphony Fantastique—A famous program symphony by Hector Berlioz.

Symphony No. 6—The Pathetique—An important Romantic period symphony composed by Peter Tchaikovsky.

Symphony No.8—Symphony of a Thousand—A famous choral symphony composed by Gustav Mahler.

Symphony of Psalms—An important work by Igor Stravinsky.

Symphony orchestra—A large European ensemble including various families of instruments but dominated by the string family of instruments.

Syncopation—An accent occurring somewhere inside a measure other than on the first beat.

Tadd Dameron—Pianist and major influence in the development of Bebop. Born in Cleveland, Ohio in February 1917, he was the most influential arranger of the Bebop era. He was also an accomplished arranger and composer for both swing and hard bop players.

Tamla Records—The original record label established by Berry Gordy before changing the name to Motown Records.

Tamla-Motown Records—Transitional period from Tamla Records to Motown Records.

Tannhauser—An important Romantic period opera composed by Richard Wagner.

Taxi War Dance—A popular swing record by the Count Basie Orchestra.

Teddy Wilson—Pianist with a sophisticated and elegant style that graced the records of many of the biggest names in jazz, including Louis Armstrong, Benny Goodman, Billie Holiday, and Ella Fitzgerald. His stint in the Benny Goodman Orchestra transcended racial barriers when Wilson was the first black musician to perform in public with a previously all-white jazz group.

Tempo—the speed of a beat.

Temptations, The—The group, Otis, Melvin, Paul and Eddie (later adding David Ruffin) pondered all day outside of Hitsville U.S.A. until they came up with the name "The Temptations." Over the next forty years, The Temptations would have top charting hits through the song-writing assistance of the Motown collection of writers. Smokey Robinson turned out some of the Temptations great hits like, "Just My Imagination" and "My Girl." The Temptations, unlike many other Motown groups, are still together and touring to this day, doing over 200 shows a year internationally.

Tenor—one of the standard range categorizations of the human voice, the fourth highest vocal range.

Ternary—A form or shape of music with a three part melodic sectional design, A-B-A.

Terry Kath—Original guitarist and vocalist for the group Chicago.

Text Painting—A musical illustration to the meaning of words in vocal music.

Texture—A term referring to the number of melodies being heard simultaneously.

Thelonious Monk—Legendary bebop pianist and eccentric composer. Monk was responsible for laying the foundation of bebop piano soloing and "comping." He was known for his unique style of improvisation and compositions, including now standard repertoire such as 'Round Midnight and Straight No Chaser. Although, in his later years, Monk's style of soloing evolved into something completely different, he is regarded as one of the founding fathers of bebop.

Theme—A melody, but a melody that is part of a larger formal structure that may contain several different themes or melodies within the whole structure.

Theme and variations—A form or shape of music with a single melodic theme that repeats employing varying accompaniment material, A, A2, A3, A4, A5, etc.

Third movement—Refers to the sonata form's third of four movement Classical period design which is usually in the form of a minuet and trio.

Thomas Alva Edison—America's greatest inventor, holding 1093 patents including: the phonograph, the electric light bulb, the electric typewriter, the Dictaphone, the mimeograph, and many others. He founded a company that merged with another to become General Electric Company.

Thomas Jefferson—An American statesman President who helped to shape Enlightenment thought in North America through his authorship of The Declaration of Independence.

Three Deuces, The—One of seven segregated jazz clubs on 52nd street, New York City, 1935.

Three O'clock In The Morning—A follow-up recording by the Paul Whiteman Orchestra that saw better sales than its predecessor, "Whispering," which sold almost two million copies.

Tonic—The first note or pitch of a scale, meaning home base or the beginning.

Tony Bennett—Born Anthony Dominick Benedetto in Astoria, Queens, New York City, he is considered to be one of the most influential singers in many American music.

Tony's—One of seven segregated jazz clubs on 52nd street, New York City, 1935.

Tower of Power—Based in Oakland, California, and responsible for the term "Oakland Soul" and possibly had more influence on the music industry than the other three horn groups. Tower of Power is the very definition of a "horn band." Boasting the largest horn section of the three horn bands discussed with two trumpets (sometimes trombone) and three saxophones, this west coast funk band has a fan base made up of fellow musicians.

Tower of Power Horns—The Horn section for the group "Tower of Power" which became more nationally and/or internationally well-known than the group as a whole.

Transcendental Etudes—An important Romantic period piano piece composed by Franz Liszt.

Treble clef—One of the most common clef indications, indicating notation spaces for pitches sounding in the upper register of human hearing, those above "Middle C."

Triad—The basic chord structure of Western music, having three notes, each a third interval apart.

Trio—A contrasting melodic section added to the minuet found in the Classical period's sonata form as the third movement to allow for contrast in the tonal scheme of the original's A-B design. The addition of the trio within a minuet provided additional balance and melodic and tonal interest when compared to the larger movements found in a sonata form.

Trio Sonata—Early instrumental music genre employing multiple short movements designed to display early instrumental music virtuosity.

Tristan und Isolde—An important Romantic period opera composed by Richard Wagner.

Trivium—the curricular aspects of a liberal education in the Middle Ages that included the subjects of grammar, rhetoric, and logic.

Trojans, The—An important Romantic period opera composed by Hector Berlioz.

Trombone—the tenor instrument (or the third highest pitch range) of the brass family of instruments.

Troubadors—12th and 13th century poet/musicians from southern France.

Trouveres—12th and 13th century poet/musicians from northern France.

Trumpet—the soprano instrument (or the highest pitch range) of the brass family of instruments.

Tuba—the bass instrument (or the lowest pitch range) of the brass family of instruments.

Tubular bells—A melodic percussion instrument.

Tune—A short, memorable melody that is complete in and of itself that needs no additional material.

Tuscaloosa Horns, The—The 10 member horn section that is the most called horn section for current touring Motown artists. The original founding members of the Tuscaloosa Horns are Chris Gordon and Mart Avant—trumpets, Ben McCoy—trombone, and Steve Black—tenor sax. Current members added for performing purposes: Shane Porter—trumpet. Kelley O'Neal, Jimmy Bowland, Rich Daviston, Jerry Ball, Jon Noffsinger, Steve Collins—saxophones. Demondrae Thurman, Jim Moeller, and Chad Fisher—trombones.

Twilight of the Gods, The—One of the four music dramas that Richard Wagner composed to create the famous Ring of the Nibelung.

Ukulele—An instrument belonging to the plucked string category of instruments.

Valkyrie, The—One of the four music dramas that Richard Wagner composed to create the famous Ring of the Nibelung.

Variations on a Theme by Haydn—An important Romantic period instrumental piece composed by Johannes Brahms.

Verdine White—One of eight original members and bassist for Earth Wind & Fire.

Vibraphone—A melodic percussion instrument.

Victor Hugo—A French poet and novelist who became recognized as a leading figure among the French Romantics through his great novels, including Notre Dame de Paris and Les Miserables.

Vietnam War—A mid-century conflict between capitalistic and communistic governments.

Vincent van Gogh—A Dutch artist and pioneer in the Expressionist movement which released his inner reactions to the world through turning, swirling, brush strokes; thick paint; and brilliant color.

Viola—the alto instrument (or the instrument with the second highest pitch range) of the string family of instruments.

Violin—the soprano instrument (or the instrument with the highest pitch range) of the string family of instruments.

Voltaire—The pen name of French Enlightenment philosopher Francois Marie Arouet.

W.C. Handy—Alabama born W.C. Handy is recognized as "The Father of the Blues." Although this declaration was self-proclaimed, his life-long support of the musical genre established the blues as a part of musical history. Handy was steadfast in his efforts of documentation and publication of blues music.

Walter Parazaider—Original saxophonist for the group Chicago.

Washingtonians, The—Duke Ellington's original group started in New York City in 1923 before it evolved into the 12 member "Duke Ellington Orchestra."

Water Music—Composed by G. F. Handel, Water Music is an orchestral suite intended to soothe the political troubles he had with the new King George I of England, handle's former employer in Germany. This is one of Handel's most popular instrumental works.

Wealth of Nations, The—An economics text which introduced the notion of a capitalist free enterprise system of economics, written by Adam Smith.

Well-Tempered Clavier, The—Two sets of twenty-four preludes and fugues each, in all twelve major and minor keys, composed by J. S. Bach over his lifetime as keyboard instruction materials for his children. The work also advocates the use of the then new tempered keyboard tuning system which served to prove that the keyboard through this novel tuning system could be functional in all available keys for the first time in history.

West Side Story—A popular and important work for the Broadway stage by Leonard Bernstein and others.

What a Wonderful World—Recorded in 1969 by Louis Armstrong Jazz All-Stars landed the number one spot on the pop charts and it was voted Billboard's "Greatest Song of the Century" in 2001.

What'd I Say—A popular record composed and performed by Ray Charles.

Whispering—A recording by the Paul Whiteman Orchestra that sold almost two million copies. This is an astounding achievement considering there were only about the same number of phonographs in the whole country at that time.

Whole step—the distance of two half-steps between two pitches.

William "Count" Basie—(1904–1984) was one of the leading figures in the swing era. He and Duke Ellington led bands that were the epitome of the big band style. Basie put together a smaller group from the Bennie Moten group, including Jo Jones and Lester Young, and became its leader. Known as the Barons of Rhythm, he began playing a lengthy appointment at the Reno Club in Kansas City. Eventually, the Barons of Rhythm would become the legendary Count Basie Orchestra.

William "Smokey" Robinson—Is noted for being one of the primary figures associated with the Motown record label/sound and second only to the company's founder, Berry Gordy. As both a member of Motown group "The Miracles" and a solo artist, Robinson recorded over 60 top 40 hits for Motown records. He served as the Motown label Vice-President from 1961 to 1988.

William Byrd—(1542–1623) a prolific English composer who wrote motets, madrigals, masses, and keyboard music.

William Harvey—An English physician born in 1578, became doctor to King Charles I of England. He discovered the function of the heart as pump and the circulation of blood throughout the body.

Wolfgang Amadeus Mozart—A Classical period composer and famous child prodigy on keyboard and violin who is important in the development of opera as well as the standard sonata forms of his day.

Woodwind——a family of instruments originally made from wood. Includes the flute, oboe, clarinet, bassoon, and saxophone groups.

Work Songs—Songs which were used as a means of expression and communication among slaves, these songs were responsible for generating a constant pulse with which the workers used for inspiration and timing.

World War I—The global conflict which marked the final break with the old world order of the absolute monarchies in Europe, in 1914–1918. Its outcome would be the catalyst for the Russian Revolution, which gave birth to the Communist ideal and encouraged others in the world to revolt, including China and Cuba, and eventually spawned the Cold War between the Soviet Union and the United States.

World War II—The second global conflict which cost between 40-50 million lives and saw the development of the world's first atomic bomb.

Wright Brothers—Orville and Wilbur Wright developed the first manned flight in Kitty Hawk, NC.

Xylophone—A melodic percussion instrument.

Yacht Club, The—One of seven segregated jazz clubs on 52nd street, New York City, 1935.

Youth's Magic Horn, The—A famous orchestral song cycle by Gustav Mahler.

Zoological Philosophy—A scientific treatise on zoological ideas which supports similar evolutionary ideas as did Charles Darwin, written by Jean-Baptiste Lama.

INDEX